HIJACKED

WILLIAM MORROW AND COMPANY, INC. ▼ NEW YORK

HIJACKED

**THE TRUE STORY OF
THE HEROES OF FLIGHT 705**

▼

▼

▼

DAVE HIRSCHMAN

It is the policy of William Morrow and Company, Inc., and its imprints and affiliates, recognizing the importance of preserving what has been written, to print the books we publish on acid-free paper, and we exert our best efforts to that end.

Library of Congress Cataloging-in-Publication Data

Hirschman, Dave.
    Hijacked : the true story of the heroes of flight 705 / Dave Hirschman.
        p.   cm.
    ISBN 0-688-15267-8
    1. Federal Express Flight 705 Hijacking Incident, 1994.
    2. Hijacking of aircraft—United States.   I. Title.   II. Title:
    True story of the heroes of flight 705.
    HE9803.Z7H53553   1997
    364.15'52'0973—DC21   96-39832
                                                                          CIP

Printed in the United States of America

FIRST EDITION

1   2   3   4   5   6   7   8   9   10

BOOK DESIGN BY GRETCHEN ACHILLES

In memory of
Captain Jimmy Price
(1954–1996)

CONTENTS

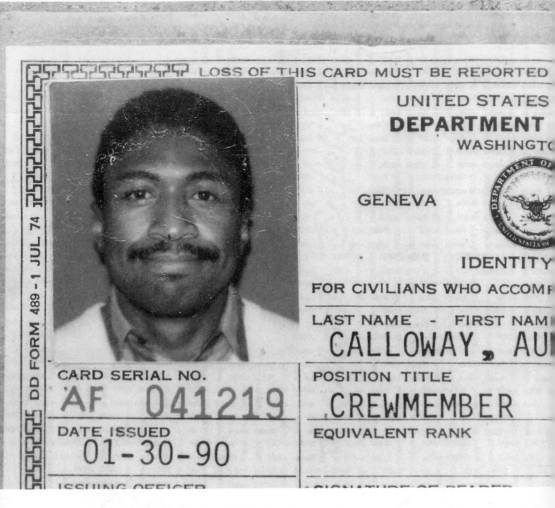

AUBURN RALPH CALLOWAY,
a FedEx flight engineer (*John L. Focht*)

CAST OF CHARACTERS

FedEx engineer **ANDY PETERSON** holds his four-year-old daughter, Anna, after the Air Line Pilots Association presented the crew with the union's Gold Medal for Heroism. (*John L. Focht*)

JIM TUCKER, the copilot of Flight 705, and his wife, Becky (*John L. Focht*)

Flight 705 captain **DAVID SANDERS** and his wife, Susan (*John L. Focht*)

HIJACKED

PART ONE

"EIGHT HOURS AND ONE MINUTE"

▼

▼

▼

APRIL 6, 1994

11:54 P.M.

FedEx captain Richard Boyle cursed the air traffic control delays that kept his wide-body jet circling in the night sky over Arkansas. The DC-10 loaded with 100,000 pounds of computer equipment from the Silicon Valley was only a few minutes away from the sprawling Federal Express Corp. package-sorting facility at Memphis International Airport. But a gaggle of purple-and-orange FedEx 727s in front of him were in the midst of their nightly slam-dunk approaches to the company's home base on the east bank of the Mississippi River.

Boyle, a twenty-one-year FedEx veteran, listened to the radio as air traffic controllers instructed pilots of the sleek "flying lawn darts" to descend at their discretion. The code meant the fliers could keep their jets moving fast and high as they approached Memphis. Then they chopped the power, pointed the long, cylindrical fuselages steeply down, and dove toward Memphis at the maximum permissible speed.

Unlike passenger airline pilots who fly flat, stable approaches with their flaps and landing gear extended miles from the runway, FedEx pilots often make steep turns and plunging descents, then toss out the speed brakes, gear, and flaps near the runway threshold. The cargo inside the FedEx planes never complains about the wild ride. All that matters to the pilots is getting the boxes to the sorting facility as quickly as possible. It's the central part of a tightly choreographed nightly ritual.

Boyle rechecked his watch—12:04 A.M. His DC-10 had been in a holding pattern for ten minutes. In the time-critical FedEx universe, it was imperative for flights from the West Coast like Boyle's to arrive in Memphis on time. More than a hundred cargo jets descended on the FedEx hub in the early hours each morning. Ground workers scurried to unload the planes, sorted more than one million packages in a furious two-hour time window, then reloaded and launched the jets again.

The nightly chaos was a miracle of modern commerce. But the system was designed so that the first FedEx plane couldn't leave Memphis until the last one had arrived. So a tardy DC-10 from the West Coast would delay a bunch of 727s bound for the East Coast— and eastbound jets lost an hour with the change in time zones. A few delays could ripple through the entire FedEx universe. And every employee knew that their company's "absolutely, positively over-night" credo meant packages delivered late were delivered free.

The air traffic controllers finally directed Boyle to follow the 727s to Runway 36 Left, but Boyle had an idea that could save some time.

"Tell them we want Runway Niner," the wiry captain said to Kathy Morton, his thirty-six-year-old copilot. Morton nodded and quickly relayed the request over the radio.

Morton, also an Air Force veteran, had been flying for FedEx ten years. An outdoors enthusiast with dark brown hair, piercing blue eyes, and handsome features, she rode horses in hunter/jumper com-petitions all over the country. The moment Boyle suggested landing on the east-facing runway, Morton understood exactly what he was trying to accomplish.

The brightly illuminated two-million-square-foot FedEx pack-age-sorting hub was at the northeast corner of the airport. If their DC-10 landed on the east-facing strip, Runway 9, it could coast to a stop next to the hub and eliminate at least five minutes of ground taxi time. That would put them right back on schedule. But FedEx made Memphis International the busiest airport in the world at night, and harried air traffic controllers denied the DC-10 crew's request to land on the east-facing strip. Boyle's last chance for an on-time arrival was gone.

Tonight, that meant his crew faced a compounded problem. Their afternoon trip to San Jose, California, had taken four hours. Now, their return trip, which usually took less time because of strong westerly winds aloft, had taken about the same amount, for a total time of eight hours. Federal Aviation Administration rules require commercial airline pilots who fly more than eight hours one day to rest at least sixteen hours before operating another flight. If Boyle, Morton, and their flight engineer—Auburn Calloway—went beyond eight hours on this trip, they would be ineligible to operate the same flight to San Jose and back as scheduled later this afternoon.

By the time the DC-10 arrived at the bustling FedEx complex and the crew shut down its three massive turbofan engines, the clocks on the instrument panel read 12:23 A.M. Boyle and his crew had flown for a total of eight hours and one minute. But when Boyle told the flight engineer to write down the exact time in the flight log, Calloway resisted. The forty-two-year-old former Navy pilot and five-year FedEx veteran seemed unusually reluctant.

"I'm looking at my clock on the engineer's panel," Calloway offered hopefully. "It says twelve-twenty-two—so technically, we didn't go overtime unless . . ."

"No way," Boyle interrupted, cutting the flight engineer off with a brisk wave of his leathery index finger. "We did our best, but the flight went overtime. That's not your fault. Those air traffic delays screwed us. By my calculations, our block time was eight-oh-one, and that's it. Now mark down the times and I'll take care of it. If anyone has a problem with what we did, they can talk to me about it."

All three pilots knew that going overtime would force FedEx schedulers to hastily put together a replacement DC-10 crew. Three pilots—a captain, copilot, and flight engineer—were going to be called in on their days off so they could operate Flight 705 on the afternoon trip to San Jose and back to Memphis.

Calloway hesitated to write down the times in the flight crew log, a book with a hinged metal cover that sat on the flight engineer's table. His round, muscular shoulders slumped.

"I don't know, Captain," he said. "I just don't feel good about it."

Boyle thought he knew the reason for Calloway's reluctance to declare the trip overtime. Just before the crew had boarded the DC-10 in Memphis, Calloway's flight manager had questioned Boyle about a delay in one of the crew's previous flights. The manager, John Wrynn, had asked all sorts of pointed questions about Calloway's performance. Why hadn't the flight engineer noticed a hydraulic leak in one of the landing gear? What was the problem with an auxiliary power unit that Calloway reported? Could it have been a faulty indication? Did the crew double-check?

Boyle had told the manager to buzz off, and later the smoldering captain had let Morton and Calloway know about his mini-interrogation. Calloway, an African American, smiled knowingly and shared his suspicions with the others. That flight manager was a racist who was searching for reasons to get him fired, Calloway had said. In fact, a disciplinary hearing would be held on Friday, April 8, to review the "historical flight time data" that Calloway had provided to FedEx when he applied for a job six years ago. The company was taking the highly unusual step of questioning him about ten-year-old flight records from the Navy.

At the beginning of their conversation, Calloway had dismissed the inquest as nothing more than a management fishing expedition. White officers had hassled Calloway in the Navy, too, so he said he made sure that every *i* was dotted and *t* was crossed. Then Calloway had become sullen and withdrawn. He had said several times—in the past tense—that he had "enjoyed" working at FedEx, that he was "sorry it had come to this." Boyle had offered to write Calloway a letter of recommendation, but then he became preoccupied with his flight's tardiness and let the subject drop.

Now Boyle, a former flight manager himself, again tried to reassure Calloway.

"Look, Auburn, I know you're worried about that hearing. But don't let these managers intimidate you. We flew the trip as efficiently as it could be flown, and we happened to go overtime. The schedulers gave us an impossible task, and now they have to deal with the consequences. The accuracy of the flight crew log is my responsibility. If any flight manager has a problem with it, they can talk to me. Now, let's all go home and get some rest.

"And I want you to relax and enjoy your day off. OK?"

Calloway sat motionless at the engineer's station behind the pilot and copilot. He rubbed his forehead. There was no sense debating Boyle. The captain wasn't listening, and he wasn't going to change his mind. And he had no way of knowing how badly he was screwing up Calloway's intricate plans. The flight engineer *had* to be on the flight to San Jose this afternoon. The fact that going one minute overtime on tonight's flight meant the crew's schedule would be altered was excruciating to him.

Time was running out—for FedEx and Calloway.

His Friday disciplinary hearing was scheduled to begin in less than thirty-six hours, and Calloway was sure he was going to be fired. Losing a job wasn't the end of the world in most occupations. But for airline pilots, whose promotions are based solely on seniority, Calloway would have to start all over again at another carrier—if he could get hired at all. The passenger airline industry was in the midst of its worst financial slump ever, and pilots were being furloughed at all the major carriers.

Plus it was doubtful any airline would take on a pilot who had been terminated at another carrier. The industry was a closed society that way. Once a pilot is out, he's locked out forever. Being fired at FedEx would haunt Calloway everywhere else. And even if he was able to land another airline job, the chance of ever becoming a wide-body captain making $200,000 a year or more was gone. It generally took twenty years to make it to the top of the seniority ladder, and by that time he would have surpassed the FAA's mandatory retirement age of sixty.

Calloway's career was over. He had to accept that.

But he couldn't accept the method, or the people, that were about to cause him and his family so much hardship. FedEx managers controlled every facet of the express transportation company, and Calloway knew they could manipulate a disciplinary hearing to bring about any outcome they desired. But they couldn't control him. They couldn't control his thoughts or his actions. And Calloway was about to teach them a lesson in the power of a single determined individual. When he was done, no one at FedEx, from founder Frederick W. Smith on down, would ever forget Auburn Ralph Calloway.

In the preceding forty-eight hours, the cornered flight engineer had hurriedly put his financial affairs in order. Now, his last will and testament was complete, his bank accounts were closed, and almost all his money was on the way to his ex-wife and two children in California. The only thing missing was money from stock and retirement funds, and he was scheduled to pick up the checks totaling about $30,000 from those accounts at 9:00 A.M. Had the money been available sooner, he might have been able to put his plan into action already. Now, due to a quirky air traffic control delay, a rare opportunity had been lost.

Calloway could still carry out his plan if he moved quickly, however.

He had fifteen hours to implement his plan. This afternoon, Calloway would turn the tables on FedEx managers. Instead of being their pawn, he would force them to deal with him as a man who had something they wanted, a man who had outmaneuvered them—and a man who could ruin them.

APRIL 7

10:40 A.M.

Jim Tucker took the call from the FedEx scheduler on his cellular phone.

The tall, athletic FedEx captain and his wife, Becky, were on their way home to Collierville with a minivan full of household goods from Sam's Club, the discount warehouse in Memphis. They planned to stop somewhere along the way for lunch, but Jim was restless.

He had hoped to fly his antique, two-seat Luscombe each of the last three days, but stormy torrents of rain, thunder, and high winds had kept him grounded. Today the skies were wide expanses of beautiful blue, and Jim was stuck in the Dodge minivan running errands around town while his sporty single-engine plane languished in a hangar at an out-of-the-way grass airstrip.

Now a FedEx scheduler was calling to find out if Jim was willing to take a DC-10 to California and back this afternoon. The out-and-back jaunt to San Jose was the FedEx equivalent of going to the corner grocery store for a gallon of milk. He might even be back in time for him and Becky to catch the end of *The Late Show with David Letterman.*

And making the offer even more irresistible, Jim would be paid 150 percent of his normal hourly rate for the eight-hour round-trip flight. It was a tempting offer. But Jim seldom volunteered for extra duty. His three children were growing up so fast that he feared he was missing out on their youth.

"Can I put you on hold for a second?" Jim asked the scheduler. "I need to talk this over with my wife."

Becky knew exactly what was happening even though she could hear only Jim's half of the conversation. She had dealt with sudden changes in her husband's flight schedule since the former college sweethearts were married in 1977. Back then, it was Navy commanders who sent Jim on sudden missions around the world; now the FedEx dispatchers did the same.

"It's an out-and-back to the West Coast," Jim said. "You think I should take it?"

Becky could see her husband was itching to fly. Whether it was his own Luscombe or a DC-10, anything that would get him airborne would suffice. She had seen the bottled-up expression on his face many times.

"Well, do you want to go?" she asked, already sure of the answer.

"Well, yeah," he confessed, grinning. "Sure I do. As long as that doesn't mess up your plans or anything."

"Look, it's no problem at all," she said. "Morgan, Andy, and Rachael all have soccer practice this afternoon. By the time they get home, clean up, have dinner, do their homework, and go to bed, you'll be on your way home. Tell the scheduler you want to go for an airplane ride."

Jim nodded. He punched the hold button on the telephone with his thumb.

"You've got a deal," Jim told the scheduler. "I'll take the trip. But I'm kind of curious why you called me. You really must be scraping the bottom of the barrel. I wonder why none of the regular volunteers took this one."

Some FedEx pilots leave their names on volunteer lists permanently in order to get as many trips at time-and-a-half pay as possible. Any of those fliers would have accepted a daytime trip to California in a second.

"I can't figure it out either," the scheduler confessed. "I would have thought this trip would be easy to give away. But all my regular customers were either sick or out of town, and we're almost completely out of DC-10 copilots in Memphis today. Thanks for getting us out of a bind."

The scheduler gave Jim the flight information slowly, just to make sure there was no confusion. "You'll be flying the right-seat copilot position on this trip. Show time is fourteen-ten Elvis Time."

Pilots were accustomed to dealing with all sorts of expressions for time. There was Greenwich Mean Time or Zulu Time. At FedEx, Elvis Time was shorthand for Central Time, the local Memphis time zone.

"Got it," Jim replied, jotting down the information on a yellow piece of scratch paper. "Thanks for thinking of me."

Becky chuckled at her husband's excitability. He was six feet three inches tall and in top physical shape. His arms were so thick from weight lifting and grueling NordicTrack endurance sessions that the sleeves of his blue uniform shirts barely fit over his biceps. Jim's pale blue eyes and chiseled features made him look like a pilot from central casting. But his restlessness and boyish mannerisms made his thoughts and emotions absolutely transparent.

That guileless disposition had appealed to her since their first date at the University of Montevallo near Birmingham, Alabama. Before she met Jim, Becky knew nothing about airplanes or pilots. But that changed when Jim was in the Navy. She helped him study by making up quiz cards and reviewing them with him. When their marathon study sessions were over, Becky would be able to recite gross weights, payloads, and performance figures for the A-7 Corsairs that Jim flew as well as most pilots.

Not long after their first child, a son, Morgan, was born, Jim and Becky began to regard Jim's long deployments at sea as a hardship on their young family. So after seven years in the Navy, Jim was ready to try something a little more settled.

Jim's first civilian flying job was at People Express, a start-up passenger airline in Newark, New Jersey. Military life had been difficult, but in many ways People Express was even harder. Housing prices in New Jersey seemed ridiculously high, and the Tuckers shared a tiny rental unit with another pilot's family. Jim was logging about a hundred hours per month of flying time while also serving as a flight dispatcher or gate agent on nonflying days. Even so, Jim made only $17,000 during his first full year at People Express. Jim and Becky had naively thought that all airline pilots were rich, but Jim was barely making ends meet.

The airline was acquiring more planes and routes all the time but seemed incapable of managing its growth. Employee morale and customer service had been high when the underdog airline started flying, but soon the planes were dirty. There were long delays in chaotic terminals, all the flights seemed full of screaming, inconsolable babies, and employees started calling the airline "People in Distress."

Jim once made a citizen's arrest on board a Boeing 737 when a New York passenger refused to pay for a flight, then punched a flight attendant when she tried to collect. On another trip, Jim's plane was forced to make an emergency descent and landing in Jacksonville when the cabin pressure system failed at 29,000 feet. After the harrowing plunge, Jim opened the liquor locker to passengers, gratis. Medicinal drinks were on the house until a replacement plane arrived to take the tipsy travelers the rest of the way to Newark.

Jim could forgive People Express for those misadventures, but he found other failures inexcusable. Once, while starting a pot of coffee in an aircraft galley, Jim found $1,200 in cash stuffed in a drawer. It wasn't unusual to have large amounts of cash on board because People Express flight attendants collected fares from passengers en route. But how could a business lose track of its revenue like that? Who was minding the store? Jim could have pocketed the money. Instead, he had taken the cash to the accounting department. No one there seemed at all surprised or concerned that bundles of money had been misplaced. The accounting office was such a shambles that, for the first time, Jim realized the airline eventually would fail.

When FedEx offered Jim a job as a flight engineer several months later, he didn't waver. Even though he was a Boeing 737 captain at People Express, Jim relinquished the prestigious left seat for a chance to start all over again at another airline. FedEx was a solid, growing company. It was part of the expanding cargo business—not the boom-or-bust passenger industry. And Jim and Becky could move back to the South. The Northeast had been like a foreign land to the native southerners.

During his first year as a flight engineer at FedEx, Jim flew less and earned more than his best year as a captain at People Express. The Tucker children, Morgan and twins Andy and Rachael, thrived in neighborhood schools. And later, when Jim was promoted to co-pilot, then captain, the family bought a large suburban home among tall pine and oak trees. Jim believed that his decision to come to FedEx was the best professional choice he had ever made. He had been with FedEx for ten years now, and already he was a captain and an instructor. No job was perfect, but this one was pretty close.

Today, Jim and Becky would have to skip the sit-down lunch they had planned at a neighborhood restaurant. Instead, they would swing by the drive-through window at Back Yard Burgers. Jim could wolf down a chicken sandwich, shower, put on his uniform, and still make it to Memphis International Airport on time.

He handed the square piece of paper with the flight information to Becky.

"This flight is supposed to get back around midnight," he said. "Can you read my writing? The flight number is seven-oh-five."

"NEAT, ROUND LETTERS"

Sitting on the green sofa in his apartment near Memphis International Airport, Auburn Calloway tried to salvage his plan for retribution against FedEx. Being replaced as the flight engineer on the afternoon trip to San Jose was a setback—but he could still carry out his plan with some last-minute modifications.

Picking up the checks from the brokerage firm at the First Tennessee Bank building downtown was his top priority. But there were other errands to run before Flight 705 left for San Jose this afternoon—and he couldn't afford to forget any of them. Calloway picked up the notepad on the small, circular table at the end of the couch. He had taken it from his room at the Tudor Hotel in New York City during a recent trip there. Using a black ballpoint pen, he printed a "to do" list by hand in neat, round letters:

1. Plan money.
2. 1st Tenn. to cash checks.
3. Shoe shop for bag.
4. Central Hardware for hammers.
5. Get dive equipment.
6. Go to 1st Tenn. to get cashier's checks.

Calloway closed his eyes and tried to think ahead, but the thunderous sounds of nearby jets made it difficult to concentrate.

Calloway had traveled so far since December 13, 1951, the day he was born in Washington, D.C. He was a father of two beautiful children—a girl, Keelah, ten years old, and a boy, Auburn junior or "Burney," who was seven years old. In the Navy, Calloway had flown jets from aircraft carriers at sea. He was the first African-American pilot to earn his wings at the Navy's air station in Mississippi, and he was a graduate of prestigious Stanford University. He was also a martial arts expert, a scuba diver, and an accomplished chess player.

He had met and surpassed the high expectations his parents and teachers at Frank W. Ballou High School had set for him. He traveled the world, spoke German and Italian, and he ordered meals in French at fancy restaurants.

Still, in many ways, Auburn Calloway regarded himself as a failure.

His ten-year marriage to Patricia Rose had ended in divorce four years ago, and now she and the kids lived in distant San Diego. Calloway had planned to be financially secure by this stage in life. He had expected to own his own home and to be planning for retirement. Instead, he lived in a dingy apartment in crime-ridden Parkway Village near Memphis International Airport. He worked overtime but still wasn't putting aside enough money to meet his financial goals.

The sparsely furnished apartment at 3630 Durand was a mess. Unclean dishes were stacked on the kitchen counter, and trash overflowed from several grocery bags on the floor. Two of the three bedrooms were vacant, and clothes were heaped in shapeless piles on the floor of the other room. Calloway had tacked some vacation pictures and drawings that his children had made to his bedroom walls, but the apartment was a lonely and depressing place.

The apartment was supposed to be a crash pad that several pilots who lived elsewhere would share during irregular layovers in Memphis. As long as the place had a stereo, CD player, TV, VCR, and beer in the refrigerator, none of the pilots complained. But after the divorce, the apartment had become Calloway's full-time residence. His constant presence and bizarre habits grated on roommates, and few kept their leases more than a few months.

Calloway was so concerned about burglaries that he put a life-sized mannequin in one of the windows to make prospective thieves think someone was home all the time. He insisted that roommates disconnect the telephone, toaster, and other small appliances and put them in the clothes drier when they left the apartment for extended periods. If burglars did get in, they wouldn't think to look for items in the drier.

Coworkers at FedEx also noticed Calloway was behaving strangely. Once, on a transpacific flight, the captain and copilot of a DC-10 heard strange, rhythmic thumping sounds emanating from deep within their aircraft. When the copilot opened the cockpit door to investigate the noises, he was surprised to see Calloway wearing a karate gi, leaping and kicking the eight-foot ceiling. The impact of each barefooted kick reverberated throughout the entire plane.

Calloway's mother, Miriam Clara Waters, had died alone in a sanitarium eight years ago after suffering for decades from paranoid schizophrenia. And Calloway had become estranged from his father, two sisters, and a brother after her death. The last time Calloway had seen his father, Earl Calloway, a retired postal worker, was on New Year's Day in 1990. Then, the two men had hugged each other and vowed to become friends and participate in each other's lives in the future.

But nothing substantive had come of their meeting.

Earl Calloway spent his days playing cards at a neighborhood bowling alley while Auburn traveled the globe as a professional pilot. Earl had legions of friends, and Auburn had always been solitary and studious. When Auburn was a teen, Earl bought his son a weight-lifting set and encouraged him to play football, basketball, and other team sports. But the only athletic activity Auburn pursued with vigor was karate—an individual endeavor that seemed more cerebral than physical.

Earl liked to spend money on fun things: motorcycles, travel, nice clothes. Auburn had always been a saver and he hid what money he had. Earl remembered the afternoon his son came home from school and discovered his mother was cleaning the venetian blinds. She was soaking them in the tub. Auburn raced to the bathroom and pulled the blinds out of the soapy water. He had stashed a wad of bills in the removable corner of the blinds, and the money was wet but salvageable.

When Auburn went away to college at Stanford, Earl loaned him a Harley-Davidson motorcycle. Auburn could use it as long as he wanted, his dad told him. With all the sunny weather in California, he could ride it year-round. Auburn drove the motorcycle across the continent to Palo Alto, then sold it. He used the money to take a European vacation after graduation. Earl Calloway had been upset with his son for selling the motorcycle, but on the day Auburn visited him in 1990, all was forgiven.

Auburn Calloway tried to maintain a closer relationship with his own children. During their recent spring break, he had brought them to Memphis and took them horseback riding and watched their tennis lessons. The family visited the National Civil Rights Museum at the former Lorraine Motel in Memphis, where Martin Luther King, Jr., had been assassinated. They toured the FedEx hub and saw the gargantuan jets that Calloway flew around the world.

But Calloway felt certain that his airline career was coming to an end. The implications for his future, and his ability to provide for his family, were grave. He had tried to help Keelah and Burney prepare to attend private schools in the hope that, someday, they would pursue lucrative professions. Now, with the disciplinary hearing that could end his flying career looming, all of that was in jeopardy. Instead of readying his children for upper-middle-class lives, Calloway feared he had set them up for deep disappointment and alienation.

Calloway's trouble at work had started on St. Patrick's Day, when FedEx founder Frederick W. Smith gave a speech to employees on the company's internal, closed-circuit TV network. Calloway was in the pilot's lounge at the company's regional package-sorting hub in Indianapolis the night the FXTV show was broadcast. When the charismatic, silver-haired chief executive began talking about the company's growth plans in Asia, Calloway got on the phone and dialed the 800 number on the bottom of the TV screen. The person who answered asked for Calloway's name and employee number. As a joke, he identified himself as Joey Johnson—a FedEx 727 captain. Moments later, Calloway was patched through to Smith on the live

TV program. He began questioning the CEO on FedEx's plans for an Asian package-sorting hub at Subic Bay in the Philippines.

"Don't you know how dangerous that place is?" asked Calloway, who had visited the area while he was in the Navy. Calloway had been disgusted by Subic Bay and the nearby town of Olongopo, a pit of prostitution, tattoo parlors, and sleazy bars. He couldn't believe the Navy tacitly sanctioned those activities by turning a blind eye to them—and he was incensed that black sailors were treated like second-class citizens. These days, anyone who read newspapers or watched TV news could see that the Philippines were in the midst of an undeclared civil war.

"In case you didn't know it, there's a revolution going on over there," Calloway said. "They'd like nothing better than to take an American pilot or his family hostage. The flying conditions are terrible, with monsoons in the summer, mountains surrounding a dangerously short runway, and unreliable navigation equipment."

Smith, a forty-nine-year-old Vietnam Marine veteran who had become an American entrepreneurial icon, listened for a few moments, then tried to break in. Calloway interrupted, and FedEx workers watching the show were shocked that any employee would dare try to talk over "Super Fred." When Smith finally was able to get a word in, he said that the show was not intended for pilots. The twenty-six hundred pilots at FedEx had recently joined a national union—the Air Line Pilots Association—after Smith and other executives had implored them to keep their company free of labor unions. If a pilot was concerned or had a policy question, Smith curtly advised him to contact his union representative.

When Calloway hung up the phone, he chuckled at his prank and bragged to other pilots that he had put the company founder "in his place." However, FedEx managers didn't see any humor in the situation. To them, the caller had deliberately set out to embarrass their leader. It was unpardonable, and they were determined to find out who the caller was and take swift punitive action. John Wrynn, a Memphis-based manager for DC-10 flight engineers, believed he recognized Calloway's voice on the program. The thirty-minute show hadn't even ended when another pilot called Wrynn from Indianapolis to confirm his suspicions. Joey Johnson, the pilot whose name and ID number Calloway had used, called the show to say that he hadn't been the one who questioned Smith so disrespectfully.

From that night on, Wrynn began scrutinizing every aspect of Calloway's performance and learning all he could about the flight engineer's history. Wrynn, also a former Navy pilot, called acquaintances in the military to find out about Calloway's military records—even though Calloway had left the service a decade ago. He wrote to the Navy personnel records bureau in Pennsylvania to obtain more information.

Wrynn, a somber, square-jawed manager, soon put together a thick file on Calloway. In it, there was a discrepancy that Wrynn found intriguing. When Calloway filled out a FedEx job application in 1988, he claimed to have logged several thousand hours as "pilot in command" of multiengine jet aircraft in the Navy. But military records showed that although Calloway had flown twin-engine S-3 Vikings extensively, he had never been certified as an aircraft commander. Therefore, he had not been the pilot in command, and he should not have been allowed to log the time.

Calloway also neglected to say in his employment application or subsequent interviews that he had worked at Flying Tigers, a transpacific air-cargo carrier based in Los Angeles, or Gulf Air, an offshore cargo airline. In fact, he was flying for Gulf Air in 1987 when he was offered a job at Flying Tigers. He started at Flying Tigers as a flight-engineer trainee. Instead of quitting the job at Gulf, however, he claimed to be on jury duty and stayed on the payroll at both airlines. When the chief pilot at Gulf found out, he called his counterpart at Flying Tigers, and they gave Calloway an ultimatum: resign immediately from both carriers or be fired.

Calloway quit, but he kept his résumé in circulation.

Federal Express offered him a job a few months later without any knowledge of this debacle.

For five years, Calloway had performed his duties at FedEx as a flight engineer on Boeing 727s and then DC-10s. He had passed one FAA examination after another and breezed through twice-annual physical fitness tests. He volunteered for charities and organized a Neighborhood Watch group in Parkway Village. He worked at the ALPA office and coordinated a "cookie drive" in which members brought homemade treats to Northwest Airlines, which allowed them to ride in their vacant cockpit jump seats.

But a few months after Calloway had been hired at FedEx, the company bought Flying Tigers. His employment records there were easily accessible to FedEx managers—including Wrynn. Calloway knew they had everything they needed to get him. Calloway earned about $80,000 annually as a FedEx flight engineer, and his future earning potential at FedEx was enviable. In a year or two, he could become a copilot with annual pay topping $100,000. Once he was promoted to captain, he'd make $150,000 his first year and more after that. But if he lost his job, there was no other airline, and no other career, that would provide similar pay or benefits.

FedEx would pay for taking that opportunity away from him.

The defining moment of Calloway's life was fast approaching. Success would depend on all the skills Calloway had developed: boldness, creativity, physical strength, and flying ability. When the time came, he vowed to show no hesitation and no mercy.

"FUNCTIONAL YET ELEGANT"

APRIL 7

12:15 P.M.

Susan Sanders used a spatula to move the warm chocolate-chip cook-ies into a plastic Baggie.

FedEx crew schedulers had notified her husband, DC-10 captain David Sanders, that he would operate the afternoon flight to San Jose. David napped in the bedroom while Susan placed the fresh-baked cookies in his black-leather flight bag. He would be gone only a few hours, but whenever David left on a trip, Susan invariably slipped a gift into his luggage. It was part of the time-honored ritual they had developed during the thousands of times they had said good-bye since they met in 1972.

At that time, Susan was an elementary-school teacher in Orange County, California, and David was a Navy pilot. Although she was raised in upstate New York and went to college in Oswego, Susan, then twenty-seven, lived in trendy Newport Beach and looked like an idealized Beach Boys version of a California girl. Petite and ath-letic, with crisp, chiseled features, large blue eyes, and perfectly aligned white teeth, she was paddling a surfboard across a saltwater canal on Balboa Island when a friend called out to her.

A Navy P-3 Orion was flying in from Maine that afternoon with a cargo bay full of lobsters, the friend said. And the arriving pilot, a real gentleman named David Sanders, needed a date. Susan wasn't eager to accept a blind date. But an airplane full of lobsters? That was an attractive proposition. Plus, the lobsters were going to be cooked on an outdoor grill in a neighbor's backyard. After a day of swimming, riding a bicycle along the crowded beaches, and dodg-ing cars jammed with tourists, a relaxing seafood dinner sounded enticing.

Susan knew that if she didn't hit it off with the pilot, she could always hop in her 1968 Malibu and make the short drive back to the apartment she shared with another elementary-school teacher. As far as she could tell, it was a no-risk proposition.

When she met David later that evening, however, Susan found herself in no rush to leave. Unlike some of her other suitors, David was calm, gracious, and unhurried. His plans were to fly back to Maine the very next day, but he acted as though he had all the time in the world. The two of them walked along the manicured residential streets of Balboa Island that night, and David surprised his date by actually stopping and smelling roses in some of the flower gardens along the sidewalk.

Susan went to New York to visit her parents later that summer, and she made a side trip to Maine to see David. He lived in a rustic 150-year-old house in Cundy's Harbor a few miles from the Navy base at Brunswick, and the place made Susan feel as if she'd stepped into a fairy tale. Meals were prepared and devoured at the nearby home of George and Alice Swallow, an iconoclastic couple whose kitchen was the town's social center. The Swallows had adopted an orphaned seal, and the fishermen who dined there brought burlap sacks full of fish for the ravenous doe-eyed mammal.

Susan was entranced by the place and by her host. Watching David in his comfortable and colorful surroundings made her appreciate his relaxed, confident, inquisitive nature. He seemed perfectly at ease dealing with all kinds of people. He could explore virtually any subject from astronomy and aviation to history and seafaring, and he usually seemed more interested in the process of arriving at answers than in the answers themselves.

David and Susan wrote to each other frequently that summer. And when he left the Navy in the autumn, David moved to California to be close to Susan. When he went to work for FedEx in a nonflying capacity and the job took him to Houston, she visited him there. And when David became a pilot and FedEx sent him to Memphis in 1975, he arranged his flying schedule so that he could get regular weekend layovers in California. In 1977, Susan came to Memphis for her first long visit. She planned to go back to the West Coast for the start of the school year, but those plans changed.

FedEx's first public stock offering was about to become a Wall Street blockbuster, and legislation was working its way through Congress that would deregulate the entire air-cargo industry. That meant FedEx would be allowed to fly large jets that carried more cargo, so the company could grow even faster. David had already begun speaking wistfully about how he would miss seeing the steam from his coffee cup freeze against Dassault Falcon windshields in the winter. To increase payloads, FedEx had removed the auxiliary power units from its small French planes—so the cockpit heaters didn't work unless the engines were running at full power.

David and Susan had been dating for five years in 1977, and they both assumed that, eventually, they would marry. They just hadn't set a date, or even a year, in which to do it. Then, on a lazy summer morning, Susan blurted out that they weren't particularly busy that weekend, so maybe they ought to get married. It was a Thursday, but if they put their minds to it, they could get a marriage license by Saturday.

Two days later, with a pair of FedEx pilots and their wives as guests and witnesses, David and Susan became husband and wife. Freeman Marr, the kindly country lawyer, city court judge, college track coach, and volunteer firefighter, performed the fifteen-minute wedding ceremony. When it was over, they celebrated with a bottle of champagne and a plate of quiche Lorraine Susan had prepared.

Three years later, David and Susan had a daughter, Lauren.

So much had changed since then. But the important things had remained on an even, predictable keel. Lauren, now thirteen years old, had inherited her father's quiet, contemplative bearing. And David's career at FedEx had surpassed all of their expectations.

David was still napping at 12:30 P.M. when Susan opened his overnight bag and placed the cookies inside. She was amused to find a worn teddy bear in the heavy rectangular case. The toy bear was tan, about three inches tall, with a squashed face and a thin red ribbon tied around its neck. Lauren had given the stuffed animal to her father a decade ago, when, as a little girl, she liked to pretend to help him pack for his trips. It was her way of getting used to her dad's frequent absences. David had kept the fuzzy memento with him through tens of millions of miles on countless flights around the globe.

Susan moved about the kitchen quietly so she wouldn't wake him.

David and Susan had sold their suburban home a year ago. They bought a twenty-acre piece of undeveloped land on a bucolic hilltop outside Memphis and were about to start construction of their permanent home. It would be functional yet elegant and have a commanding view of their property and a nearby lake. During the year that it would take to build the house, the family had moved into a mobile home on their property.

The mobile home had a living room, a fireplace, and a small office with a computer, fax machine, and multiple phone lines. There was even a small piano for Lauren. But it was a tight squeeze for the family of three and their black cat, Janie. The walls were thin, the floors creaked, and Susan took her shoes off in order to step quietly.

They laughed at the fact that, for all their success, they were living in a fourteen-foot-wide trailer.

"Maybe someday we'll get a double-wide," Susan would add jokingly.

They wouldn't have to step lightly once their new house was complete. Crews were scheduled to grade the site later in the month during David's three-week vacation. In May, they would pour the foundation, and framing could start after that. The family's permanent home would contain a billiard room, private offices, a built-in aquarium, and a hot tub. A wooden porch would wrap all the way around the lower floor of the two-story structure.

David quietly emerged from the bedroom dressed in his blue pilot's uniform. Four stripes on the shoulder showed his rank as captain.

Trim, physically fit, about six feet tall, with wavy brown hair and a graying mustache, David projected a calm, dignified bearing. His professorial appearance was heightened by the dark-rimmed reading glasses he had begun using to read cockpit instruments and small print. Articulate and thoughtful, the forty-nine-year-old pilot's words carried a faint trace of a southern accent, a faded remnant of his hardscrabble West Texas roots.

David's father had to quit school after the eighth grade to work on the family farm. He raised his children to expect hard, physical labor. But he also taught them that education was their key to a better life. David took the message to heart. He started playing the trumpet in the sixth grade, and during college, he planned to become a music teacher.

When David began college in West Texas, the band director at Abilene Christian University, a Navy reserve officer, got him interested in joining the Navy. The military draft was a fact of life then. And if a young man was going into the service, it would seem a lot more pleasant to be an officer giving orders than an enlisted man receiving them. As an added incentive, a Navy recruiter who visited the campus offered anyone who took and passed the Navy flight-aptitude test a ride in a two-seat T-34 trainer aircraft.

David took the two-hour test on a whim and received an extremely high score. The thirty-minute airplane ride that followed convinced him that his future in the Navy should be in airplanes— not ships. After graduating from college, David began flight training in Pensacola, Florida.

David had done well academically in college, and he had shown himself to be a capable musician. But he recognized others possessed far more talent and native ability in those fields than he. Flying seemed different, though. David found within himself a talent for operating aircraft that he never suspected he possessed. At the beginning of flight school, other students bluntly told him they doubted a music major could compete with all the young engineers, mathematicians, and physicists in the program. But flying seemed to David more art than science. He performed with ease in areas where supposedly more qualified candidates struggled and failed.

Instructors required students to memorize the positions of every switch, dial, and lever in the cockpits of the planes they flew. For part of their final exams, each student was required to sit in the cockpit blindfolded. Then, on command, the young fliers had to reach out and identify each instrument without looking. The blindfold cockpit checks were like learning to play new instruments. New airplanes were like different keyboards, and touching the instruments was like playing musical scales. David's memory, dexterity, and creativity helped him master complex aircraft cockpits.

David considered applying to fly the Navy's supersonic attack jets, but his pragmatic nature ruled against it. He planned to become an airline pilot when he left the Navy, and multiengine transport planes flew missions that were similar to passenger jets'. He opted to fly four-engine P-3 Orions, submarine hunters with multiperson crews like airliners. Orions flew long missions that allowed pilots to log thousands of hours of flying time.

His choice of airplanes seemed to pay off when he left the Navy and American Airlines offered him a job as a flight engineer. It was the first step on what promised to be a long, lucrative career. The day the offer came, however, David surprised the company by turning it down. His Navy friends couldn't believe it either.

American had scores of applicants for each pilot position. The company offered a tremendous opportunity. Very few airlines were hiring pilots in the early 1970s, and fewer still were likely to start. But David didn't want to be stifled by any large company's monolithic culture. It didn't matter to him which airline was the biggest, the most profitable. David had just come from the Navy, a bureaucracy unlike any other. He wanted to take entrepreneurial risks and try things that hadn't been done before. Better opportunities would come along, he assured himself. All he had to do was be patient.

David had saved some money during his years in the Navy, and since he was accustomed to Spartan living, he could make that savings last. He delved into music again by buying a neglected piano at a garage sale, taking it totally apart and rebuilding it. When the instrument was finished, it was as good as new. For extra money, David hired himself out as a piano tuner.

Then one day in 1973, a friend told David about a small, start-up company in Memphis that was looking for pilots. The company, something-or-other express, had this nutty idea about flying Dassault Falcons around the country at night, picking up small packages, bringing them all to Memphis for sorting, then delivering them around the country the next morning. The company had begun its network with twenty-five cities, mostly in the Midwest. Now, it was expanding. Someday, it might even cover the entire country. The concept intrigued David.

He called American Express in Memphis and asked for the flight department. The receptionist assured him that American Express did not fly airplanes. He finally got in touch with Federal Express, though, and the company sent several sales brochures. David thought their business concept was brilliant. He came to Memphis and spent his own money getting flight instruction in Falcons. FedEx was losing $1 million a month at the time, but David was undaunted. He believed the company's unique business concept eventually would prevail. And when it did, David was convinced it would succeed fantastically.

FedEx had temporarily stopped hiring pilots at the time David first came to Memphis, but the company offered him a job as a ground instructor in the flight-training department. The pay was dismal, but as soon as FedEx began expanding again, the company's hire-from-within policy would ensure that David got a regular flying job.

David wasn't quite ready to move to Memphis if he couldn't fly airplanes right away. But FedEx was planning to expand to the West Coast, and Sanders proposed that FedEx hire him as a salesman. He would sell FedEx to California companies. Then, when more flying positions opened up, he would move into the cockpit. FedEx managers quickly agreed.

"Hello, I'm David Sanders and I'm with Federal Express," he had said thousands of times at the beginning of cold sales calls.

"You're with the government?" was a frequent reply.

"No, Federal Express. It's the biggest venture-capital enterprise in history. We'll pick up your urgent packages, fly them to their destinations, and have our own people deliver them by noon the next business day."

"Doesn't Airborne do that?"

"No, sir, we're the only company in the world that transports packages from doorstep to doorstep overnight. We use our own people and all our own equipment. We guarantee on-time performance."

David learned the FedEx network from the inside out. A few months later he was promoted to manager of large accounts in Houston and made sales calls at Exxon and other giant oil companies there.

Finally, in 1975, a pilot position opened, and David moved to Memphis. He had to take a pay cut of $200 a month as a starting copilot. But after the first year his wage would jump to $15 an hour. By working overtime, a FedEx copilot could expect to make $1,500 per month or more.

When David joined FedEx, the parcels were sorted by hand in an old hangar at Memphis International Airport. Executives spoke dreamily of the day FedEx volume would top 100,000 packages a night. All the pilots, indeed all the employees, checked the package count daily for signs of growth. Everyone knew an expanding package count meant job security. Now, twenty years later, FedEx moved more than two million packages a day and operated the largest fleet of cargo planes in the world. FedEx was the biggest, most dynamic transportation company anywhere, and it operated in 171 countries.

David fondly remembered the freezing, drizzly day in January 1978 when FedEx took delivery of its first Boeing 727. Hundreds of employees came to the airport on their day off just to stand outside and cheer the big purple jet as it taxied to the FedEx ramp. A bagpipe band escorted the plane, and founder Fred Smith gave a rousing pep talk. The spirit, dedication, and vision of those early employees built FedEx, and the three-engine jet represented their future. Two years later, the company bought its first DC-10s, widebody jets that dwarfed the 727s. Then it bought an entire fleet of

DC-10s and still couldn't keep up with surging demand. The future seemed limitless.

FedEx had always operated under founder Smith's "People-Service-Profit" philosophy. PSP turned the traditional, adversarial manager-employee relationship on its head. Employees were responsible for providing customers the absolute best service. In turn, the primary task for managers was making sure employees had the proper tools and training they needed to serve customers. As long as employees and managers worked closely and harmoniously, customer satisfaction, job security, and profits would naturally result.

In the 1980s, David dedicated himself to making the system work. FedEx pilots elected him chairman of their Flight Advisory Board, a group of pilot representatives who met with managers to decide schedules, work rules, and other issues. In the top FAB post, David had been an advocate for pilots. Still, his approach to dealing with managers was quiet, well-reasoned and took customers into consideration.

David didn't lose his temper or pound the table. Such histrionics, he was sure, would be unconvincing and ultimately counterproductive. By listening, thinking, and staying as informed as possible, David was able to gain and maintain the trust of pilots and managers alike. The system had performed admirably—until now.

The trouble started in 1988 when FedEx bought Flying Tigers, an international air-cargo company based in Los Angeles. A paragraph in the FedEx pilot handbook assured company fliers that if FedEx ever purchased another carrier, the additional pilots would be placed at the bottom of the existing FedEx seniority list. Seniority is critical to pilots because it determines the type of aircraft pilots fly, their choice of routes and schedules, and indirectly, how much money they earn.

Flying Tigers pilots were members of the Air Line Pilots Association, the nation's oldest and largest pilots' union. ALPA lawyers threatened to scuttle the $880-million acquisition unless the two seniority lists were merged. ALPA refused to allow its members to be tacked on to the end of the existing list. FedEx executives leaned on David and other members of the Flight Advisory Board to change the pilot handbook and to use binding arbitration to settle the seniority dispute.

FedEx managers argued that the career expectations of FedEx pilots would be met and exceeded in the merger. Flying Tigers had vast international routes in Asia and Europe. Acquiring them would greatly expand FedEx's reach and spur the purchase of bigger, more technologically advanced airplanes. Pilot careers would advance faster than ever, managers promised, because FedEx would duplicate its highly successful next-day deliveries overseas. Business leaders in France, Germany, Japan, and China would find FedEx products as irresistible as Americans—and FedEx pilots would be the big winners.

FedEx flight engineers would move up to copilot "window seats," and copilots would become captains. Everyone would add stripes on their uniforms and digits on their W-2 forms. David and other FAB members agreed with FedEx managers and turned over the seniority list to a neutral arbitrator. Pilots would live with the arbitrator's decision.

Meanwhile, FedEx poured hundreds of millions of dollars into replicating its U.S. overnight delivery network in Europe. The company built massive facilities and hired and trained thousands of new employees. But European shippers resisted American faster-is-better business habits, and FedEx overseas losses mounted. An international economic downturn also reduced the volume and price of international freight shipments.

Instead of rapid pilot advancement, there was stagnation. If not for the company's no-layoff policy, FedEx pilots would have been furloughed. Then, when the arbitrator published the merged pilot seniority list, it seemed no one was happy. David and other FedEx pilot leaders were vilified and accused of selling out to unscrupulous managers. The intra-European delivery network was scrapped in 1992. But bitterness among pilots remained, even when the economy finally turned around and FedEx international operations were headed toward sustained growth and profitability.

In 1993, FedEx pilots seemed to abandon their founder's People-Service-Profit philosophy. In an extremely close union representation election, pilots rejected Smith's approach and voted to form the only union in the company's domestic workforce. Now, the union was just beginning contract talks—and David hated it. In the old days, pilots could walk into Fred Smith's office anytime they had a prob lem. If fliers were being short-changed, Smith would fix it.

David couldn't understand why pilots were willing to jeopardize all the gains FedEx employees had made together. Bringing a national union into the close-knit FedEx family would divide loyalties and destroy close working relationships between managers and employees. And the potential for a destructive strike could ruin FedEx. David knew from his time as a salesman that FedEx reliability and customer service meant everything. The company could not survive if it was only as good as the competition. It had to be noticeably, empirically better.

David was appalled by the confrontational tone that pilot union leaders were taking. They asked for the moon—raises, signing bonuses, and improved pensions at the expense of other employees. Pilots seemed to have no idea how competitive their industry was becoming, with United Parcel Service, Airborne Express, and others cherry-picking the biggest and must lucrative FedEx accounts.

Smith had offered to debate union leaders during the representation campaign, and they rebuffed him. Now the company was ignoring legitimate pilot concerns and using textbook stall and delay tactics. Instead of acting like forward-looking, imaginative problem solvers, FedEx executives were behaving more like boorish union busters of the 1920s.

To David, the entire situation was a disgrace. His position at FedEx was degenerating into just a job at a giant, multinational conglomerate. He had walked away from American Airlines twenty-one years ago because he wanted to be more than a bit player in a huge corporation. To David and other FedEx veterans who remembered more noble times when their company was a cause, the current in-your-face way of doing business was insulting.

David refused to join the Air Line Pilots Association and did his best to keep the sordid labor situation out of his mind. He had been a leader among pilots for many years. But now he wanted to be anonymous again. He would do his job, then leave. He would dedicate himself to building his family's new home.

The five thousand-square-foot, four-bedroom structure would enable them to entertain guests whenever they chose, as many as they chose. Lauren would be able to play her piano upstairs on the second floor in complete privacy. David immersed himself in details of the project. And he arranged his flying schedule so that he could be at the construction site on key days to oversee the subcontractors and coordinate the work. He did much of the labor himself and used the best materials available. His family intended to live there forever.

In just over ten years, he would retire from FedEx. By that time, virtually all his professional and financial goals would be met.

In the meantime, David would focus on the more pleasant aspects of his job, and flying across the country on a beautiful spring afternoon was one of them. Years earlier, David had heard a fellow FedEx pilot remark that every airline captain, copilot, and flight engineer had the first-, second-, and third-best jobs in the world. Despite the recent labor conflict, David still believed that.

"Don't wait up for me," he told Susan. "I probably won't be back until one A.M. or so."

These words, too, were part of their preflight ritual. He always said not to wait up for him, and she always said she wouldn't. But Susan was a light sleeper, and she would open her eyes as soon as David's car pulled into their long gravel driveway. How could she not? His twelve-year-old Chevrolet Caprice broke the stillness of country nights. He insisted on keeping the old relic, though, pointing out that it made no sense to park a fancy vehicle at Memphis International Airport for the two weeks each month that he traveled. The pilot parking lot was full of brand-new BMW, Mercedes, Lexus, and Cadillac luxury cars—all collecting dirt and grime at the same rate as David's tired old Chevy.

When David came home from a trip, no matter how late the

hour, he would get a beer out of the refrigerator, pour the contents into a frosty mug, and drink it while reading his mail and the newspapers he had missed. Tonight, Susan had intended to turn in early. She and her friend Kelly Roberts—also the wife of a FedEx pilot— planned to go antique shopping the next morning. Their outing had been set a week ago.

Susan kissed David on the cheek as he gathered up his overnight bag. She knew all the statistics about how safe commercial jets are and how rarely accidents happen.

But each time her husband left on a trip, she made sure to tell him good-bye—just in case.

"ALL SEATS ARE OPEN"

APRIL 7

1 2 : 1 8 P.M.

"Jump seats, this is Daphne, may I help you?"

"Hi," Auburn Calloway told the FedEx reservationist over the telephone. "Has the afternoon flight to San Jose got any jump seaters?"

She recognized Calloway's voice and didn't have to ask his name or employee number. Calloway frequently commuted to and from California on FedEx planes, and he was notorious among reservationists for making last-minute changes in his flight schedules. Daphne Null would make reservations for him, but the normally friendly, singsong quality in her voice disappeared.

"From where?" she asked.

"From Memphis. I think the flight number is seven-oh-five, but I'm not sure."

"For what day?" She assumed he was asking about today's flight. FedEx pilots always seemed to make their travel plans at the last possible moment, but the reservationist wanted to be certain.

"Today," Calloway said, a hint of exasperation in his voice.

"All right, let me pull that up for you."

Calloway had returned to his apartment after running his final errands. The checks from the brokerage house had been waiting at the front desk when he got there. Now they had been cashed, and money orders were on the way to California via Express Mail. Calloway never used FedEx for his personal shipments, even though employees got a discount.

He purchased several hammers from a Central Hardware store. The only new problem took place at the neighborhood shoe store, where the latch on his garment bag had not been repaired on time. The bag had been sent elsewhere, so it wasn't available to Calloway at all. The flight engineer was furious at the clerk when she gave him the news. He cursed the woman behind the counter, then slammed the door on his way out. The garment bag may have seemed like a small matter to the clerk. But it was essential to Calloway's plan for retribution against FedEx. Calloway had to regain his composure.

But now as he waited for the FedEx reservationist to give him the passenger information, his heart was pounding. Flights to California were popular among FedEx employees, virtually all of whom were allowed to ride company jets for free. And daytime trips like this were especially likely to draw riders. There was a long pause, and Calloway could hear Null typing on her computer keyboard.

Then the information appeared on her screen.

"We have no one on that flight," she finally said. "All seats are open."

"No one at all?" Calloway could scarcely believe his good luck. He needed a break, and maybe this was it.

"No one," Null repeated.

"OK. What's the showtime for that flight?" Calloway asked.

Pilots are generally required to show up about an hour prior to departure. Calloway wanted to arrive even earlier.

"It's two-ten."

Null asked if Calloway wanted to reserve a jump seat on the afternoon flight, but he abruptly declined. Calloway had to keep his name out of the FedEx computer system as long as possible. If FedEx managers somehow learned he was going to the West Coast the afternoon before his disciplinary hearing in Memphis, he might arouse their suspicions.

Instead, he would appear in person a few minutes before the scheduled showtime. That would give FedEx managers no notice at all.

"OK, thanks," Calloway told the reservationist.

"You're welcome," she said reflexively. "Bye-bye."

"CONSTANT MOTION"

APRIL 7
1:30 P.M.

Andy and Susan Peterson had just started clearing out their attic when a FedEx scheduler called Andy to assign him to Flight 705, the afternoon trip to California and back.

The flight engineer and his expanding family had decided to convert the attic of their two-story, 1,650-foot home into a fourth bedroom. The change would allow four-year-old Anna to have her own room, a prospect that thrilled seven-year-old Mary Margaret. The youngest Peterson child, William, was sixteen months old.

The towheaded kids showed the Scandinavian genes they had

inherited from their father. Their rambunctious, outgoing disposi-
tions, however, came straight from their mom. Susan Peterson had
been one of the youngest finance executives in the country. After
graduating from the University of Mississippi in three years, with a
business degree and a straight-A average, she became vice president
of a small bank in Jackson, Mississippi.

Now thirty-three years old, Susan had put her profession aside
to devote all her energy to her growing young family. The life she
had chosen was not glamorous, but Susan found it satisfying. She
outfitted herself in jeans and cotton sweatshirts most mornings and
kept her light-brown hair short enough that she didn't need to waste
time drying or curling it. The children's school, church, and gym-
nastics kept her in constant motion.

"Hey, Andy," she said, opening the attic window and looking
down at the driveway and carport below. "Instead of carrying these
boxes downstairs, I'm going to start pitching them out the window."
Seconds later, the cardboard rain began.

It was a gorgeous spring day, just crisp enough to make working
in long sleeves comfortable. Susan was born in Atmore, Alabama, a
town of fifteen thousand a stone's throw from the Florida panhandle.
Her father, Doug, moved the family to Mississippi when she was
eleven years old. She and her two brothers were the fifth generation
of the Hall family born in Alabama, and her parents planned to
return there when they retired. Maybe, in a few years, Andy and
Susan could buy a vacation home there. Lots of FedEx pilots had
second houses or condominiums outside Memphis.

For now, however, the Petersons had to watch their spending.
Andy would do all the carpentry on the attic conversion himself.
Their house was only six years old, and the added room would certainly increase its value as well as make it more comfortable for the
kids. The Petersons lived in Olive Branch, Mississippi, a fast-
growing Memphis suburb. A new high school was under construction a few blocks away. When their kids were old enough, they could
walk or ride bicycles to class there.

William, or Will, as his parents called their son, was asleep when

Andy slipped by the open bedroom door and quickly donned his FedEx uniform, the short-sleeved blue shirt with three stripes on each shoulder.

Susan was still bombarding the driveway with boxes when Andy slid into the 1978 Datsun 280Z he had purchased new and backed out of the carport. The car had 155,000 miles on it but still ran smooth and strong. Andy did all the tune-ups, oil changes, and maintenance himself. Susan liked to joke that Andy fell in love with the sports car before he fell in love with her. Memphis International Airport was only ten miles away, and Andy would be at work in less than twenty minutes.

As Susan watched the shiny gold Datsun negotiate the speed bumps on their residential street, she caught herself feeling slightly perturbed that Andy had been called away on such short notice. He had worked at FedEx five years and still had to spend endless months on "reserve" status, meaning that he could be assigned trips like this without warning. Unlike more senior pilots, Andy didn't have a set schedule. He was on call for two weeks each month, then off for two weeks.

Susan chuckled at herself for thinking such a schedule was onerous. At his previous job as a pilot for an air-charter company in Dallas, Andy would be on duty nine days in a row, then off for three. He would frequently be called in the middle of the night to transport donor organs across the state or across the country. Sometimes, when rock bands went on tour, they would rent the private jet and its crew for the duration. Andy once took guitarist Eric Clapton and his entourage blitzing around North America for two weeks. This would have been fine for a bachelor, but the extended road trips were tough on the Petersons. For six months, while Susan worked in Jackson and raised their first child, and Andy flew out of Dallas, they seemed to see each other only in passing.

Now Andy had a job that allowed him to spend time with Susan and their kids. They lived in a place that, despite its close proximity to the city of Memphis, had a small-town feel they enjoyed.

Susan remembered the first time she and Andy met, in 1980.

She had come home for spring break when an uncle died unexpectedly in Alabama. She drove there with the family, but Susan had to return to Mississippi quickly to avoid missing school. Her father arranged for Susan to fly back on his company's corporate plane, a twin-engine King Air.

Andy, who was then twenty-five years old, was the pilot.

Susan had been crying all morning at the funeral. Then Peggy Bullock, a family friend whose husband worked with Susan's father at Mississippi Chemical Co., told her to cheer up for the trip home.

"I want you to put on some lipstick," she told Susan. "There's this really cute pilot flying the airplane today. You'll want to look your best."

When their car pulled up to the airport tarmac at Montgomery, Alabama, Andy was waiting by the door of the airplane. He had wispy blond hair, brown eyes, and a quick smile. About five feet ten inches tall with broad shoulders and sturdy workman's hands, he quickly loaded their baggage in the plane and made the passengers feel at ease. Once the plane was airborne, Peggy suggested that Susan walk up to the cockpit and say hello to the pilot. When Susan hesitated, Peggy marched to the front of the plane and asked the copilot to come back to the passenger area.

"I've looked all over," she said helplessly, "but I just can't find the Cokes anywhere. Or the ice."

"They're in the refrigerator at the very back of the plane," the copilot replied. "The glasses are there, too."

"Show me," Peggy insisted.

When the copilot left the cockpit, Susan unbuckled her seat belt and stepped forward.

"I've never been in a small plane like this," she said to Andy.

"Go ahead and sit down," he offered, motioning toward the vacant copilot's chair. "It's a lot of fun."

Susan slid into the cockpit and smoothed her black dress as she sat down. The twin-engine turboprop airplane was quiet enough that they could chat without raising their voices. Peggy kept the copilot busy in back to make sure he wouldn't try to reclaim his seat in the cockpit. Susan asked a few questions about flying, while Andy inquired about her. Had she and her uncle been close? Where did she go to school? How old was she?

"I'll be a junior next year," Susan said, intentionally vague about the fact that she was nineteen and in the midst of trying to complete her freshman and sophomore years simultaneously. She asked Andy if he had ever been to Montgomery before.

"A few times on company trips," he said. "My parents met in Montgomery during World War Two. In fact, I'm sure my dad could show you the exact spot."

During this ninety-minute flight back to Mississippi he told her that he loved to water-ski and that he had his own boat. He also owned a two-seater airplane, a Citabria capable of taking off and landing on the small grass strip at his parents' farm in Goodman, Mississippi. Susan later realized that Andy was able to buy the boat and airplane on his meager corporate pilot's salary only because he didn't pay any rent. He lived in Canton, Mississippi, with his doting Aunt Lina. The boat was relatively new, but the airplane was hardly a showpiece. The fabric-covered plane had been stored outside and was in fairly rough shape when Andy bought it. He had re-covered the steel-tube fuselage, wings, and control surfaces with new material and inspected every bolt, brace, and wire to make sure the plane was airworthy.

Before they landed, Susan decided that she wanted to see Andy again. He seemed handsome, intelligent, and entirely without pretense. She dropped a few hints about her availability, but when the corporate King Air touched down, Andy still hadn't asked to see her again. During the short drive to her house from the airport, Susan feigned anger at her friend Peggy.

"Why didn't you tell me that cute pilot has his own 280Z, an airplane, and a ski boat!" Susan demanded. "We've got to get to work on him immediately."

A few weeks later, Susan invited the Bullocks to her parents' house for dinner—along with pilots Andy and Fred. She explained the dinner to her parents as a way to thank the pilots for voluntarily giving up their Easter weekend to make the unscheduled flight to Montgomery. Andy pointed out that evening that the water in area lakes had warmed with the May sunshine, and to Susan's delight, he invited her to go water-skiing when the semester was over. They began dating that summer. When Susan's family went on vacation at Greers Ferry, a deep blue-water lake in central Arkansas, all she thought about was Andy.

One day, she noticed a bright orange windsock marking a grass runway near the lake. She called Andy that night and invited him to fly over. The next day he appeared in his Citabria. And Andy and Susan flew back to Goodman to meet his parents.

That autumn, Andy flew the small plane to the University of Mississippi at Oxford on weekends, circling Susan's sorority house and banking the wings to announce his arrival. He did it dozens of times during the two years they dated. As soon as she heard the Citabria overhead, Susan would get in her car and drive to the nearby airport to pick him up.

Andy and Susan were married two weeks after Susan graduated from college. The newlyweds spent two nights at the Peabody Hotel in downtown Memphis, then two weeks in the Virgin Islands. When they came home, they moved into an apartment in Jackson. Andy was flying a Learjet for the Mississippi Chemical Co., which had recently purchased the sleek $3 million plane. And Susan got a real estate license and began selling houses.

Soon she landed a job with a mortgage company. And then small Republic Bank hired her as vice president of its fledgling residential-mortgage division. They bought a house of their own, then moved into a larger house that they planned to fill with children. Their first, Mary Margaret, was born in 1987.

Then, in December, Andy called from work with some unsettling news. Mississippi Chemical Co. was going to sell the Learjet and eliminate Andy's job. Luckily, the Dallas air-charter company that bought the jet offered Andy a job on the spot. If he accepted, he would keep flying the same sleek airplane. As an extra incentive, the company promised to let Andy remain a captain, rather than work his way up from the bottom.

Andy moved to Dallas immediately. But Susan stayed in Jackson with their daughter.

Susan was busy with her banking job, and the real estate market was awful. They tried to sell their house but no offers came. When Andy drove home to see Susan and young Mary Margaret, he could spend a maximum of thirty-six hours before he had to drive back to work in Texas. Each good-bye was wrenching. In Dallas, Andy got an interview with American Airlines, but the giant passenger carrier ultimately rejected him. He was convinced the fact that he wore contact lenses had cost him the job. He applied at FedEx, too, but heard nothing from the company.

In 1988, Susan moved to Dallas. The Petersons sold their house in Jackson at a steep loss.

Then, in June 1989, exactly a year after Susan had moved to Dallas, FedEx offered Andy a job in Memphis. It was a godsend. Susan was pregnant with their second child, and the FedEx job would bring them closer to family, and offer more financial stability and a better schedule. Starting pay at FedEx was $40,000 annually—the best of any major airline.

Moving back to the Memphis area would be like old times for the Petersons. They could take vacations together, and if they felt like visiting their old haunts, the University of Mississippi in Oxford was just an hour away by car. They could even bring the ski boat back to some of their favorite lakes. In a few years, their kids would be old enough to learn to slalom.

The couple had been through some trying times, but they persevered. Now they were doing exactly what they had set out to do in the place where they wanted to do it.

"ANOTHER UNUSUAL REQUEST"

APRIL 7

1:40 P.M.

"Hello, this is Auburn Calloway, employee number double eight, triple seven."

"Yes, sir, Mr. Calloway," answered Shirley Parker on the FedEx crew-scheduling department's telephone line. "What can I do for you?"

Calloway was at his apartment preparing to go to the airport. His preparations were nearly complete, but he wanted more information. Specifically, he wanted to know which pilots had been assigned to operate Flight 705 to San Jose.

"Listen, I've got a letter that needs to be hand-delivered to San Jose," Calloway said, inventing a scenario by which he could be expected to show up at the airplane without a reservation. "I was hoping you could tell me who's scheduled to fly Flight seven-oh-five today. I want to give something to the crew."

"Sure thing," Parker said, typing a code into the computer terminal on her desk. "The replacement flight engineer on Flight seven-oh-five is Andy Peterson. Do you know him? He's a real nice guy."

"Yeah, he sure is, isn't he?" said Calloway, busily jotting down the name on his notepad. "How about the copilot?"

Parker was a little surprised that Calloway asked for the copilot. Usually, flight engineers ask favors of other flight engineers. They seldom impose on more senior pilots.

"Um, let me see," Parker said, typing more codes on her computer keyboard. "The copilot on that trip is Jim Tucker."

"Tucker?" Calloway mused. "I don't know him. How about the captain?"

Another unusual request, Parker thought. She had the full crew list on the screen in front of her.

"The captain is Sanders, David Sanders."

"OK. I understand," Calloway said. "Thanks a lot."

Calloway examined the list of names. Peterson, Tucker, Sanderson, he wrote, mistakenly adding an extra syllable to the captain's last name. Calloway couldn't picture them in his mind. Maybe he would recognize them when he saw them in a few minutes at Memphis International Airport.

Calloway went to his bedroom and put on his summer pilot's uniform: blue slacks, a belt, and a short-sleeved blue polyester shirt. On the bed, he left a FedEx Overnight Letter envelope with a neatly typed document inside.

"The Last Will and Testament of Auburn R. Calloway" had been notarized on April 5, 1994.

"GLAD TO BE HERE"

APRIL 7

2:00 P.M.

Becky Tucker answered the telephone in the kitchen.

Jim just calling to let her know that he had arrived at Memphis International Airport on schedule, and he had a few extra minutes before he needed to start reviewing plans for the flight to California and back. It was a little peculiar for Jim to call the house from FedEx. Usually when he was at the hub, it was the middle of the night.

But because Jim had altered their plans for the day so suddenly by volunteering to operate Flight 705, Jim wanted to make sure everything was under control at home before he got on the plane. Becky assured him that she would take their three children to soccer practice when they came home from school, and all the ingredients of the beef stew she was preparing for dinner were in pieces on the cutting board. There might even be some left if he was hungry when he returned.

"Hey, since I'm going to be close to San Francisco," Jim added, "I'll try to bring back some of that sourdough bread—the kind they sell down on Fisherman's Wharf."

Jim's voice sounded even more exuberant and full of life than usual. Becky was about to say good-bye, but Jim said something that made her pause.

"You know, I'm really glad I'm here," he told her.

Did he mean that he had had car trouble on the way to the airport and was glad that he made it on time? Becky silently wondered. Was he saying that it was a beautiful day and he was glad to be at the airport? She wasn't sure, and it didn't matter. She was warmed by the pure joy in his voice. Jim made a good living as a pilot, but Becky was convinced that he would fly airplanes for nothing.

"I'm glad that you're glad," she laughed. "Have a good time, and don't worry about us. We'll be fine. See you tonight."

Becky put the stew in a large metal pot, and the smell of the bubbling meat and vegetables soon filled the kitchen. She still had thirty minutes or more before the kids came home, so Becky went to the living room and put some of "her music" on the CD player. The kids didn't enjoy folk songs, but since she was alone in the house, she picked out *Smoky Mountain Hymns,* a collection of instrumental songs she hadn't heard in many months, and cranked up the volume. Accompanied by the soothing sounds of dulcimers, violins, and guitars, Becky sang along with the spiritual melodies that she had always found uplifting and reassuring.

She lay on the carpet and stretched for a few minutes. Then, organized by the music, Becky returned to the kitchen and took on a new job—cleaning out the walk-in pantry. If she hurried, she could finish by the time Morgan walked home from Collierville Middle School. Andy and Rachael usually got home a few minutes later from Crosswind Elementary.

So far, this had been one of those "Mommy days" when everything was going so smoothly that Becky felt nothing could ever upset or bother her. And nothing bad would ever happen to her young family.

"FULL OF ANTICIPATION"

APRIL 7

2:10 P.M.

The three Flight 705 pilots assembled in the FedEx crew room about ninety minutes before their scheduled departure time. Captain David Sanders greeted copilot Jim Tucker by the tall wooden counter where the flight dispatchers gave their calculations to pilots. A manila folder with their flight number written in oversized numerals had been left there for the crew to find.

"Looks like a great day for flying," David remarked.

"Couldn't ask for anything better," the copilot replied cheerfully. "The weather en route looks good, too. I don't think there's a cloud between here and California. And the visibility in San Jose is clear and a million."

David had never met Jim Tucker before. With 2,600 pilots, FedEx had grown far beyond the old "purple flying club" days when most members of the group knew each other as well as their wives, kids, and neighbors. He shook hands with Andy Peterson, the engineer on Flight 705, and Andy quickly excused himself from the crew room.

Most of the engineer's preflight duties had to be performed at the airplane, and he wanted to get an early start. David and Andy had flown together once before at FedEx on a trip to Paris. Captains regarded the younger engineer as a sort of "Radar O'Reilly" of *M*A*S*H* fame. Andy seemed always to be one step ahead of the captains he served, anticipating their requests even before they made them.

David was pleased with the crew that schedulers had assigned him to lead. Even the trip to San Jose seemed fortunate. David was on "reserve" status for the month of April, so if schedulers decided to send him on a grueling ten-day odyssey through Anchorage to Asia and Europe and back, that was their prerogative. An afternoon out-and-back to California was a gift. David knew San Jose well. During his Navy flying career, he had frequently been sent to Moffett Field there.

The captain hoped the rest of the flight would be as routine as its planning. The DC-10 would carry 120,000 pounds of cargo to the Silicon Valley, and the trip was scheduled to take just over four hours. Ground crews in California would unload the plane, then fill it again with computers, electronic equipment, and other high-tech gadgets for the return trip. A strengthening tailwind would carry the plane back to Memphis around midnight. That would give FedEx workers just enough time to unload the cargo, sort the packages, and put them on other planes. All of them would be delivered Friday morning. Each of the pilots knew the drill by heart.

Andy rode a FedEx van out to the massive airplane while the other pilots took care of last-minute preparations in the crew room. The half-mile trip across the FedEx ramp was short but treacherous. FedEx workers drove compact tugs pulling long trains of shipping containers, and the tug drivers were under intense time pressure. The tugs were supposed to follow white lines painted onto the airport tarmac, but in their haste they sometimes ran stop signs, and near-misses and accidents were common. Andy's van deferred to the tugs as it cautiously made its way to the DC-10—number 306. The plane's wide cargo doors were still open, and a yellow truck was pumping fuel into the tanks in the left wing.

Andy's first task was the "walk-around," a methodical preflight task of visually inspecting the outside of the aircraft. On a mild day like this, it was an enjoyable job. Andy had done his share of walk-arounds on windy, subfreezing nights in Chicago, sweltering after-noons in Dallas, and snowy mornings in Anchorage. Today, he felt the sun on his face and the breeze on his bare arms.

Andy, who was now thirty-nine years old, had been fascinated with flying as long as he could remember. He grew up watching cropdusters spray cotton fields and dodge trees and power lines at his parents' farm in central Mississippi. A cropduster gave Andy and his twin sister, Sandy, their first airplane rides when they were seven years old.

Andy had been a star halfback on his high school football team, and he retained a compact, powerful build. He had decided when he was a junior in high school to seek a career in aviation. Poor vision might have kept him grounded, but contact lenses corrected his sight to 20/20, good enough to become an airline pilot. He washed and refueled airplanes during high school to pay for flying lessons, then attended Northeast Louisiana University in Monroe, where he quickly advanced through instrument and multiengine ratings.

Shortly after Andy was hired at FedEx and moved to Memphis, however, the company bought Flying Tigers and absorbed all 940 of its pilots. When the two companies merged their pilot seniority lists, Andy was pushed to the very bottom. Of all the pilots at FedEx, he was fourth from the end of the DC-10 flight engineer seniority list. But Andy didn't complain.

This was the job he had always wanted. When he gazed up at the massive jet that was about to carry him to the West Coast and back, the sense of wonder he had felt watching planes as a boy re-turned. He checked the tires, twelve of them, for proper inflation and signs of unusual wear. He looked for hydraulic leaks and in-spected the control surfaces for cracks. It was all quite routine and all quite wonderful.

This particular DC-10 was nine years old. Unlike many cargo planes that came to FedEx second- or thirdhand, this DC-10 model F for "freighter" had been purchased brand-new from the manufac-turer. It had been a cargo plane since the day it rolled off the

McDonnell Douglas assembly line in Long Beach, California. FedEx DC-10 number 306 arrived in Memphis on January 24, 1985—the first of nine new company airplanes. In an industry where cargo planes were expected to last more than thirty years, it was still a young machine.

Andy lingered outside for a moment, breathing in the familiar airport fragrance he found so full of anticipation: fresh spring air mixed with the kerosene scent of jet fuel.

This DC-10 carried the name JOHN PETER JR. in purple script beneath the cockpit. FedEx named all its airplanes for the sons and daughters of company employees. The practice was so popular that each year FedEx held a lottery, and the winners got to have one of the planes carry their child's name. Each kid also received a certificate on FedEx stationery showing "their" airplane, its serial number, and some facts about how much cargo it carried and how fast, how far, and how high it flew.

Andy bounded up the three flights of metal stairs that ended at the plane's passenger door and stepped inside. He was surprised to find Auburn Calloway waiting in the airplane. The printed manifest Andy had picked up in the crew room didn't list any jump-seat passengers.

Calloway was sitting in one of two rear-facing jump seats in the galley area between the cockpit and the cargo bay. He was in uniform and wore his company ID badge on his short-sleeved blue shirt. Calloway was about three inches taller than Andy, stockier, and heavier by about twenty-five pounds. Calloway had the current issue of *Business Week* magazine on the seat next to him, along with a book and a yellow legal pad.

"I just checked in with the jump-seat reservationist," Calloway said when he noticed the replacement flight engineer looking at the printed manifest. "It may take a few minutes for the paperwork to catch up."

Andy didn't know Calloway but found it a little strange that he had boarded the aircraft before the crew. Jump-seat passengers, even if they are off-duty pilots, typically board the plane after the crew. It's a small thing, a common courtesy.

But Andy was too busy to take offense. He wanted to run the preliminary aircraft systems checks from the cockpit before the captain and copilot arrived. One of the items on the engineer's checklist reminded Andy to ensure that all the circuit breakers above the instrument panel were in their proper positions. He reached up with his left hand and moved it over the breakers.

Strangely, the breaker that controlled the cockpit voice recorder had been disconnected. Without this breaker, the audiotape inside the plane's "black box" would be shut off. In case of an accident, there would be no record of what took place in the cockpit. Andy pushed the circuit breaker with his index finger and it snapped back into position.

Maybe it had vibrated loose, Andy thought. Maybe a surge in electrical current tripped the breaker in flight. Sometimes technicians pulled breakers during ground inspections, and maybe they forgot to put it back in place. He didn't worry about it. That was the reason for double-checking the electrical connections in the first place.

Andy's next task was to check the cargo compartment, the cavernous bay in the fuselage behind the cockpit. If the cargo was improperly loaded, it could alter the plane's center of gravity and make it unstable. Also, FedEx sometimes carried containers of radioactive material and hazardous chemicals. Andy made sure the dangerous substances were secure and all the required paperwork was in place.

A nylon cargo net and a green vinyl smoke wall separated the cargo compartment from the forward section of the airplane. Andy unzipped a section of the smoke wall and began to walk into the cargo bay. He almost tripped over a black guitar case when he stepped through.

"You want me to move that?" Calloway asked, pointing to the case.

"No, no, that's a good place to leave it," Andy replied.

"Yeah, that's where I usually stow my gear," Calloway said. "Never had a problem yet."

The galley area behind the cockpit measured eighteen feet nine inches wide from one side of the plane to the other. It was about six feet in depth, and a hard rubber mat covered the metal floor. Andy checked to make sure the leather flight bag that stayed with the airplane was properly bolted to the center of the floor. The suitcase contained up-to-date aeronautical charts for every airport in the world. Company rules dictate that when planes leave Memphis, they have to be ready to go on unscheduled trips virtually anywhere on the planet.

Andy left the airplane briefly to make sure the exterior strobe and position lights were working properly. Then he climbed the stairs again and walked forward, past the galley and the airline-style lavatory, through a narrow passageway and into the cockpit. Some pilots would be huffing and puffing after the exertion of trotting up and down the metal staircase. But Andy found the activity invigorating.

Captain David Sanders and copilot Jim Tucker were boarding the airplane now, and they met passenger Calloway inside. David introduced himself while Jim went straight to the cockpit. The van had taken longer than expected to cross the tarmac, and time pressure on the crew was beginning to build.

"You don't mind if I ride with you today, do you?" Calloway asked the captain.

"Not at all," David said as he shook the passenger's hand. "Everything looks good for our trip today. We don't anticipate any problems. The weather looks like it's going to give us clear sailing the whole way."

"Good deal," Calloway nodded submissively. "I'm going to try and get some sleep back here. The smoother the ride, the better."

"Make yourself comfortable," David said before he turned and entered the cockpit.

Andy was seated at the metal flight engineer table in the cockpit.

He glanced at the electrical panel above the instrument panel and, strangely, the circuit breaker that controlled the cockpit voice recorder was out of place again. That was really weird.

The circuit breaker was a simple five-dollar item, but it was critically important. Without it, the microphones in the cockpit wouldn't pick up a sound. There would be no audio record of the flight. Andy made a note to check the circuit breaker at the end of the trip. If it was faulty, he would make sure to get it replaced.

PART TWO

''AIRCRAFT WITH EMERGENCY''

▼

▼

▼

APRIL 7

3:02 P.M.

Eight minutes before their scheduled departure time, the Flight 705 crew called the FedEx control tower that monitored aircraft ground movements on the ramp.

Unlike bustling night operations when scores of FedEx jets came and went, daytime flights were relatively uncomplicated. The DC-10 would taxi to nearby Runway 27 for departure and start heading toward California the moment it began its takeoff roll.

Despite the apparent simplicity, however, there was a sudden rash of foul-ups. First, the pilots discovered that some papers that were supposed to be in the cockpit had inadvertently been left in the crew room. The pilots called FedEx dispatchers, and a company van rushed out to the airplane to deliver the documents. Then, when the pilots called the airport ground controller for taxi instructions, they got a baffling series of directions.

Copilot Jim Tucker examined a diagram of Memphis International Airport and still couldn't figure out the directions the crew had been given. They were told to proceed via taxiway Victor to a holding point called Victor One, which was located next to a turnoff called One Victor. Adding to their bewilderment, the taxiways had recently been renumbered, so the old airport diagram they were looking at was virtually useless. The pilots could see where they wanted to go, however. The runway they were supposed to use was just a few hundred yards away. And they could plainly see that their path to the runway was clear.

All of this took four minutes to resolve, so Flight 705 wouldn't get an early start after all. The crew took the delay in stride, however, and the pilots laughed about the Keystone Kops confusion.

"Are they trying to tell us we can't get there from here?" Tucker asked, chuckling.

"A total goat rope," Captain David Sanders replied, using the old Navy term to describe the snafu. Then, as the plane neared the runway, the pilots got another call from FedEx flight dispatchers. They wanted to know the aircraft number for Flight 705.

"I can't believe it," Sanders said. "What airplane is this?"

"It's number three-oh-six," Tucker said, spotting the number on the instrument panel.

Sanders relayed the information to the FedEx ramp.

"Do you want to fly this leg of the trip, or would you prefer the return?" Sanders asked Tucker. Airline captains customarily take turns flying trip segments with their copilots.

Tucker was about to tell the captain to fly the first leg of the trip to San Jose, but impulsively he changed his mind. It was such a glorious day, and he was looking forward to getting off the ground so much that he volunteered to fly right away. "You never know when you'll get another chance," Tucker added with a wry smile.

No sooner had the plane arrived at the west-facing runway than air traffic controllers called again to say Flight 705 was cleared for an immediate takeoff. A light wind was blowing across the concrete strip from right to left, but it was unlikely to complicate the departure. Once the airplane started rolling, the pilots would barely notice the breeze.

Since Tucker was going to make the first takeoff, it became Sanders's duty to make the radio calls. "Express seven-oh-five, cleared for takeoff," Sanders acknowledged over the radio while Tucker adjusted the instruments on the panel.

"Clocks if you want 'em," Tucker said as he pressed the button on a stopwatch to measure elapsed time during the trip. "Lights are coming on," he added, flipping the switches that illuminated the external landing lights and strobes. The bright beacons signaled to onlookers that the DC-10 was about to roll.

"We'll get the vertical speed wheel here," Tucker said as he set the flight guidance computer at the center of the console for an initial climb rate of 2,500 feet per minute. Tucker loosened his shoulder straps in order to lean forward and reach across the instrument panel, but he kept the lap belt tight around his waist.

"How's the checklist look?" Sanders asked flight engineer Peterson, who sat at the rear of the cockpit, his seat facing forward for takeoff.

"Once the flight guidance has been set, we'll be complete," Peterson answered.

"All right," Tucker said. "It's set."

"All right," Peterson replied with finality. "Before takeoff checklist is complete."

"Your airplane," Sanders told Tucker as he used the tiller at the left side of the cockpit to align the DC-10 with the runway centerline.

"I have the airplane," Tucker confirmed, rocking the yoke back and forth. "Set standard power, please, before they change their minds."

"Power is set," Sanders said.

"OK." Tucker pushed the three throttle levers forward with his left hand. Once he advanced them to 40 percent power, the on-board computer kicked in, automatically moving them all the way up to the preprogrammed takeoff setting. The steady acceleration pushed the pilots firmly against their seat backs.

"Eighty knots," Sanders called out, letting his copilot know the airspeed indicator was working properly and the heavily laden aircraft was gaining speed at the proper rate. Flight 705 weighed 520,000 pounds, slightly less than its maximum allowable takeoff weight of 565,000 pounds.

"Vee one," Sanders announced when the plane reached the speed at which the pilots could not safely abort the takeoff. "Rotate."

Tucker pulled back on the control yoke. Even though the day outside was crystal clear, Tucker watched the gyroscopic gauge in front of him to make sure the plane's wings were level and its pitch was exactly 15 degrees. Periodically, he glanced outside to confirm the information the instruments were giving him.

"Positive rate," Sanders said, letting the copilot know the plane was indeed climbing at the proper rate and that it was all right to raise the landing gear.

"Gear up, please," Tucker replied.

Sanders lifted a lever at the right center of the instrument panel, and the plane's hydraulic system gave its customary series of creaks and groans as landing gear retracted. Four lights on the instrument panel turned from green to red, indicating the wheels were up and locked.

Flight 705 accelerated smoothly as it climbed into the afternoon sky.

"HIS OWN DESTINY"

APRIL 7

3:12 P.M.

In the galley area behind the cockpit, Auburn Calloway picked up the guitar case he had hidden behind the nylon smoke wall at the entrance to the DC-10's cargo bay.

Calloway had owned a guitar for years, but until this morning, he hadn't figured the instrument's worn case would play any role in his plan. He intended to use a garment bag to smuggle weapons onto the DC-10. The guitar case was a last-minute substitution when he learned the garment bag was unavailable. Calloway worried the guitar case might arouse suspicion from FedEx security guards. He feared he would look as obvious as a mafioso with a violin case. But the guards casually waved Calloway through their security checkpoint. No one else knew the contents of the guitar case as he boarded the plane.

In the galley area of the DC-10, Calloway opened the two silver latches and lifted the lid.

Four brand-new hammers of assorted sizes, a speargun, and a sheathed scuba diver's knife were inside the velvet-lined carrying case. These were the only weapons he needed to accomplish his objective—hijacking a FedEx jet.

Calloway had developed his plan for revenge against FedEx over many months. It began as an abstract question, a puzzle: How can I get back at my boss and make my family rich at the same time? Calloway considered every possibility. And like a good chess player, he anticipated his opponents' reactions.

Traditionally, airline pilots have used an arsenal of weapons to get back at managers when fliers felt they were being treated unfairly. A Boeing 747 captain could burn up a $100,000 set of wheels and brakes with a couple of quick stops. If an airline crew wanted to strand a multimillion-dollar jet in a remote corner of the world, they could always find a "safety-related" maintenance reason to do so.

Countless times in the history of commercial aviation, pilots had proven their resourcefulness at creating costly headaches for managers. By the time airline owners began tabulating the price of increased maintenance, lost revenue, and sudden epidemics that kept crew members unavailable for duty, the wage increases pilots sought usually seemed like bargains. The most successful passive-aggressive pilot job actions had always been waged by hundreds of fliers acting in concert.

There was frequent banter among newly unionized FedEx pilots about how just a few of them could bring the company to its knees any night they wanted. Simply flying "by the book" and approaching the Memphis hub with their landing gear down and flaps extended a few miles out could stack up arriving jets from Nebraska to Rhode Island. If five 727 captains coordinated their actions on any given night, the flying lawn darts behind them would have nowhere to go. Tens of thousands of shipments would arrive late, and angry customers would force managers to relent to pilot demands.

But for Calloway, the timing at FedEx was all wrong. Contract negotiations were just beginning, and they were likely to drag on for months—maybe years. Calloway's impending disciplinary hearing on Friday, April 8, meant he had to act now. He wouldn't have the luxury of safety in numbers. He had to formulate and implement his plan alone.

Calloway's first priority was to force FedEx to make his family financially secure forever. Calloway had tried to save money for Keelah and Burney during five years of flying at the cargo airline. But if managers he believed were racists insisted on ending his career, Calloway would find a way to make them pay.

John Wrynn and his cohorts might succeed in firing him, but Calloway refused to be bound by their rules. In the Navy, flight instructors had accused Calloway of incompetence and tried to boot him out of the jet-training program several times. They blocked his chances for promotion with poor performance reviews. Calloway figured the good-old-boy system got him again when the chief pilots terminated him at Flying Tigers and Gulf Air. This time, however, Calloway was going to strike back. He had to think beyond the disciplinary hearing. He had to look ten or fifteen years ahead to make sure his children could go to elite colleges, marry the right kinds of people, and settle into comfortable professional careers.

Hijacking a FedEx jet was the first step in accomplishing Calloway's objectives.

From the flight engineer's seat behind the pilot and copilot, taking over the aircraft would be a simple proposition. As a karate expert, Calloway figured he might be able to kill or incapacitate the two other pilots in a single, furious assault. And FedEx had inadvertently made his task even simpler. The company didn't require pilots to pass through metal detectors in Memphis before they boarded FedEx planes. So smuggling weapons onto an aircraft would be a no-brainer. The other pilots would never know what hit them.

A zealous head of security at FedEx had tried to institute metal-detector screenings for pilots in the 1980s, but the FedEx chief pilot at the time angrily refused. The chief pilot told everyone that he would personally instruct fliers to disregard the metal detectors. And if security guards wanted to push the issue, the pilots would simply go home. Then the chief pilot and the head of security could go to

Fred Smith's office the next morning and explain why the airplanes didn't fly the previous night.

Pilots, the chief argued, suffered enough indignities. They had to take random drug and alcohol tests, proficiency checks and regular medical exams. Then, some paranoid security boss proposed letting a bunch of rent-a-cops rummage through the pilots' pockets and personal belongings. Didn't fliers deserve any privacy? Finally, FedEx security relented.

Once Calloway commandeered the airplane, he could demand ransom for the DC-10 and its crew. He could land somewhere and insist the jet be refueled. A full tank of jet fuel would allow him to take the plane across an ocean, to another continent. He could seek political asylum in the country of his choosing.

But the more complex his plan became, Calloway knew, the more limited its chance for success. Ransom, refueling, political asylum created too many variables. The final outcome would depend on cooperation from too many people. Police could shoot out the DC-10's tires when it landed. What would Calloway do then? Maybe no other country would allow him to land or give him permanent refuge. If Calloway failed, he would be seen as a common extortionist, a terrorist. He wouldn't want his children to have to live with that stigma.

The most meaningful thing that Calloway could give Keelah and Burney was his life. He wouldn't always be there for them. He couldn't be. The urgent reality of his family's financial situation called for Calloway to sacrifice now. And offering anything less than his life would seem cowardly, selfish.

The only thing he hadn't provided for his son and daughter was economic security—and that was about to change. If Calloway died while he was employed at FedEx, his heirs would receive $1.3 million from a company life insurance policy. If he perished in a work-related accident, the policy would pay double. And that was only the beginning. FedEx would likely provide additional benefits. Maybe Patricia could even sue the company for negligence in his untimely death. She could manage the money for the kids. By the time the children grew into adults, they would be multimillionaires.

From his seat at the flight engineer's panel of a DC-10, Calloway knew he could easily cause the massive plane to crash. The tricky part was making it seem like an accident. As the flight engineer, Calloway could quietly dump all the DC-10's fuel as the plane flew across the country. The other crew members wouldn't notice the fuel streaming away until it was too late to save the plane.

That solution was flawed, though. The other pilots would surely declare an emergency on the radio when the engines stopped running. And if the plane was at high altitude, air traffic controllers might be able to guide it to a safe landing. There would be many radio transmissions, and all of them would be recorded by audio equipment in the cockpit and on the ground. Even if the pilots died in the crash, investigators would find the engines were stopped and the fuel tanks empty. It wouldn't work.

Calloway could reach up after takeoff, grab the three fire handles on the ceiling, and shut down the DC-10's three engines simultaneously. There would be no way for the plane to recover. It would crash in a fiery heap a few miles from the airport. But radio transmissions were a problem there, too. Even if only a few seconds passed from the time the engines were shut down until impact, that was too much time. The other pilots would see what had happened, they might broadcast the information over the radio, and the wreckage would confirm foul play. Calloway had to be bolder, more creative.

Calloway had qualified as an expert marksman with handguns while he was in the Navy. It was a standard part of the training at Aviation Officer Candidate School in Pensacola. Sneaking a gun onto the plane would be easy. Bullets created their own unique problems, though. Crash investigators and forensic experts would certainly be able to identify bullet holes in the plane's aluminum skin and gunshot wounds in the bodies they found in the wreckage. That was clearly unacceptable.

Calloway could smuggle explosives aboard FedEx planes. Like

bullets, however, bombs left too many clues behind. Crash investigators combing through the debris of the Pan Am 747 that was blown out of the sky over Lockerbie, Scotland, were able to pinpoint the location of the bomb, the radio that concealed it, the store where it was purchased, and the Libyans who planted it. Calloway couldn't leave such telltale clues.

He would commandeer a DC-10 in flight without any high-tech weapons or explosives. The captain and copilot sat with their backs to him virtually the entire time the plane was airborne. Calloway could dispatch them with a blunt instrument. A single crushing blow would incapacitate each of them almost immediately. And the fractured skulls and head injuries that would result were consistent with injuries likely to be sustained in an airline crash.

Each U.S. airline cockpit contains a "crash ax"—a steel hatchet designed to rip through metal and break thick Plexiglas in case the crew has to tear its way out of a burning cockpit. The ax could be a devastating weapon. But the crash ax was located in a thin and sometimes cluttered closet behind the captain's seat. Surprise had to be a central part of Calloway's strategy, and if he had to fumble for the crash ax, or if it had been inadvertently left off the plane, his attack might fail. Calloway decided to use hammers instead.

He could purchase hammers at any hardware store, and the wounds they inflicted would be as debilitating as gunshots. Best of all, if security guards asked him why he was bringing hammers on board an airplane, he could tell them carpentry was one of his hobbies. There's no law against bringing simple hand tools on an airplane, is there?

Even if crash investigators found the hammers, they wouldn't be able to prove they played a role in the catastrophe. The more Calloway thought about it, the more fantastic yet attainable his low-tech plan seemed.

A FedEx jet would crash. The pilots would perish in the conflagration. Meanwhile, FedEx would have to explain why a multimillion-dollar jet and its valuable cargo hit the ground for no apparent reason. John Wrynn and a few other managers might have their suspicions. They would believe that Calloway was involved. But they would never be able to prove it.

When Calloway saw his schedule for early April, he couldn't believe his good fortune. He would fly all week with a pair of ideal victims. Kathy Morton, a copilot, was probably as tough pound-for-pound as anyone at FedEx, but she weighed only 120 pounds. Richard Boyle, the captain, was a combat veteran, but without the F-4 Phantom jet he had flown in Vietnam, he was a small, middle-aged man who had spent thousands of sedentary hours in the overstuffed captain's seat of wide-body jets.

When the original crew was bumped from Flight 705, Calloway faced new obstacles—but not insurmountable ones. Instead of a small captain and a female copilot, Calloway would have to overcome three men: Sanders, Tucker, and Peterson.

Peterson, the flight engineer sitting at a table behind the pilot and copilot, would have to be the focus of the initial attack. Calloway had to take him out quickly and incapacitate the other pilots before they got out of their seats. If one or two of the crew were able to unbuckle their seat-belt harnesses and move around the cockpit, Calloway's task would become far more difficult, messy, and time-consuming.

But the speargun would solve that problem. If any of the men stood up, Calloway would point the fearsome weapon at them and order them to sit down. Airline crews are trained to cooperate with hijackers. Surely the pilots would do what Calloway told them.

Another potential barrier was the cockpit door itself. Now that he wasn't a member of the crew, Calloway occupied a jump seat in the galley area behind the cockpit. His weapons were back there, too. He had to walk rapidly through the narrow corridor, past the door, and into the cockpit to preserve his element of surprise. It was a short distance, but he had to cover it fast.

The cabin doors leading to FedEx cockpits are always open during takeoff and landing. The Federal Aviation Administration requires it. But once airborne, crew members sometimes close the doors to diminish noise in the cockpit. If the door was closed, Calloway knew that it still wasn't much of a barrier. All FedEx crew members are aware that a key hangs in each plane within easy reach above the lavatory. And the key itself is insignificant because, even if the cockpit door is locked, a sharp pull from the outside will jar it open.

Passenger airline crews have made it their policy to leave the cockpit doors closed since 1987. That year, a disgruntled former ground employee smuggled a gun into the passenger cabin of a Pacific Southwest Airlines jet. Once the plane was airborne, he shot his former manager as well as the two pilots. The former employee and forty-two others perished in the ensuing crash. But Calloway's plan had the potential to be far more destructive.

Once he accepted the prospect that his life was over, Calloway's willingness to sacrifice himself opened up tremendous possibilities. Yes, it was true that he couldn't run away from his problems at FedEx. But if he hijacked an airplane, it was equally true that FedEx couldn't run away from him. A fully loaded DC-10 with twenty thousand gallons of fuel on board would be an awesome weapon. Calloway could plunge it into the FedEx package-sorting hub at Memphis International Airport and instantly turn the sprawling complex into an inferno. He had flown hundreds of simulated bombing missions in Navy jets. By coming in fast and low, on about a 3-degree trajectory, he could knock out the entire FedEx facility. The blast would destroy the company's computerized labyrinth of conveyor belts and irreplaceable components of its global telecommunications system. The impact would wreck scores of millions of dollars in computer equipment and priceless data.

Dozens of jet aircraft parked on the FedEx ramp would be reduced to aluminum shrapnel. The blast would ignite massive underground jet-fuel storage tanks, which probably would burn for days. FedEx executives would get the message that a catastrophe had happened when the explosion blew out windows in their three-story headquarters less than five miles away. FedEx could never recover from such a blow.

In addition to the psychological shock, there would be insurmountable logistical problems. FedEx satellite operations in Los Angeles, Oakland, Indianapolis, Newark, and Anchorage had grown in recent years. Yet there was no way the regional hubs would be able to accommodate the sudden surge in package traffic they would experience if the Memphis facility went up in flames. Replacing the ruined infrastructure in Memphis would take years—if the company could ever do it.

Fred Smith would be on the phone to rival chief executives at UPS and Airborne Express begging them to take care of FedEx customers. Even if they wanted to help, Smith's competitors didn't have enough airplanes and they didn't have enough manpower, no matter how much FedEx was willing to pay. And what about the prized FedEx name? In an instant, the logo recognized throughout the world for efficiency and teamwork would become synonymous with an unexplained disaster, massive loss of life, and unprecedented destruction.

Calloway tried to imagine the confusion and panic in the FedEx Command and Control Center when flight dispatchers got a call from air traffic controllers wondering why a FedEx DC-10 seemed to be returning to Memphis without talking to them on the radio.

"Hey, what's up with seven-oh-five?" they would surely ask. "Why isn't he following his flight plan? Why isn't he talking to us? Where's he going?"

If FedEx managers were really smart, they'd figure out who was on the plane and what was happening, and they would evacuate the hub. On a midweek afternoon when the daytime sort was complete, about four hundred FedEx ground workers or "hubites" would be there—far fewer than at night when five thousand employees showed up for work.

Many hub workers were college students with part-time jobs. Most of them were African Americans. Maybe managers would clear the place out in time. But if they didn't, Calloway concluded, that was their fault, too.

"Do you know the difference between involvement and commitment?" one of Calloway's karate instructors used to ask rhetorically. "It's like a bacon and eggs breakfast: The chicken is involved. But the pig, he's committed."

Now Calloway was committed. The moment the wheels of Flight 705 left the ground, there was no turning back.

The final new hurdle to Calloway's modified plan was the cockpit voice recorder. There was no way for him to know in the galley area whether the replacement flight engineer had reconnected the circuit breaker before takeoff. But even if the tape recorder inside the CVR was working properly, it created only a temporary complication. The CVR audiotape is a thirty-minute loop that constantly records over itself.

Once Calloway wrested control of the plane from the three crew members, he could check the circuit breaker himself. If it had been reset before the flight, all Calloway needed to do was fly around without saying anything. If he did that for half an hour, all that anyone listening to the tape would ever hear was the humming, throbbing sound of three huge jet engines.

In the galley of the DC-10, Calloway chose his weapon: a twenty-ounce Stanley framing hammer with a long yellow neck. His thick right hand closed tightly around the gray rubber grip. He closed the lid of the guitar case, stood up, and took several deep, cleansing breaths.

In Calloway's mind, he was already dead. The only unfinished business was bringing down the FedEx aircraft and thereby meeting his family's financial needs forever. He stepped forward, into the narrow corridor that led to the cockpit. The door to the airplane's nerve center was wide open, and Calloway moved toward it.

Calloway's belongings were piled on the rear-facing jump seat next to the passenger door. There was a stack of magazines, a manila folder full of letters, and a book—*The Seven Habits of Highly Effective People* by Stephen R. Covey.

The best-selling 318-page paperback was one of Calloway's favorites, and he had recommended it to many friends and acquaintances. The author urges readers to examine "new paradigms"—new patterns of thinking. Peak performers, he says, have the ability to visualize the methods and outcomes they use to succeed. Effective leaders see and affirm their goals and techniques, which flow from a wellspring of well-ordered principles.

In one of the book's early chapters, the author quotes Max Frankl, a Holocaust survivor, who said individuals "detect" rather than "invent" their missions in life. Calloway underlined the paragraph with Frankl's words:

"Everyone has his own specific vocation or mission in life. Therein he cannot be replaced, nor can his life be repeated. Thus, everyone's task is as unique as is his specific opportunity to implement it."

"A MAGNIFICENT VIEW"

APRIL 7

3:15 P.M.

Even with a full load of cargo and fuel, FedEx Flight 705 climbed at the fairly rapid rate of 2,500 feet per minute. Copilot Jim Tucker turned slightly right to the assigned compass heading of 275 degrees, almost straight west, as the DC-10 passed over the Mississippi River. Downtown Memphis, with its waterfront buildings and bridges, passed by the right wing.

The pilots could see the The Pyramid with the afternoon sun glinting off its stainless-steel exterior. The distinctive 320-foot-tall arena where the University of Memphis basketball team played its home games was a handy navigational beacon for pilots. On hazy summer days, bright reflections from the metal building were visible fifty miles away or more, and pilots flying to Memphis International Airport could steer toward it, knowing they were precisely on course.

The crew of Flight 705 had a particularly good airplane for sight-seeing. While the cockpits of most other airliners had small panes of Plexiglas, their DC-10 was fitted with large picture windows that provided panoramic vistas, especially on clear days like this. Tucker glanced at the instrument panel but looked up frequently to take in the magnificent view as the aircraft crossed into Arkansas.

There had been a few turbulent bumps from columns of warm air rising over Memphis. As the plane climbed, however, the air became still and placid. The outside temperature dropped about 3 degrees for each 1,000 feet the airplane rose. By the time they reached their cruising altitude of 31,000 feet, the external temperature would be 20 degrees below zero.

"Right turn to two-eight-zero degrees; track the two-seventy-five-degree radial outbound," Captain David Sanders said, repeating instructions from air traffic controllers.

During the past thirty years, the FAA had built throughout the United States a vast network of radio navigation beacons resembling white dishes about twenty feet in diameter. The beacons were about fifty miles apart, and pilots used cockpit instruments to guide them from one navigational aid to the next. Flight 705 would track a westerly course of 275 degrees from the Memphis beacon.

"Check," Tucker acknowledged, beginning a shallow right turn.

"Two-seventy-five radial outbound," Sanders confirmed on the radio. "Express seven-oh-five."

Controllers instructed the DC-10 crew to climb from their current altitude of 2,500 feet to 6,000 feet.

"Climb power," Tucker said, as Sanders pushed the three throttle levers forward, then confirmed the instructions from air traffic controllers.

"Express seven-oh-five, two thousand five for six thousand. Express seven-oh-five."

So far, so good.

"You want to use CWS?" Sanders asked, referring to the "control wheel steering" mechanism that allows DC-10 pilots to fly the plane using a sensitive sort of power steering. Normally, the DC-10 control yoke is heavy and requires two hands to manipulate. But with CWS, the control movements become smaller, and almost effortless.

"Well, we appear to be safely airborne. Why not?" Tucker answered. "Set the vertical speed to a thousand feet per minute, please, or thereabouts."

Sanders turned a dial on the flight management system, and the gyroscopic instruments in front of Tucker showed him the precise path the plane should follow. If they wanted to, the pilots could fly all the way to California just by turning the knobs on the flight management system and following the sensitive instruments. With the power-steering mechanism engaged, Tucker guided the massive jet with only one hand on the control yoke.

As he flew the airplane, Tucker went back to thinking about all the confusion they had left on the ground in Memphis. He still couldn't believe it.

"What a goat rope back there. Jeez!"

The others chuckled. Then he turned back to the business of flying the jet. The airplane was high enough and fast enough for them to retract the flaps, and raising the flaps would increase the plane's speed even more.

"Retract the flaps, and let's get out of here," Tucker said. He turned his head to the left and addressed Peterson. "After-takeoff checklist?" he asked, wanting to know if the crew had complied with all their proper procedures.

"We're down to the line on the after-takeoff," the flight engineer replied, meaning the crew had completed all the items on the list.

"All right, OK," Sanders said.

Tucker glanced at the navigation instrument that tracked the radio signal in Memphis and noticed the DC-10 was slightly south of its intended path. "I'll come over and get that radial," he said, referring to the correct course over the ground.

As the plane continued west, air traffic controllers allowed the jet to keep climbing. Jet engines burn less fuel and planes travel faster in the thin air at high altitudes than in the more dense air near the ground. On the trip to California, the plane would climb to 31,000 feet, far shy of its service ceiling of 42,000 feet.

"Express seven-oh-five is at ten three for sixteen thousand," Sanders reported on the radio, meaning the plane was at 10,300 feet climbing to 16,000, where it would wait for clearance to an even higher altitude.

Then, the comedy of errors that surrounded them on the ground began to take place in the air. Controllers told Sanders to switch to another radio frequency for more instructions. When he made the change, however, no one answered on the new frequency.

"They're out to lunch," the captain muttered before switching back to the original radio frequency. Then the DC-10 crew received contradictory instructions about which flight path the controllers wanted them to follow.

"Gee whiz," Tucker said, slightly exasperated. Then the miscues were resolved and Flight 705 received instructions to resume climbing all the way up to 23,000 feet.

"Flight level two three zero for Express seven-oh-five," Sanders confirmed on the radio as he dialed the new information into the plane's flight management computer. "Leaving one six thousand, direct Razorback. Express seven-oh-five."

Tucker planned to fly the airplane by hand until it reached its cruising altitude. He pulled gently back on the yoke with his right thumb and index finger.

"Here we go," Tucker said as the DC-10 continued its steady ascent.

"THE STRANGEST SOUNDS"

APRIL 7

3:28 P.M.

"That's Crowley's Ridge," said FedEx DC-10 captain David Sanders, craning his neck to see over the nose of the climbing aircraft.

Flight 705 was about thirty-five miles west of Memphis, climbing through 18,000 feet. All three crew members were sightseers now, taking in the spectacular scene. From this height, they could see the patchwork of green farm fields and trees that spread out like a quilt below them. The landscape changed abruptly at Crowley's Ridge, however, a few miles straight ahead.

Arkansans pronounced it "CROW-lee's" ridge, with the accent on the first syllable.

"That's it right there," said Sanders, pointing left to right. "See those trees? That's Crowley's Ridge. Sometimes you'll see gliders riding the updrafts along the length of it. The ridge is a natural fault line."

"Oh, is this the New Madrid fault?" copilot Jim Tucker asked. The New Madrid fault had been in the news two years before when author Iben Browning claimed there was an increased chance that a catastrophic earthquake was about to rock the area along the Mississippi River from Memphis to Cairo, Illinois. In the early 1800s, an earthquake struck the region so powerfully that it caused the Mississippi River to temporarily reverse its course.

"Well, it's part of it, but it's much higher in elevation," the captain said, sitting back in his sheepskin-covered padded chair. "And the climate is different. If you drive in Arkansas, you drive right over it."

"I wondered about that," Tucker said amiably, remembering a trip to the area he had made in his two-seat Luscombe a year ago. "I went to Wynne, a small town in this general area, and the geography was flat on the east side. But on the west side of this ridge, it changed quite noticeably."

"Altimeters," said Andy Peterson, breaking into the conversation with an item from the checklist. Aircraft altimeters are adjusted for barometric pressure that changes from one weather system to another. Above 18,000 feet, however, all aircraft use a standard barometric pressure setting of 29.92.

"Nines and twos here," Tucker said, making the adjustment on the altimeter in front of him while Sanders did the same.

"OK," Peterson said, closing the notebook that contained the checklists. "After-takeoff checklist is complete."

The two pilots in the front of the cockpit resumed their conversation. Peterson went back to making handwritten entries in the plane's flight crew log at the flight engineer's table behind them. Peterson called FedEx dispatchers on the shortwave radio to let them know the plane's exact departure time and the estimated time en route to San Jose.

Flight 705 reached 19,000 feet and continued its steady ascent.

"Dave, do you live in Arkansas or . . ."

"Naw. I live in Fisherville."

"Fisherville! Great spot . . ." Tucker said. He was about to add that he lived nearby in Collierville, but Tucker's thoughts were broken by a loud thud and a metallic banging sound behind him. It was as though a melon had fallen from a tall shelf onto a piece of sheet metal. Jet airplanes could make the strangest sounds sometimes. The copilot wasn't concerned, though. He had heard jet engines disintegrate, cabins lose pressure, and electrical systems fail during his years in aviation. So he knew the bizarre noise wasn't a mechanical failure.

Tucker was turning around to ask Peterson if he could identify the peculiar sound when a blinding, ear-splitting jolt shocked him from the top of his head to the base of his spine. Tucker's head jerked forward involuntarily. His hands reflexively lifted up, but not in time to cushion the impact of his face slamming against the instrument panel.

"God!" Tucker groaned, the pain unbearable. His eyes wouldn't focus. His limbs were rubbery. He felt blood streaming down his face and into his eyes. "Oh, shit."

Sanders turned toward the copilot when he heard the loud thumping noise. There was Tucker, his head bowed and a stream of blood turning his short-sleeved blue shirt to wet crimson. Out of the corner of his eye he could see Andy Peterson slumped against the engineer's table behind them, blood spouting from his head like a strawberry fountain.

"God Almighty!" Sanders shouted in horror as he looked straight into the determined brown eyes of Auburn Calloway. The passenger seemed focused and dispassionate. He was standing behind the captain and copilot and holding something in his right hand. He moved rapidly toward Sanders, who was still strapped into his chair.

Sanders raised his hands defensively just in time to partially deflect a blow from the claw hammer that whizzed by his face. The stunned captain reached down to unbuckle his seat belt and shoulder harness, then ducked as another hammer blow crashed into the right side of his head, cutting him and spraying the cockpit with more blood. Calloway swung again, but the hammer clipped the metal fire handle on the cockpit ceiling, deflecting the blow.

"What the fuck are you doing?" Tucker shouted at the attacker. The impact of the first hammer blow had shattered the left side of Tucker's skull. He knew he had to resist, but how? He couldn't move from his seat. Tucker watched in stunned disbelief as the attacker took one swing after another at Sanders, who was still a captive of his seat-belt harness. Each time, Sanders managed to duck or raise his hands at the last instant.

Another blow nearly severed Sanders's right ear and sent the captain's reading glasses flying off to the side of the cockpit. Then, without saying a word, Calloway retreated from the cockpit as suddenly as he had appeared.

Tucker tried to assess the situation. Even though Calloway hadn't said anything, it was clear to Tucker that the off-duty flight engineer was intent on taking over the airplane. Calloway could have caused the plane to crash any number of ways, but he hadn't done that. He wanted to seize control of the airplane, and Tucker knew implicitly that the crew would die if they let him have it.

The crew had no weapons with which to fight back. No one on the ground could help them.

Memphis was the only city in the area with a runway long enough to accommodate a DC-10. But the crew had to disarm the attacker before they tried to land there or anywhere else.

The pilots had to take the initiative somehow.

"Get him, get him, get him!" Tucker yelled to Peterson, urging the flight engineer to pursue Calloway as he left the cockpit. But the engineer remained motionless in his seat.

Peterson hadn't noticed anything unusual about the passenger's entry into the cockpit until he felt the stupefying impact of one colossal hammer blow, then another. The flight engineer's head had been fractured in several places. The temporal artery under his scalp was severed, and blood was gushing out at an astonishing rate. Without treatment, Peterson would bleed to death in less than one hour.

"He's going to kill us!" Sanders shouted, dazed and horrified.

"Get up and get him!" Tucker again commanded Peterson.

The copilot didn't realize that the strange sounds he had heard a few moments ago meant that Peterson's skull was being crushed and smashed against the sharp metal corner of the flight engineer's table.

"I can't," Peterson groaned, struggling to remain conscious. "God!"

"TAKE THE OFFENSIVE OR PERISH"

APRIL 7

3:30 P.M.

Auburn Calloway stormed back into the DC-10 cockpit, a hammer in his right hand and a loaded scuba diver's speargun in his left.

He had been gone less than ten seconds, but in that time his demeanor had changed. During the initial stages of the assault, Calloway had been deliberate and methodical. Now his eyes were wide, fearful—on the verge of panic. He had hit the pilots with murderous strength and precision. The flight engineer had been pounded with two unobstructed blows, the copilot was struck once, and the captain several times. Calloway expected them to be unconscious, if not dead, from the beatings. But instead, they were alert, shouting, moving, and exhorting each other to fight back.

The speargun was Calloway's trump card. He retrieved it for the purpose of quelling any resistance from the injured pilots. The shaft of metal was nearly three feet long, and a powerful pneumatic air chamber inside the black-metal gun was primed to launch it forward.

The tip of the stainless-steel shaft was barbed and razor sharp.

"Sit down! Sit down!" Calloway yelled at Captain David Sanders, who had disconnected his seat-belt harness and risen from his seat. "This is a real gun, and I'll kill you."

There was a momentary pause as the crew considered the new threat. Should they listen to Calloway's demands? Could they talk to him? Reason with him? No, they decided independently. There was no time left. The crew had to take the offensive or perish.

Andy Peterson's hands were pressed against his bleeding face and head. Between his fingers, he noticed the gleaming point of the spear a few feet away. His field of vision was so narrow that he could not see the nearby attacker. But he could distinguish the outline of the speargun as it moved forward, deeper into the cockpit. Peterson focused on the tip of the spear. Then, all at once, he grabbed it a few inches behind the barb with both hands and allowed himself to slide out of his chair toward the cockpit floor. Peterson held on to the weapon with all the strength he could summon as he redirected the shaft downward.

Copilot Jim Tucker's right side was growing numb, but he knew he couldn't stay passive. If he was going to be killed, he would die fighting. Tucker grabbed the sensitive DC-10 control yoke in front of him with his left hand. Abruptly, he jerked the control column back toward his chest as hard as he could.

The plane was traveling at 372 miles an hour, and the sudden onset of gravitational or G forces slammed the DC-10's occupants down toward the floor at three times their normal weight. Peterson held firm to the speargun, preventing the attacker from aiming the lethal tip at the other pilots.

"Get him, get him, get him!" Tucker yelled to Peterson and Sanders.

This was their chance.

Tucker turned the control yoke all the way to the left and rolled the nearly half-million-pound aircraft. The DC-10 passed 60 degrees of bank—the maximum amount that airliners are normally allowed to fly. He held the yoke against the stops as the plane rolled passed 90 degrees, or perpendicular to the ground. He held it through 120 degrees, and still the plane kept rolling onto its back.

Peterson held on to the speargun and Sanders lunged for the hammer. As the three men grappled for advantage, the wild gravitational forces and extreme nose-high position of the aircraft pushed them rapidly out of the cockpit, through the narrow passageway and into the wide galley area. Tucker's wild maneuvering turned the DC-10 into a huge gravity chamber, a cavernous roller coaster slicing an undulating track through the sky. The three struggling men slammed into the nylon smoke wall, then floated weightless as they fought for control of the weapons.

A computerized voice in the cockpit automatically warned

Tucker the airplane was exceeding its maximum angle of bank, something the designers never intended it to do. But Tucker ignored the warnings. The upside-down plane reached 140 degrees angle of bank, and it was 19,700 feet above the ground.

(Bank angle, bank angle, bank angle . . .)

"I'm gonna kill you!" Calloway shouted. "Hey, hey, I'll kill you!"

(Bank angle, bank angle . . .)

Tucker had allowed the crew to take the offensive. Now he tried to rally them as he flew the plane.

"Get him, get him, get him! Andy! I got the plane!" the copilot shouted, assuring the crew that he could fly the airplane alone while they fought Calloway.

(Bank angle, bank angle . . .)

Tucker stopped the airplane's roll when the wings were nearly level upside down. If he continued rolling, he knew he could eventually right the aircraft. But continuing the roll was too predictable. Calloway could simply wait until the maneuver was over, then resume his attack. The purpose of the extreme maneuvers was to fly erratically and keep the attacker off balance. If Tucker was successful, he thought he might be able to prevent the attacker from getting back on his feet and returning to the cockpit.

As the plane rolled inverted, Tucker considered shoving forward on the control yoke to bring on a sudden spike of negative Gs that would throw the occupants against the ceiling. Tucker was still strapped into his seat-belt harness, so he would remain in his seat.

But the cargo in the back of the plane would shift, too. And if Tucker pushed too hard, he knew that dozens of boxy, metal freight containers, or "cans," in the back of the plane would lift off their tracks and slam into the thin top of the aluminum fuselage. A single can puncturing the cylindrical fuselage would create a rapid and destructive decompression throughout the aircraft. The explosion would break up the DC-10 in flight, and thousands of metal pieces would rain down on the ground almost four miles below.

Tucker pulled on the yoke, and the inverted plane fell into a vertical dive. When he looked straight ahead through the windshield, he saw a patchwork of distant green and brown farm fields. The plane was gaining speed at an incredible rate, and Tucker faced a dilemma: If he hauled back on the control yoke to pull out of the dive, the sudden increase in G forces would rip the wings off the airplane. But if he tried to gently coax the plane out of its dive, the plane would build up so much speed that it would become uncontrollable. He had to find the fine line between overstressing the DC-10 and overspeeding it.

The yoke began shaking automatically and a series of loud clicks warned Tucker the plane was accelerating past its "never exceed" speed. At its current altitude, the plane's maximum allowable speed was 378 miles an hour. But Flight 705 was moving almost 500 miles an hour—and still it continued to accelerate. If the DC-10 continued gaining speed, sonic shock waves on the wings and tail would break the plane into pieces as it approached the speed of sound. Even if it held together, it would become completely unresponsive as an aerodynamic phenomenon known as Mach tuck pushed the nose down even more.

G forces pinned the three struggling men to the galley floor at three times their normal weight. They could feel the massive plane rumble and shake as the airspeed surged far beyond the maximum permissible level. But in the windowless galley area, they had no idea if the DC-10 was upside down or right side up. They knew only that invisible forces were shoving them down against the hard, matted floor.

Tucker tried to use his right thumb to pull the electronic trim mechanism on the yoke downward. The power steering system was still on, but the yoke was abnormally heavy and difficult to manipulate. The trim button could lighten the load and help accomplish the same purpose as pulling back on the yoke. But Tucker's right thumb was paralyzed, numb and unresponsive.

Then Tucker noticed to his horror that the three throttle levers were still in their automatic climb setting. As the nose of the aircraft fell toward Earth and the plane accelerated through 510 miles an hour, the three jet engines made matters worse by continuously churning out maximum thrust. Somehow, he had to reduce the throttle setting. But he could reach the throttles with his left hand only—his good hand—and he needed to keep pulling on the control yoke.

Tucker decided he had to let go of the control column momentarily. He reached over to the center console with his left hand and clicked the throttles into the manual setting. Then he yanked all three levers back to idle. His left hand was back on the yoke again two seconds later, and Tucker pulled back on it smoothly. As he was doing this, he could see the green fields in front of him getting closer and closer, bigger and bigger.

The DC-10 was heading straight down at a faster air speed than the instruments on the plane were capable of registering. The plane was diving through the air at 517 miles an hour. Never before had a DC-10 flown this fast.

Tucker kept pulling. There was nothing else he could do. Gradually, almost reluctantly, the massive airplane began to emerge from its plunge. By the time its wings were level, the plane had fallen more than one mile.

"Center, center emergency," Tucker called on the radio while he tossed the plane into another steep turn, still trying to keep the attacker from reentering the cockpit.

(Bank angle, bank angle . . .)

APRIL 7

3:32 P.M.

The breathless male voice came through loud and clear on air traffic controller Kent Fleshman's plastic earphone.

The pilot's urgent, determined tone jarred Fleshman out of the doldrums of what had been a routine, totally uneventful afternoon. He was tutoring a new controller and monitoring planes from Memphis to Little Rock and north as far as Missouri. Despite the large geographic area, there were relatively few aircraft in the radar sector, and since the weather was crystal clear, most of the pilots were flying under visual flight rules that required no radio communication with the Memphis Air Route Traffic Control Center.

"Aircraft with emergency, go ahead," said Fleshman, a twenty-seven-year-old air traffic controller, as he took over from the student. Fleshman waved to get the attention of his nearby supervisor, and he flipped a switch on his console that made the radio communications audible on a speaker as well as his earphone.

Fleshman scrutinized each of the tiny green blips on the radar screen in front of him. Each blip represented an airplane, and all of them were right where they were supposed to be. None of the planes was off heading. None of them was off altitude.

"Aircraft with emergency, say again," Fleshman repeated.

Still no reply. The only unusual sound was the infrequent click of a microphone being keyed and some indistinguishable background noises. Then silence.

"Aircraft with emergency, say again."

Wait. Express 705 was supposed to be heading west and climbing to 23,000 feet. Fleshman had just confirmed those instructions with the cheerful-sounding captain of the FedEx jet. Now Fleshman's radar showed the wide-body jet veering sharply to the north.

"Express seven-oh-five!" the breathless voice came through loud and clear again in the air traffic controller's ears. But this time the pilot's voice was grave and purposeful. "I've been wounded. There has been an attempted takeover on board the airplane. Give me a vector, please, back to Memphis . . . Hurry!"

The news was alarming, but the request was simple. The pilot, Jim Tucker, was asking for a vector, or compass heading, back to Memphis International Airport.

"Express seven-zero-five, fly heading zero-niner-five direct Memphis," Fleshman shot back.

Then, a few seconds of uneasy silence.

Fleshman wrote down the exact time of the emergency radio call and marked the paper strip showing the DC-10's flight plan. About a hundred air traffic controllers were at work in the ground floor of the Memphis center, one of twenty such facilities around the country that monitor and direct airborne planes. The Memphis center coordinated air traffic among hundreds of airports in nine states.

"Alert the airport facility!" Tucker told Fleshman. "Are you still with me?"

"Affirmative, seven-zero-five," Fleshman said reassuringly. "Descend and maintain one zero thousand."

If the plane got below 10,000 feet, a bullet could pierce the aluminum skin of the aircraft without causing an explosive decompression, and the pilots could breathe at that altitude without supplemental oxygen, the controller reasoned. Fleshman was about to ask the pilot if anyone had been shot, but another voice broke through on the radio frequency.

"Navajo one four three seven yankee, over."

Fleshman couldn't believe it, but the pilot of another plane—a twin-engine Piper Navajo—was interrupting. Certainly the pilot could hear there was an emergency in progress on this radio frequency. Don't get distracted, the controller told himself. Just ignore him.

"Navajo, one four three seven yankee, over," the clueless Piper pilot repeated.

Then there was the sound of a microphone being keyed again, and this time the transmit button was being held down. Maybe the FedEx pilot wanted controllers to be able to hear for themselves what was happening aboard the DC-10. Fleshman listened intently to the horrific sounds of men screaming.

The yells weren't fearful, such as might be made by people stuck in a plane they knew was going to crash. These shouts were indescribably violent, like nothing the controller had ever heard.

"OK, one zero thousand," Tucker said, holding the microphone close to his lips again. "Listen, I'm hand-flying the airplane."

There were more shouts and noises, and Fleshman could barely make out Tucker's words through the din.

"Hey, center," the copilot said. "Give me a vector back to Memphis."

Fleshman stared at the solitary blip that showed Flight 705 on his circular radar screen. The digital readout next to it showed the plane was traveling at more than 500 miles an hour—far faster than it was designed to fly at its relatively low altitude and almost twice the normal FAA speed limit of 250 nautical miles an hour below 10,000 feet. The plane was moving at Mach .86—or 86 percent of the speed of sound.

"Fly heading zero-niner-zero direct Memphis," said Fleshman, realizing that even with more than one million dollars of navigational equipment in his plane, the pilot had completely lost his bearings. The airport was exactly east of him, or 90 degrees on the compass. More than anything else that had been said in their brief communication, the pilot's disorientation alarmed Fleshman.

"Zero-niner-zero, roger," the wounded pilot repeated.

The stricken DC-10 now turned to the northeast. And the next radio call proved the pilot was still confused.

"Express seven-oh-five," Tucker said. "Where is Memphis?"

"Fly heading zero-niner-five," Fleshman answered as he watched the plane on his screen. "You are heading eastbound at this time. The airport is forty-three miles at your twelve-thirty–one o'clock."

The DC-10 was pointed almost directly toward Memphis International Airport. The pilot would have to turn slightly right for the shortest course.

"Look, just keep talking to me, OK?" Tucker said.

"Express seven-zero-five, affirmative. If you need an ambulance, stand by and we'll get that for you," Fleshman volunteered.

"Yeah, we'll need an ambulance," Tucker replied. "And we'll need armed intervention as well."

Fleshman's palms were suddenly so moist with perspiration that it was difficult for him to hold his pen. "Armed intervention" meant the situation inside the plane was so dangerous that the pilot wanted commandos to storm the plane or take other drastic measures to keep it on the ground after landing. The term let controllers know that the crisis on the plane was so great that the pilots would rather face bullets than allow the situation to continue.

Fleshman turned to face his supervisor. "Make sure and notify the SWAT team. He's asking for armed intervention."

The supervisor picked up a nearby telephone and called the Memphis Police.

Fleshman turned back to his radar screen. He wanted to get the plane lower as it raced toward Memphis International Airport.

"Express seven-zero-five," Fleshman said. "Descend to five thousand feet."

"Down to five thousand, roger."

APRIL 7

3:38 P.M.

"Let go of it!" Andy Peterson yelled. "Let go of the spear!"

In the cockpit, Jim Tucker heard the shouts. But he had no idea what was happening in the galley area behind the cockpit. Was Auburn Calloway winning the struggle back there? Were the maneuvers helping the other crew members or hurting them? What if the attacker killed Peterson and David Sanders and then came back into the cockpit with those damn weapons? How could Tucker fight back?

In the galley area, Sanders and Peterson fought to disarm their attacker. Peterson charged headlong into Calloway, the former football player's legs driving in short, choppy, powerful steps. Peterson pushed the larger man backward and pinned him against the side of the plane at the passenger door. Then they both lost their balance and slid to the floor.

Peterson's skull had been fractured during the initial moments of the attack, and with each heartbeat, blood gushed from the torn artery on his scalp. A deep half-moon slice was carved above his right eye where his face had collided against the sharp metal corner of the flight engineer's table. But in his desperation, Peterson ignored his injuries and directed his full fury at Calloway.

As the two men grappled on the floor, Peterson held on to the metal shaft of the speargun in Calloway's left hand. Somehow, the long steel shaft had been ejected from the gun. At the same time, Sanders tried to pry the hammer out of Calloway's right hand. But the weapon was coated with warm, slippery blood.

The three men were piled against the locked passenger door on the left side of the aircraft. Calloway's back was against the wall, and Peterson pushed against him, his back to Calloway's chest. Calloway sank his teeth into Peterson's left shoulder, but Peterson refused to relax his grip on the spear.

Sanders held Calloway's right arm, the one with the hammer, but the attacker's moist hand kept slipping loose. Then a sharp crashing sound rang in Sanders's ears as Calloway's hand broke free and smashed him on top of the head with the hammer. For the first time, it occurred to the captain that the crew might lose the struggle. Momentarily dazed, Sanders tried not to black out.

A sudden spike of G forces pushed the hammer in Calloway's right hand to the floor, and Sanders pounced on it. He pulled the hammer free and stood up.

Peterson and Calloway still wrestled for the spear. Peterson had two hands on it, and Calloway held it with his left hand.

"Let go of the spear!" Sanders yelled, grabbing the metal shaft with his left hand.

The captain pulled on the spear as hard as he could, and Calloway and Peterson slid down farther onto their sides, both of them still clinging to the weapon.

"I said let go of the spear!" Sanders bellowed.

When Calloway refused, Sanders stepped over him, raised the hammer, and delivered two punishing, downward blows. The impact dazed the attacker and opened a deep, curved wound on top of his scalp.

"Don't hit me," Calloway pleaded, loosening his grip on the spear. "Don't hit me. I give up."

"AN ATTEMPTED TAKEOVER?"

APRIL 7

3:40 P.M.

Air traffic controller Kent Fleshman pressed another button on his radar console and was automatically connected via a telephone line to Paul Candalino, an air traffic controller in the ground floor of the fourteen-story control tower at Memphis International Airport.

Candalino was coordinating aircraft arrivals from the west when Fleshman called. The urgency in the young man's voice was unmistakable.

"We have an emergency," Fleshman said. "Express seven-zero-five. He's had an attempted takeover on the aircraft, and he is wounded at this time."

For Candalino, forty-four years old and a veteran air traffic controller, a hijacking was uncharted territory. He'd handled his share of tense situations—planes with landing gear that wouldn't come down, failed engines, smoke in the cockpits. But a hijacking?

He cleared his throat.

"He's had an attempted takeover?" Candalino asked incredulously, pronouncing the words slowly and deliberately as he considered the implications. Why in the world would anyone want to hijack a cargo plane in Memphis?

"Affirmative," Fleshman answered, stretching the first syllable ("Ay-firmative"). "He's north of Forrest City about eight miles at this time. He's descending . . ."

Candalino spotted the fast-moving blip on his radar screen and got busy.

"OK, radar contact," he said, letting the young controller know he had identified the target. "Put him on nineteen one [the approach control radio frequency]."

"He's requesting emergency medical assistance. . . ." Fleshman continued.

Candalino, anxious to establish his own dialogue with the crew, cut Fleshman off. "Thanks, radar contact."

Fleshman disconnected the landline to Candalino and called the FedEx plane on the radio. There was no immediate reply. He repeated the call.

"Express seven-zero-five, contact Memphis Approach on [radio frequency] one one niner point one. They know about your emergency. They'll have a lower [altitude] for you and assistance."

Still no answer. Fleshman tried again.

"Express seven-zero-five, contact Memphis Approach on one one niner point one. They're aware of your emergency."

The controllers around Fleshman looked at each other and their radar screens helplessly. Without radio communications, there was nothing they could do for the wounded pilot.

Finally Jim Tucker replied to the repeated radio calls.

"Request a single-frequency approach," Tucker said tersely. The radio shorthand meant the pilot was too busy to switch radio frequencies. He wanted controllers to guide him to the airport using the frequency they were already on. But Fleshman knew the radio transmission tower he was using to talk to the DC-10 was located sixty miles away in Walnut Ridge, Arkansas. As the FedEx jet descended and approached Memphis, Fleshman was concerned that it would move out of range.

"A single-frequency approach, roger, we'll pass that along," Fleshman said, prodding the wounded pilot again to switch frequencies. "One one niner point one."

"Nineteen one," Tucker replied, confirming his intention to change radio stations.

Then sixty seconds passed slowly, and to their dismay, controllers were unable to reach the stricken plane on any frequency. Fleshman and Candalino spoke into the microphones mounted on their headsets but the stricken jet didn't answer. The controllers watched their radar screens helplessly as the speeding DC-10 turned away from the airport and began climbing.

Another minute passed by, and still no word from the injured pilot.

Maybe they're circling and dumping fuel, Fleshman hoped. But he also considered the possibility that the pilot was disoriented again, or that he had succumbed to his injuries, or that the hijackers had taken control of the jet. There was no way to know.

Candalino wasn't completely sure what type of aircraft he was trying to reach. But the generic term "heavy" covered all wide-body jets including DC-10s, MD-11s, and the new Airbus A300s that FedEx had recently acquired

"Seven-zero-five heavy," Candalino called out. "How do you hear?"

Still nothing. He picked up the landline and spoke to Fleshman again.

"Did you shift seven-zero-five heavy?" Candalino asked.

"Affirmative. Nineteen one. He was on a ninety . . ."

"I don't know what's going on now," Candalino said curtly. "He's heading northeast-bound, not talking to me."

"He's been wounded. He sounds like he's in bad shape," Fleshman said. "If he comes back over on my frequency, I'll try and get him directed to the airport."

Candalino was getting frustrated. "Did they subdue the assailants or what?"

"They're not sure," Fleshman said. "I heard some noise in the background, hollering. Sounded like he'd been, he said he'd been injured. He didn't say if he'd been shot. But he said he needed assistance toward the airport."

"OK," Candalino said, exasperated. "If he comes back to you, tell him to expect [to land on] Runway niner and put him on me."

For several more agonizing minutes, the controllers were unable to communicate with the FedEx jet. They watched in consternation as their radar screens showed the DC-10 making a lazy turn to the north, then the west, and finally southwest—away from the airport.

"EXTREME GYRATIONS"

Auburn Calloway eased his grip on the spear but he wouldn't let David Sanders take it away.

The captain now grasped the spear with his left hand and held a twenty-ounce Stanley framing hammer in his right. Sanders had struck Calloway so hard with the hammer that he thought the blows might be fatal. Sanders began to stand up straight, but he was so winded that he could barely do it. The struggle had been exhausting. Then he heard Andy Peterson howl in pain as Calloway clamped down with his teeth on the flight engineer's left arm.

"Help!" Peterson shouted. "The son of a bitch is biting me!"

"Andy!"

Sanders lifted the hammer again and struck Calloway twice more in the head. The impact fractured his skull and left a deep, circular indentation in his forehead. Calloway writhed on the floor. His eyes were half open and seemed not to focus. Blood flowed steadily from a round crater in Calloway's scalp.

Just then, Sanders yelled to Tucker, "Put it on autopilot and come back here!"

"Keep him back there, guys. I'm flying," Tucker replied, misunderstanding the command.

"Hurry up, Jim!" Peterson shouted in pain. "Jim!"

"Jim, is it on autopilot?" Sanders yelled toward the cockpit.

Tucker could hardly believe that they were asking him to leave the cockpit. All airline pilots are drilled that someone has to actively fly the airplane at all times, especially during emergencies. It's an FAA violation for two members of a three-person crew to leave the cockpit during any flight. In his Navy training, when pilots were taught to recover from spins—situations where aircraft actually tumbled out of control—Tucker learned never to let go of the controls,

even though it had been conclusively proven that releasing the stick
could bring about quicker spin recoveries. Instead, Navy pilots were
taught to neutralize the controls. Letting go of the stick, instructors
decided, would make students too passive. They had to be imbued
with the notion that they were the masters of their aircraft at all
times.

However, this was clearly a situation where rules didn't matter.
Tucker would do as his fellow pilots asked. He tried to engage the
autopilot, but before the mechanism would start operating, Tucker
would have to fly the airplane straight and level for several seconds.
The extreme gyrations the plane had been through had confused the
gyroscopic device, and the autopilot refused to take over. Tucker
clicked it on again, but it wouldn't hold.

"Jim, put it on autopilot and come back here," Sanders ordered.
He had to make sure Calloway was under control. If that meant
leaving the cockpit vacant for a while, it was a small price to pay.

"Quick, Jim," Peterson pleaded.

"Hurry, Jim," Sanders commanded. "Come back here now!"

"Wait a minute," Tucker said, making sure the autopilot was
working and that the trim was properly set. If he made a mistake,
the plane might resume its descent. It could hit the ground before
any of the pilots in the back realized they were going down. Tucker
programmed the autopilot to hold the plane's current speed and
altitude. He clicked the mechanism again, and this time it engaged.

"I'm coming." Tucker yelled.

"Jim, do it now!" Sanders shouted as Calloway writhed on the
floor.

"Hurry!" Peterson yelled. "Hurry!"

"WEAKER BY THE MINUTE"

APRIL 7

3:44 P.M.

The autopilot held the FedEx DC-10 at ten thousand feet while copilot Jim Tucker prepared to enter the dim galley area.

Tucker reached down to unhook his seat belt and shoulder harness, but the useless fingers on his right hand couldn't grasp the latch. Using his left hand, he unhooked the belts and pushed the electrical switch on the side of the seat that allowed him to slide back away from the instrument panel.

He was almost overcome with dizziness as he stood up. He felt as if a vast weight was pulling down on his numb right arm and shoulder. The passageway was narrow, and Tucker brushed against the bulkheads as he stumbled toward the galley area about four strides from the cockpit door.

When he got to the galley, Peterson was lying on top of Calloway. Sanders stood over both of them, huffing and puffing—a hammer in one hand, the pointed metal spear in the other. All three men were soaked in blood. There was so much blood that none of the pilots could determine whom it was coming from.

Someone was going to have to attempt to land the aircraft. Sanders, the captain, decided that he should be the one. In an emergency situation the captain was supposed to fly the airplane. The safety of the aircraft and everyone on it was his responsibility, and Sanders felt capable of bringing Flight 705 home. Also, Tucker, a bigger, stronger, and younger man, would be better able to restrain the attacker while Sanders went up front. Sanders had no idea how seriously Tucker had been hurt.

"If you can keep him contained, I'll land the airplane," Sanders told Tucker.

"OK," Tucker replied. "Go up and get the airplane."

"I'm going."

Blood streamed down Calloway's face from the deep gash on the
left side of his forehead. He was lying on the floor, his eyes half
closed, back pushed against the passenger door on the left side of
the aircraft. The guitar case he had carried onto the plane had been
knocked open during the melee, and several hammers and an oversized scuba diver's knife were scattered around it.

"Can you take these?" Tucker asked, pointing to a pair of hammers that had fallen on the floor. Sanders grabbed the weapons,
carried them to the cockpit, and dropped them by the engineer's
seat where the attacker couldn't reach them. Then Sanders strapped
himself into the captain's chair and clicked off the autopilot.

In the galley area, Tucker knelt down to steady himself. Blood
poured from an open wound on the left side of his head just below
the part line on his scalp. There was no way Tucker could stop the
flow, and he felt himself getting weaker by the minute. He wasn't
sure if he had been shot with a gun or struck with a hammer. He
only knew that he was hurt in a way that he had never experienced
before. But Tucker knew the blood loss must be taking a toll. His
body was like an engine with an oil leak, and the oil pressure was
getting dangerously low. Unless something happened soon, the engine could seize and die. He had to hold on.

Tucker glanced at Peterson, noting that the flight engineer's
complexion, fair under normal circumstances, was now blanched
white from blood loss. Tucker wondered what he would do if Peterson faded. Could he handle Calloway alone? He didn't think so.

Tucker took the spear that Sanders had wrested from their attacker. He straddled Calloway, then squatted on top of him, poking
the sharp metal barb against the soft flesh under Calloway's chin.
"You move and I'll kill ya," Tucker growled, his voice low and
guttural.

It was a bluff but only Tucker knew that.

Tucker's right hand was numb, and he couldn't make it grip
the metal shaft of the spear unless he looked directly at his hand. As
soon as he looked away, his entire right arm would fall limply to his
side. It was maddening.

Calloway had kept a calm, focused look about him during the initial stage of the attack. Then he was afraid. After Sanders struck him, Calloway was momentarily dazed. Now his eyes were sharp again and he started squirming on the floor, wriggling toward the two passenger jump seats.

"Let me up, let me up," Calloway pleaded. "I won't fight anymore. Let me up. Please. I can't breathe."

Calloway's movements, small at first, became bolder. He would take a few deep breaths, concentrate his energy, then move in quick concentrated spurts. Each burst of energy became more explosive and more difficult for the wounded pilots to contain. Tucker and Peterson didn't know how much longer they could hang on.

"TOWARD THE AIRPORT"

APRIL 7

3:44 P.M.

David Sanders picked up the microphone in the cockpit and tried to make a radio call, but his mouth wouldn't move.

The captain's jaw had somehow become dislocated, and now he couldn't talk. It was impossible for him to form words. Sanders closed his mouth hard, but his teeth no longer fit together. He pushed against the side of his face with his right palm, and all at once, his jaw snapped back into place. He could hear the bones, muscles, and tendons click into the proper position.

Sanders reached again for the microphone that was connected to the left side of the instrument panel by a coiled, stretchable cord. "Memphis, can you hear me?" he asked, glad to finally be able to get the words out.

"Is this seven-zero-five heavy?"

"Seven-oh-five, yes!"

"Seven-zero-five heavy, Memphis, roger, I do hear you," air traffic controller Paul Candalino told him. "You can proceed direct to Memphis if able, expect Runway niner. Emergency workers are waiting for you."

"Do you understand we're declaring an emergency?" Sanders asked, sounding as though he had just run a marathon. "We need security to meet the plane. We'll stop it on the runway if we can."

The pilot was obviously fatigued and under enormous stress. He sounded coherent, though. Maybe the guy could get back to the airport and land the giant aircraft.

"Express seven-zero-five heavy, that's affirmative," the controller said soothingly. "All that's been taken care of. Security will be available as well as medical assistance. Proceed direct Memphis. Descend at your discretion."

"We're headed that way now, I think."

Wrong. The plane was headed southwest, still going away from the airport at more than 350 miles an hour. Candalino wanted to tell the pilot to turn left, but he resisted. Maybe the pilot was trying to tell him something. Maybe he was trying to fool the hijackers into thinking they were coming back to Memphis when in fact the pilot had another plan.

"Express seven-zero-five heavy, is the situation under control or is it still in progress?" Candalino asked, trying to determine the pilot's real intentions without further endangering the crew.

"We appear to have it under control," the pilot said.

That was the answer Candalino needed. The pilot wasn't trying to trick anyone, he was just disoriented.

"Express seven-zero-five heavy, are you able to turn toward the airport?"

"Yeah. Give me a vector."

"Express seven-zero-five heavy, fly [compass] heading one zero zero vectors Memphis."

"We're turning toward the airport now."

"CAN'T IT WAIT?"

APRIL 7

3:45 P.M.

Don Wilson tried to pay attention to the distant voices on the telephone conference call, but his mind wandered. The forty-eight-year-old chairman of the Air Line Pilots Association and FedEx DC-10 captain gazed out his twenty-ninth-floor office window. From the Clark Tower office building in suburban Memphis he could clearly see Memphis International Airport just eight miles to the southwest. Watching airplanes come and go sometimes made the white-haired Wilson wish he were at the controls of a wide-body jet instead of the wooden desk that cornered him today.

FedEx pilots had elected Wilson chairman of their fledgling union, however, and Wilson was determined to complete ALPA's first collectively bargained contract with FedEx. At the snail's pace company managers were moving, a contract seemed many months, if not years, away.

Wilson was one of the few FedEx pilots who grew up in Memphis. He joined FedEx shortly after leaving the Air Force in 1972, where he flew C-141 cargo planes. Wilson got involved in FedEx pilot politics from the outset. He was elected to leadership positions on pilot/managment advisory committees. And he moved into management for a couple of years as an executive in the flight operations department. He had helped write many of the rules that still governed pilots and the way the company conducted its enterprise.

Wilson's two years in management had been turbulent, however. Other executives regarded him with suspicion because Wilson behaved like a pilot advocate—not like a manager whose primary responsibility was increasing the company's value to shareholders. Wilson sided with pilots time and again on issues of pay and work rules. Finally, after frequent clashes with other executives, Wilson was unceremoniously dumped as a manager. He was abruptly sent back to regular line flying.

Like the other FedEx pilots of his era, Wilson began his career flying Dassault Falcons before moving up to Boeing 727s and finally DC-10s. Wilson was one of the first "purple" FedEx veterans to support a pilots' union. He worked on the ALPA organizing committee at FedEx in 1991 and 1992 and was elected ALPA chairman when the union won a representation election in 1993.

Many of the "silver" former Flying Tigers at FedEx wanted to elect one of their own as a leader. No one at FedEx had ever negotiated a collective-bargaining agreement before. At Flying Tigers, they were used to hard-nosed, confrontational tactics. A decade earlier, they had faced down Stephen Wolfe, one of the shrewdest airline managers in the industry. Wolfe threatened to put the air-cargo carrier's assets—including airplanes—up for sale if pilots refused to make pay concessions. Flying Tigers aircraft were a few hours from being auctioned to the highest bidder when the two sides came to terms. Pilots reluctantly accepted 40 percent pay cuts.

At FedEx, the silver pilots wanted to avoid alienating the purple FedEx veterans. They needed pilots from all backgrounds to join the union if they were going to create enough solidarity to make collective bargaining successful. During a marathon meeting in San Francisco, purple and silver FedEx pilot representatives deadlocked on four ballots before they chose Wilson over a former Tiger. Wilson was smart, he knew the managers the union would face across the bargaining table—and as a twenty-year FedEx veteran, his purple credentials were impeccable.

The union job kept Wilson off flying status and in the Memphis office full-time. The stress of trying to build the union while preparing to negotiate against a large multinational corporation was taking a toll, though. Wilson had undergone open-heart surgery in the mid-1980s, and now he was gaining weight. His morning runs with the family dog were becoming less frequent, and sometimes he had trouble sleeping.

The divided FedEx pilot group seemed to be pulling itself apart. Wilson had thought he could unite them. Now, four months after his election, he was having doubts.

On beautiful clear afternoons like this, Wilson wished he was flying a jet to Alaska, Europe, or Asia. Anything would be more enjoyable than listening to this disjointed telephone conversation. The staff was bickering over the wording in an upcoming ALPA newsletter. Someone wanted to run it by the legal department. Someone else wanted the public relations staff in Washington to take a look. Couldn't they come to any conclusions without his intervention? Wilson expected to make tough decisions as ALPA chairman. It was the seemingly never-ending series of trivial, mundane decisions that bothered him.

Then he heard a real voice instead of a telephonic one.

"Hey, Don, get off the phone."

It was Dennis Higgins, an ALPA organizer and former Continental Airlines captain, who had entered through Wilson's open office door. "One of your planes has been hijacked."

The chairman frowned and pushed the mute button on the speakerphone.

"I'm on a conference call," Wilson said, exasperated. "Can't it wait?"

Higgins was notorious for playing practical jokes, and Wilson was sure the supposed hijacking was just a ruse to get him off the phone. Maybe one of the office secretaries was celebrating a birthday today. Higgins probably wanted Wilson in the room when she blew out the candles or something.

"I mean it, Don," Higgins insisted. "Hang up. Get off the call right now."

Higgins's broad, normally jovial face was deadly serious. Wilson begged off the call.

"It's all over the radio and TV," Higgins said brusquely. "There aren't a lot of details so far, but a FedEx plane has had an attempted hijacking—and it's returning to Memphis right now."

"Who's on it? Does anyone know who the crew is?"

"No one's sure," Higgins said. "They think the flight originated in Memphis this afternoon, so it's probably a DC-ten. But we don't even know that for sure."

Higgins had been a sheriff's deputy in his native Oklahoma before learning to fly in the early 1960s. His tone was matter-of-fact.

"What's the flight number?" Wilson asked. If he knew the number, Wilson could call the company's automated crew-scheduling telephone number and find out the names of the pilots assigned to the trip. Wilson stepped out of his office and began walking down the long corridor to the receptionist's desk. The phone lines on the switchboard suddenly were jammed with incoming calls. Pilots and their spouses, FedEx employees and news reporters from all over the country, suddenly were calling the ALPA office asking for more information about the hijacking. Wilson wished he had something to tell them.

Then a FedEx pilot at the package-sorting hub in Memphis called Wilson. The receptionist handed him the phone. The pilot said the hijacked plane was a DC-10 bound for California. It was Flight 705.

Was he sure?

Positive.

Wilson and Higgins ran back to the chairman's office and Wilson picked up his phone. He knew the FedEx automated-crew information number by heart. He punched in his employee identification number and the computerized voice read a menu of options. Did the caller want to find the phone number for a particular FedEx pilot? Address? Did the caller wish to volunteer for additional flights or trade trips? Wilson kept pushing buttons and a few seconds later the computerized voice gave Wilson the information he sought.

"Captain David Sanders, Captain James Tucker, Second Officer Andy Peterson."

"NO RUSH"

"Express seven-oh-five, I'm going to descend down to seven thousand feet and proceed into Memphis," said David Sanders, his voice stronger and more authoritative.

Air traffic controller Paul Candalino was encouraged. The last few transmissions had been so normal that it seemed the situation on the airplane must be under control.

"Express seven-zero-five heavy, roger," the controller replied. "Descend at your discretion."

Air traffic controllers had closed Memphis International Airport to all other airplanes. Fire trucks, ambulances, and police were assembling near the FedEx hub where Flight 705 planned to land. Airport workers turned a radio navigation signal, a localizer, to the west so the plane could follow it to the runway.

"Express seven-zero-five, if able, you can pick up the localizer for Runway niner and track it inbound."

"Give me that frequency, please," the pilot responded.

"Yeah, the Runway niner localizer is one zero niner point five."

"One oh nine five, thank you."

Please? Thank you? These courtesies were a good sign. If the pilot had the time and presence of mind to use them, then it was likely that the situation in the cockpit had improved.

The pilot still had to get that massive jet back on the ground, though. And with a full load of cargo and fuel, the plane was sure to be far above its maximum allowable landing weight. The DC-10 would have burned more than forty tons of fuel during the long flight to California. Now all that fuel and the full load of cargo were liabilities.

An overweight plane would have a higher landing speed than normal, and a longer landing roll. The added strain could cause tire blowouts and make the plane impossible to control on the ground. At the very least, it would probably roll off the far end of the runway. The east-facing strip was 8,936 feet long, the second-longest of the three active runways at Memphis International Airport.

"Express seven-zero-five heavy, if able, when you can, I'd like to know your fuel on board and number of persons on board."

"OK," the pilot responded. "I'll get that to you in just a second."

"Roger, no rush."

"ALERT III"

APRIL 7
3:49 P.M.

The long ring of the telephone and an electronic buzz interrupted paramedic David Teague's afternoon nap. The code signified the call to Fire Station 33 was coming from the control tower at Memphis International Airport.

Teague picked up the telephone and was told that an Alert III— the highest-level emergency—was in progress at the airport. There had been an attempted hijacking aboard a large jet, controllers said, and the plane was going to attempt to land in Memphis with injured victims, and the possibility of a crash was very real.

Teague, forty-three years old, was taking night-school classes at the University of Memphis to earn a bachelor's degree, and he had been studying for upcoming exams since his shift began at 7:00 A.M. Then, after a fast-food lunch, he had turned on the TV and fallen asleep.

"This has got to be a drill," he wearily assured his partner. Nothing ever happened at Station 33, which is located on the airport property. The three-day rotations paramedics and firemen put in there were like paid vacations. The two paramedics hopped into ambulance number nineteen and drove quickly to the east end of Runway 9, the place they were told the jet would come to a stop.

On the way, the fire chief told them on the radio that this was not a drill. A real hijacking attempt was under way, and they had to be ready to assist the victims. But the paramedics were instructed to let armed police board the aircraft first. The situation on the plane might still be dangerous.

When Teague arrived at the east end of the runway, a large group of fire trucks and police cars had already assembled there, and all eyes were searching the sky to the west.

"THERE'S SOMETHING THE MATTER WITH ME"

APRIL 7

3:51 P.M.

FedEx captain David Sanders took stock of his surroundings. The DC-10 was descending through 8,000 feet. OK, he would go lower. All three engines were running normally. Good.

Had the violent maneuvers damaged the aircraft? From the left seat of the gargantuan plane, Sanders couldn't tell. The handle on the number-three fire lever had been torn off during the fight in the cockpit, yet the lever itself was in its proper position flush with the ceiling. The DC-10 felt solid and stable, and Sanders pushed the throttles forward to the stops. He would get the leviathan back on the ground as fast as possible.

"Dave!" Tucker called from the rear of the cockpit.

"Yes!"

"Are you OK?" the copilot wanted to know.

"I'm OK. Are you? Do you have him under control?"

Several seconds of silence followed; then Sanders heard a commotion in the galley area behind him.

"Talk to me, Jim," Sanders commanded, deeply concerned about his fellow crew members. "Do you have him under control?"

Back in the galley area, Tucker was fading quickly.

The hammer had smashed through his skull and into his brain, and the injury was causing the organ to bleed and swell. As swelling increased the pressure inside his head, normal brain functions began shutting down one by one. Tucker was losing vision in his right eye, and the right side of his body was almost completely paralyzed. Tucker couldn't tell Sanders how desperately ill he felt, however, without encouraging Calloway. And Calloway seemed to be gaining strength with each passing moment.

"I'm OK," Tucker finally answered weakly and unconvincingly. Silently, the copilot willed himself to carry on until the plane touched down. He had to hold on that long. Failure was not an option.

In the cockpit, Sanders saw that the sheepskin cover of Tucker's seat was stained deep red. The engineer's table was covered with sticky blood, and the pages of Peterson's flight crew log were soaked. Strangely, the Crystal Geyser soft drink Peterson had been sipping from a plastic bottle was still upright despite the violence that had exploded around it. The bottle was wrapped in a white paper napkin. The center console of the plane's instrument panel was covered with a slick coat of oily blood. And red handprints were smeared across the ceiling.

Sanders had to concentrate. He would have only one chance to make this approach and landing. The plane weighed 460,000 pounds and had 100,000 pounds of fuel in its massive wing tanks. The DC-10 far exceeded its maximum landing weight, but Sanders knew he couldn't do anything about that. The switches and levers for dumping fuel were all on the engineer's panel about six feet away; he couldn't reach them.

Sanders twisted the heading bug on the gyroscopic compass until it showed 100 degrees. As he turned the knob, the airplane automatically began a 30-degree banked turn toward the desired heading. The captain was beginning to feel more comfortable. He was flying the airplane again. He was doing the job he had trained his entire adult life to perform. He was back in his element.

"Dave!" Tucker asked from behind the cockpit. "Can ya get her on the ground?"

"Yeah!" the captain replied without hesitation.

Then, concerned about the continuing sounds of struggle from the galley area, Sanders told the crew to use Calloway's weapons against him.

"Listen," Sanders shouted to Tucker and Peterson. "Put that [spear] in his throat. I don't give a shit if he's dead or not. Don't kill him, but hold him. You got him, Jim?"

There was no answer from the galley.

"Jim, are you under control?"

Still, no audible reply.

"Jim, are you under control?" Sanders screamed. "Jim!"

Tucker was trying to grip the spear but couldn't hold it. He tried to stand but couldn't get his balance. The spear fell harmlessly to the floor.

"Jim, are you under control?" Sanders asked urgently.

The copilot wanted to say yes, but Sanders had to know the truth.

"No, no!" Tucker yelled. "There's . . . there's something the matter with me!"

"There's something the matter with him!" Sanders shot back.

"No!"

"You keep him down, hear!"

"I can't!"

"You can keep him down, put that thing in his . . ."

"No!" Tucker yelled, fearing he was about to pass out at any moment.

Calloway resumed thrashing around. Most of the hammers had been tossed or carried into the cockpit to keep them away from the attacker. But one of the weapons—a two-pound sledgehammer with a wooden handle—was still on the floor just out of Calloway's reach. He arched his back, bridging his shoulders off the slick rubber matting, then rolled away from Tucker and Peterson. The wounded pilots tried to hang on, but they were dizzy and weak and bleeding at an alarming rate.

Tucker and Peterson piled on top of Calloway, and this time he went totally limp. Calloway relaxed every muscle in his body and took short, panting breaths. The wounded pilots held the attacker on his back. But when Calloway had rested enough to speak, he pleaded with them to let him up.

"I'm not going to hurt you," he promised. "You win, you win. Just let me up so I can breathe."

Tucker wanted to believe Calloway, but he suspected the conciliatory words were a ploy. The attacker would continue to come after them. They had to continue their resistance. Peterson clung to Calloway's midsection and Tucker wrapped his long left arm around the attacker's waist for leverage. Tucker snaked his left leg between Calloway's ankles. He and Peterson had to keep the attacker immobilized.

The DC-10 was heading east toward Memphis at more than 370 miles an hour. The airport was thirty-five miles away. At this speed the plane would arrive in six minutes.

"FOUR SOULS ON BOARD"

APRIL 7

3:54 P.M.

"Express seven-zero-five heavy, is that localizer coming in now?" Paul Candalino asked. The air traffic controller wanted to know if the pilot was able to track the radio signal to the airport.

"Yeah," David Sanders replied. "We're on the localizer now, descending."

The localizer showed pilots if their aircraft were aligned with the runway, but gave no indication whether the planes were coming in too high or too low. Candalino asked if the pilot wanted to fly an instrument or a purely visual approach. The weather at the airport was clear and the winds were calm.

Sanders said he would watch the aircraft instruments until he got within sight of the runway, then trust his instincts the rest of the way to the ground.

"OK, you're three one, thirty-one miles west of the airport," Candalino reported.

"Thank you, sir."

A minute later, Candalino called again.

"Express seven-zero-five heavy, you're about twenty-five miles from the airport and I'll be making a transmission to you every thirty or forty-five seconds just to stay in touch."

A double click of the microphone told Candalino that Sanders understood.

"Express seven-zero-five heavy, you're twenty miles from the airport. And do you have that fuel and passenger information?"

"We've got four souls on board," Sanders said, using the nautical term that airline crews had adopted long ago. "We've got eighty-six, uh, eighty-five thousand pounds on the fuel."

That put the plane's gross weight at 18 tons over its maximum landing weight. It was approaching fast and there was no way to dump the excess fuel in time. Candalino doubted the pilot would be able to stop the hulking aircraft on the runway.

Police wanted to know how many hijackers were aboard the aircraft. Were they stowaways? Was a FedEx employee involved? Company officials gave police a manifest that listed the crew and passengers, and according to them, there were four pilots on the plane—three crew members and Auburn Calloway, an off-duty flight engineer.

Candalino tried to find out about the hijacker or hijackers.

"Express seven-zero-five heavy, how many people should security be looking for?"

"Four."

Sanders had misinterpreted the question.

"OK. I mean how many involved in the action?" Candalino asked.

"Everybody has been injured," Sanders said. "There is one person that lost it. . . . The jump-seat passenger is the one who attacked the crew."

"A JUMBLED HEAP"

As Jim Tucker and Andy Peterson grew weaker from blood loss, Auburn Calloway seemed to gain strength. He reached for the sledgehammer on the floor, but Peterson pinned his arms.

"You hang in there now!" Sanders yelled toward the rear of the plane. The captain could hear them struggling again.

The plane was eighteen miles from the airport. Just four minutes away.

Calloway had been resting, totally limp, for several minutes. But Tucker noticed the attacker was breathing more slowly and deeply now. Calloway's muscles began to tense for what Tucker suspected would be a final, furious assault.

Seconds later, Calloway gritted his teeth and bridged his shoulders off the grooved, matted floor. He rolled away from Peterson and climbed onto his hands and knees. Tucker and Peterson were draped across his back, but Tucker was unable to gain his balance. Peterson could see that Tucker was on the verge of losing consciousness, so the flight engineer took the lead.

"Stay down!" Peterson yelled at Calloway, still trying to hold his arms.

"Is he still down?" Sanders asked from the cockpit.

"I don't know," Tucker replied, barely able to turn his head. "Yeah, he is."

Calloway pushed himself against the two rear-facing jump seats and used the chairs to pull himself off the floor, dragging the two clinging crew members with him. Just then, Calloway reached back with his right hand and found Tucker's face. With his thumb, Calloway gouged the copilot's eyes, scratching and digging with his sharp thumbnail. But with all the blood lubricating Tucker's face, the attacker's fingers slipped each time he pressed and Tucker turned his head away.

As they struggled, the upholstery that Calloway was using to support himself began to tear. He grabbed more fabric with his left hand. But it, too, began peeling away from the seat cushions. Then the fabric gave way, and Calloway fell back to the floor in a jumbled heap with Peterson and Tucker.

The plane was fourteen miles from the airport.

In the cockpit, David Sanders searched for familiar landmarks. He could see the winding Mississippi River and the bridges and office buildings of downtown Memphis in the distance. He aimed slightly south of the skyline. He knew from years of experience that the airport would soon appear there.

Blood from the open wounds on his head kept clouding the vision in Sanders's left eye. He tried wiping it away with his arm every few seconds, but it was pointless. He couldn't stop or even slow the flow, and he couldn't allow the annoyance to distract him. He had to stay focused. The approach and landing were critical phases of any flight, particularly this one.

The captain thanked God for the clear day. Poor visibility or high winds would have made his task more difficult. As it was, the plane would be almost perfectly aligned with the east-facing runway. He planned to come straight in and brake to a halt directly in front of the FedEx hub.

There were no aircraft on the runways or taxiways, and Sanders reasoned that the facility must be closed to handle the ongoing aerial emergency. He expected to see the flashing lights of police cars, ambulances, and fire trucks on the ground at any time.

Then the struggle erupted again behind the cockpit, more violently and ferociously than ever. The situation was intolerable. Sanders had to decide whether to put the airplane back on autopilot so that it would maintain altitude and go back to the galley area and reenter the brawl, or remain alone in the cockpit and try to land the airplane right away. He had to protect his crew, his airplane, and himself.

Sanders decided it was time to permanently end the struggle behind the cockpit. If that meant he had to kill Calloway himself, so be it. He was prepared to face the consequences. He set the autopilot so that the DC-10 would hold its current altitude of 7,000 feet. Then he slid his chair back, unfastened his seat-belt harness, and stood up. The claw hammer that Calloway had used in the initial attack was on the floor next to the engineer's table.

Sanders would use it to end the attacker's life.

"SORT OF UNDER CONTROL"

APRIL 7

3:57 P.M.

Just as David Sanders was about to leave the cockpit of the DC-10, copilot Jim Tucker yelled from the galley area that Auburn Calloway was under control again.

Sanders decided to remain in the cockpit and attempt a landing. His crew was badly injured, and getting medical treatment for them as soon as possible was his top priority. He quickly sat down at the controls again, slid his seat forward, and disengaged the autopilot. He would fly the airplane manually the rest of the way. Sanders pushed the nose of the DC-10 downward and began a speedy descent into Memphis.

"Express seven-zero-five heavy, verify the situation is still under control," Candalino called on the radio.

"Well," Sanders replied cryptically, "it's sort of under control."

That was the best he could do for now. The plane should be visible to spotters in the control tower at Memphis International Airport at any moment.

"Express seven-zero-five heavy, you are fourteen miles from the airport," Candalino said. "Advise when you get it in sight."

"I have it in sight," Sanders replied.

"Express seven-zero-five heavy is clear to land, visual approach, Runway niner."

"Cleared to land," Sanders confirmed.

"TOO HIGH, TOO FAST"

APRIL 7

3:58 P.M.

"Express seven-zero-five heavy, you're about six and a half miles from the runway threshold. If able, when you're on the ground, advise when you're on the ground," air traffic controller Paul Candalino said from his windowless ground-floor office. "I won't make any more transmissions to you at this time."

A double click of the DC-10 microphone acknowledged the message. These were critical moments and Candalino wanted to let the injured pilot concentrate. Upstairs, workers gathered at the west side of the control tower and all eyes focused on the gigantic plane coming from that direction.

It was about 4,000 feet high and coming in fast—too fast.

"COMING AROUND TO THREE-SIX LEFT"

APRIL 7

3:59 P.M.

There was more commotion in the galley area behind David Sanders. He had to let the crew know that they needn't suffer anymore.

"Kill the son of a bitch!" Sanders shouted toward the galley area, giving the orders and accepting the responsibility. "Kill him, kill him, kill him, kill him!"

Calloway had rolled onto his side and was thrashing his arms and legs. Peterson tried to hold the attacker's arms down, but couldn't. Calloway's teeth locked down on the flight engineer's shoulder, tearing the skin.

"Jim, Jim, Jim!" Peterson shouted in pain. "Jim, help me!"

Even though the pain was excruciating, Peterson didn't move. He decided it was better to let Calloway keep biting him than pull back.

Tucker sprawled across Calloway's waist. But the tall copilot had lost virtually all of his strength, balance, and coordination. He was exhausted, barely able to move or breathe.

"Stop fighting!" Peterson pleaded.

In the cockpit, Sanders realized that leaving the plane on autopilot at 7,000 feet for those critical seconds had made his approach to the east-facing runway too high and too fast. The plane was traveling at 365 miles an hour—almost double its normal approach speed. Even if Sanders pulled the three throttle levers all the way back to idle, there was no way he could descend while slowing the overweight plane to its normal approach speed of 190 miles an hour.

A straight-in landing on the east-facing runway would make it impossible to stop the airplane in time. The DC-10 would roll off the pavement at a high rate of speed with possibly catastrophic results. There were fences, a deep gully, and a busy four-lane street at the far end of the runway. Sanders had to do something else, quick.

"I'm coming around to Three-six Left!" he told air traffic controllers.

Sanders's short statement informed air traffic controllers that he had changed his mind and now intended to land on the nearer of two parallel north-facing runways. In order to get there, he had to turn sharply right, then make an immediate 180-degree left turn to align the fast-moving airplane with the two-mile-long concrete strip.

The maneuver might be possible for a cropduster. But for an overweight DC-10 being flown by a single, injured pilot, it seemed like too much to ask.

"ALL HE COULD DO"

APRIL 7

4:00 P.M.

"Clear to land," Candalino replied from his station below. "You are clear to land, visual approach, Runway Three-six Left. Wind is [from the northeast] at eight [miles an hour]. All the emergency equipment will be on one two one point niner."

Another double click of the microphone.

Candalino lowered his face to his hands. He had done all he could do.

But somehow, it didn't feel like enough.

In the Navy, David Sanders had made scores of high-speed, high-angle approaches. But they had been done decades ago, mostly in single-engine trainers—not wide-body jets.

Still, an airplane is an airplane, Sanders reasoned. All it knows is airspeed. An ironing board will fly if it's got enough wind going over it. So would the DC-10 if he could keep the speed up.

There was no time to wait.

Sanders turned steeply to the right and pulled hard on the yoke. The plane passed 35 degrees angle of bank, an unusually steep turn this close to the ground, but Sanders could see he needed to turn even harder to avoid coming too close to his intended touchdown point. At 45 degrees angle of bank, the same was true. Sanders turned the yoke all the way to the right and held it there as the DC-10 reached 60 degrees of bank. It was virtually on its side when he began to roll out of the descending turn.

(Bank angle . . . bank angle . . .). The automated voice sounded whenever the plane exceeded 60 degrees angle of bank. Sanders ignored it.

"Ow! Jim, he's biting me!" Peterson yelled in the galley area.

"Stay down!" Tucker warned.

(Bank angle . . . bank angle . . .)

The runway was off the left wing of the aircraft now. Sanders would have to make an extremely hard 180-degree left turn in order to get there. He reached out with his right hand and instinctively grasped the speed-brake lever on the center console behind the throttle levers. He pulled it backward abruptly and instantly felt the deceleration as the plane slowed from more than 300 miles an hour to 270.

Without his glasses, Sanders found the gauges on the instrument panel slightly fuzzy. But his distance vision was good, especially in the daytime. And Sanders could tell by the sound and feel of the airplane that everything was working properly. He wanted to keep the plane moving as fast as possible and make the approach as tight as he could. Reducing speed meant more time in the air. That would put the crew at risk for additional seconds.

At 260 miles an hour, Sanders reached to the copilot's side of the instrument panel with his right hand and immediately found the round landing-gear handle. All those blindfold cockpit checks that Sanders had done to familiarize himself with different aircraft cockpits were paying off. He pulled the knob sharply down and was gratified to hear the familiar sound of four massive landing gear groaning and clanking into position. Four green lights on the instrument panel confirmed the wheels were down and locked.

Next came the flaps.

Under normal conditions, DC-10 crews add flaps a little at a time to smoothly slow the aircraft. Sanders did the same this time. If he lowered the flaps or the landing gear when the plane was traveling too fast, he could damage them. A mistake now could cause the landing gear to fail or not to extend all the way. That might make the landing gear collapse when the plane touched down. Extending the flaps too soon could crack them or rip them off the airplane. He couldn't take those risks.

Sanders dropped the flaps to 15 degrees, the standard approach setting, and he noticed the deceleration immediately. He glanced at the airspeed indicator. The moment the needle registered 210 miles per hour, Sanders pushed the flap handle all the way down. As the plane slowed, the flaps would automatically extend to their maximum setting of 50 degrees. The hulking plane responded as though he had tossed out an anchor.

Flight 705 was 2,200 feet above the ground, and Sanders began a 180-degree turn toward the runway as the flaps continued to extend.

(Bank angle . . . bank angle . . .)

The DC-10 was making an impossibly tight turn, and its rate

of descent became excessive. Halfway through the turn, Flight 705 had dropped 1,000 feet. It was just 1,200 feet above the ground and dropping like a rock.

"He's after the hammer, Andy!"

The wooden-handled sledgehammer was on the floor just out of Calloway's reach. Tucker tried to kick it farther away, but his legs wouldn't respond.

(Altitude alert, one thousand!)

"Where's he going?" Peterson asked.

Tucker could see that the hammer was just beyond the attacker's outstretched fingers. Peterson probably could reach it, but he was lying across Calloway's chest and couldn't see the weapon.

"The hammer's by your leg," Tucker tried to tell Peterson, but he was so breathless the words came out in gasps. "Your left leg. You have to grab it, Andy. You have to grab it. And you have to hit him with it."

Keeping his chest against Calloway's belly, Peterson reached back with his left hand and located the hammer. His wet, sticky fingers wrapped around the wooden handle.

Calloway continued to struggle. Pulling his arms and legs in close to his body, he rolled onto his side with Peterson still sprawled across him. Tucker was too weak and too dizzy to provide any meaningful assistance.

"Andy," Tucker began again in a low stern voice, as if trying to communicate an important point to a child. "Andy, you have to take the hammer. And you have to hit him with it. Do you understand? You have to hit him, or he's going to kill us."

(Pull up! Sink rate! Pull up! Sink rate!)

Sanders was allowing the aircraft to descend far faster than normal. The plane banked 35 degrees in a steep, descending left turn. Sanders would have to wait until the last possible moment before leveling the wings in order to line up with the runway. If he kept the plane in a turn too long, it would strike the ground with enough force to kill everyone on board.

The paved runway surface was 9,600 feet long. Under ideal conditions, a DC-10 at its maximum allowable landing weight needs 6,130 feet of runway to stop from the point it touches down. Flight 705 was far above its maximum landing weight. It would need even more distance.

Sanders glanced at the airspeed indicator as he drove the nose of the airplane toward the concrete runway surface. The DC-10 was traveling 200 miles an hour—far above the normal landing speed of 140 miles an hour. The speed was on the verge of being too high for the DC-10's tires. If the wheels touched down at more than 200 miles an hour, the impact could make the ten main landing-gear tires disintegrate on touchdown. If that happened, the plane would instantly careen out of control.

Sanders intended to slow the plane to 190 miles an hour at touchdown. He had practiced emergency landings with high approach speeds many times in computerized flight simulators at FedEx. Every six months, captains were required to perform simulated landings without flaps, and the recommended touchdown speed was 190 miles an hour. The captain was confident that if he brought the plane in at that speed, the tires would hold and he could bring the overweight jet to a stop on the runway surface.

Sanders aligned the plane with the segmented white stripes that marked the runway centerline. He looked into the distance. It was easier to judge the plane's rate of descent by looking far off toward the horizon rather than close in under the nose. White lines passed underneath the cockpit in a blur. Sanders rolled abruptly out of the turn and stopped its rapid rate of descent all at once.

The flaps were extended 40 degrees, and the resistance of the passing air hadn't allowed them to reach their full travel of 50 degrees. The plane was moving 212 miles an hour and it was over the runway.

The crew was almost home.

"PRELUDE TO DISASTER"

APRIL 7

4:02 P.M.

ALPA chairman Don Wilson and Dennis Higgins stood by the window at the southeastern edge of the chairman's office and scanned the cloudless blue sky to the west. From the picture window on the twenty-ninth floor of the office tower, they watched a dot on the horizon as it quickly grew into the familiar form of a DC-10 moving fast toward Memphis International Airport eight miles to the southwest.

Higgins carried a portable radio about the size of a walkie-talkie, the kind that had become so popular among general aviation pilots. He tuned it to the Memphis Approach frequency: 119.1. Maybe they could hear the plane's radio transmissions as it arrived. From the ALPA office so high above the ground, the reception was excellent.

"Is that them?" Wilson asked. "Is that seven-oh-five?"

"It's got to be," Higgins said. "They've got the airport closed to all other traffic."

Wilson thought about his friend David Sanders. He and Sanders had started flying for FedEx about the same time, and they had worked together in a variety of administrative posts. Both had served on the company's Flight Council and later the Flight Advisory Board, committees made up of pilots and managers who wrote and amended company aviation policies. Wilson and Sanders had also served together on the controversial "merger committee" during the 1989 Flying Tigers acquisition.

Wilson regarded Sanders as a thoughtful, unflappable pilot who played a valuable devil's advocate role on rule-making committees. Wilson and his staff used to draft policies, then take them to Sanders, who had a knack for being able to find the most minuscule loopholes in them. Sanders could anticipate ways pilots and company managers would try to bend the rules in their favor. Through their combined efforts, Wilson and Sanders came up with precise contract language designed to guard against abuse from either side.

The other pilots on Flight 705 weren't as well known.

Wilson recalled that Tucker had been the instructor during Wilson's most recent six-month test in the DC-10 simulator. Wilson knew Tucker to be a quick thinker and an imposing physical presence.

"I can't believe anyone would try to hijack a plane with Tucker on it," Wilson thought. "The guy is built like a tank. I'd hate to have him mad at me."

The ALPA chairman didn't know Andy Peterson. Wilson had been told that Tucker and Peterson were both union members. Sanders wasn't, but that came as no surprise since very few purple veterans had joined the union. Union affiliation no longer seemed important, however. These were all fellow aviators, and they were in peril.

What were those pilots going through right now? How many hijackers were on the plane? If they attacked a three-man crew that included the burly Tucker, they had to be armed. They would probably shoot the big guy first. Still, why would anyone try to commandeer a cargo plane in Memphis of all places? Was the DC-10 carrying something particularly valuable?

Broadcast news reports were repeating what reporters had heard on their police radio scanners: that a FedEx jet was returning to Memphis after the crew had been attacked by a jump-seat passenger. Wilson assumed it was a disgruntled FedEx ground employee. There were wackos in every workplace. This was probably some nutty hubite who had finally come unglued after hefting too many boxes in the middle of the night. The automated crew-scheduling list didn't keep track of jump-seat passengers, though, so there was no way Wilson could check over the telephone.

There was another quick radio transmission. The pilot said something about the runway but it was garbled. He was talking very fast.

Wilson and Higgins held their breaths as the massive plane banked sharply right and descended. Its landing gear came down.

But the plane seemed to be moving too fast, losing altitude too quickly, to have any hope of a safe landing. The two pilots watched in astonishment as the half-million-pound airplane dropped out of sight.

The scene the pilots witnessed from the office window seemed like a prelude to disaster. At any moment they expected to see the telltale black smoke from an airplane crash rising over Memphis International Airport.

Kent Fleshman walked out the south side of the air traffic control center and looked to the west. He had done everything he could to redirect Flight 705 toward the airport. Now he wanted to see the DC-10 land with his own eyes.

But when the plane came into view, it seemed far too high and too fast. Fleshman and several of his coworkers watched in awe and disbelief as the wide-body jet made a sharp, 90-degree turn to the south, its white belly facing him. Then, with its landing gear down and flaps extended, it began an equally sharp 180-degree turn to line up with Runway 36 Left. Without a radio, Fleshman had no idea what the pilot was trying to do.

A moment later, the DC-10 disappeared from Fleshman's view behind a row of buildings.

Paramedic David Teague watched from the right seat of his ambulance as the FedEx jet turned as steeply as a fighter plane. He could see the top of the fuselage and the planform of the plane's swept-back wings as it seemed to hang in the air while making a 180-degree turn toward the runway.

Teague had assumed the hijacking attempt had occurred on a passenger jet. But air traffic controllers assured emergency workers that the injured pilots were aboard the FedEx jet, and the police and firefighters were told over the radio that they could cross any runway and any taxiway to get to the plane—wherever it came to a stop.

Teague's partner, William Hammond, drove their ambulance at more than seventy miles an hour down Runway 36 Right, the two-mile-long strip of concrete that ran parallel to the runway where Flight 705 planned to touch down.

"CAVALRY CHARGE"

APRIL 7
4:04 P.M.

The DC-10's main landing-gear tires touched down at 208 miles an hour on the grooved runway surface, and all ten tires remained intact.

In the cockpit, David Sanders pushed forward on the control yoke immediately to bring the nosewheel to the ground. He pulled the three throttle handles all the way back into reverse and stood on the brakes. He didn't care if he burned them up. He had to stop the airplane right here, right now.

The DC-10's antilock brakes kept the tires rolling. Sanders straightened the plane with the rudder pedals; then, with his left hand, he found the tiller that steered the nosewheel. The plane lurched to a halt on the east side of the runway surface about a thousand feet from the end.

Sanders watched the cavalry charge of emergency vehicles screaming toward him from the other side of the airfield. On the radio, the pilot of a small airplane who was listening to the emergency unfold congratulated the controllers on their handling of the emergency, but to Sanders, it wasn't over yet.

"Get the crews over here now!" he yelled into the microphone. "Get 'em over here in a hurry!"

There was more commotion behind the cockpit.

"Stop the jet, help us!" Peterson pleaded from the galley area. "Stop the jet on the ground and help us!"

Sanders rushed out of the cockpit. Tucker, Peterson, and Calloway were a pile of intertwined arms and legs by the left passenger door. Calloway was lying on his back with Peterson on his chest. Tucker sprawled across the attacker's side. The three men were gasping for air, but none of them moved. They were totally spent.

The jump seat that Calloway had occupied was covered with blood. The seat next to it had most of its upholstery ripped off.

The black guitar case that Calloway had brought onto the plane was open, a plastic speargun cover with the product name "Magnum 70 by ScubaPro" lay inside. A diving knife with an eight-inch stainless-steel blade was still in its black plastic sheath next to the guitar case. A leather penny loafer that had been pried from Tucker's left foot rested by the passenger door on top of a heap of bloody magazines, financial brochures, and books.

"Have they got the emergency equipment out here yet?" Peterson asked breathlessly.

"They're on the way," Sanders said.

The captain started to reach for the emergency handle by the left passenger door, but the three injured men were too close to it. He didn't want the crew members to fall to the ground more than twenty feet below.

"Blow the other door!" Peterson yelled.

"Yeah!" Sanders went to the cockpit and shut down the engines. Then he ran back to the right side of the DC-10 and yanked the red emergency handle. The door opened with a bang, then a hiss as the yellow slide inflated all the way to the ground. Fresh cool air swirled into the plane.

Calloway was still conscious, still writhing, still gnashing his teeth and trying to bite.

"Don't get close enough that he can grab anything," Peterson warned the captain.

"Don't move!" Sanders yelled furiously to the attacker, picking up the speargun. He held the black metal gun, but the spear was loose on the floor.

"Shut the engines down," Peterson said to Sanders. "Did you shut the engines down?"

"Yeah. Don't let him move!"

Tucker tried to rise but collapsed on the floor, his chest heaving with each labored breath.

"STILL DANGEROUS"

APRIL 7

4:07 P.M.

Paramedic David Teague kept the siren blaring as ambulance number nineteen approached the FedEx jet from behind.

A swarm of police cars encircled the DC-10, and the ambulance stopped in the grass near the right wingtip of the jet. White smoke rose from the wheels and brakes, and an emergency slide inflated below the right passenger door. As Teague approached the DC-10, he was amazed at its sheer size. Wide-body planes look big enough when they fly overhead, but seeing the behemoth up close he wondered how anything so huge and so heavy could ever get off the ground.

Teague could see a man in a pilot's uniform, his face and shirt stained with blood, standing in the doorway. He held a speargun in one hand and a hammer in the other. Uniformed police officers, firefighters, and paramedics gathered below the inflated emergency slide on the right side of the airplane.

"Get up here right now!" David Sanders yelled to the emergency workers. "Hurry!"

Three police officers tried to go up the emergency slide, but it was covered with a slippery white powder that made it difficult to climb. One after another, they slid like cartoon characters to the bottom. Teague, who ran his own roofing company during the summers, was in better physical condition than the police officers and he was accustomed to climbing. With a thirty-pound medical bag slung over his shoulder, Teague started up the slide. His movements were slow and steady. One hand, one foot at a time. Teague pressed his feet against the sides of the slide, and kept looking forward, resisting the urge to glance at the ground far below. A police officer ahead of Teague lost his grip and fell toward him. The falling police officer passed between Teague's legs, and knocked the radio off the paramedic's belt.

As Teague neared the open door of the DC-10, he began to slip. Sanders reached down and grabbed the back of the paramedic's shirt, pulling him the final few feet. Sanders immediately pointed at Auburn Calloway lying on his back on the floor.

"That's the attacker," Sanders said. "That's the guy who attacked the crew."

Jim Tucker was sprawled across Auburn Calloway's legs and Andy Peterson clung to his arms. The three men were still heaped against the passenger door on the left side of the aircraft. They were barely moving, gasping.

"Have you got handcuffs?" Sanders asked the paramedic. "If not, you'd better get some. This son of a bitch is still dangerous."

Teague yelled to the police officers on the ground. One of the officers threw handcuffs to him in the doorway. The paramedic fumbled with them awkwardly. He had never had to restrain anyone like this before. It took a few seconds for Teague to clamp the handcuffs on Calloway's slippery wrists. The paramedic told Sanders to stand on the chain holding the bracelets together so Calloway couldn't move.

Sanders put his right foot on the handcuffs and pinned them to the floor.

"Can you move your foot?" Calloway asked the captain. "You're hurting my hands."

Sanders didn't budge.

Several police officers were still trying to climb the slide, but it was beginning to deflate, and that made it even more difficult to ascend. Inside the plane, Teague quickly assessed the four men's injuries. Sanders's face and the back of his head were bloody. His right ear seemed to be dangling from the side of his head, and he had a deep gash in his right forearm. The FedEx captain was alert and walking around, though. He would be all right for now. Calloway had deep cuts and swelling on his forehead, but he was conscious, moving.

Tucker tried to talk, but his words were garbled and nearly impossible to understand. He was bleeding heavily from a deep wound on the left side of his head. And Peterson was lying in a pool of his own blood that flowed freely from the left side of his head. He was breathing but seemed on the verge of collapse.

"I've got to get him down the slide right away," Teague told Sanders, motioning toward Peterson. "You keep standing on those handcuffs and I'll move him."

Teague normally would have immobilized the patient by putting him on a back board and making sure movement didn't aggravate possible spinal injuries. But Teague didn't have the equipment, he didn't have help, and he could see the patient was likely to die if he waited much longer. He grabbed Peterson by the shoulders, pulled him to the right side of the aircraft, and sent him down the emergency slide feet first.

Police officers and firefighters at the bottom of the slide loaded Peterson into an ambulance.

Next came Tucker. He was still conscious, barely. In a slurred, drunken-sounding voice, he mumbled that he was unable to control the right side of his body, and he couldn't feel his legs. It was obvious to the paramedic that Tucker couldn't move the right side of his mouth, either.

Teague looked into the tall man's eyes and noticed they were turned to the left. That was a bad sign. Teague had seen elderly stroke victims with the same symptoms. The eyes always pointed in the direction of the head injury, and paralysis set in on the opposite side.

Even through the blood-soaked hair, Teague could see that Tucker's scalp was deeply indented. Such "depressed" skull fractures were particularly dangerous because germs and foreign objects could be pushed into the brain, leaving the fragile organ susceptible to infection. This man was in deep trouble.

Tucker tried to get to his feet but couldn't. Teague struggled to lift him, and was able to half drag the wounded copilot to the slide. Tucker came down on his back, feet first, too, his right arm flailing behind him.

Teague told Sanders to leave the airplane but the captain refused.

"I'm not going until everyone is taken care of," he said. "Let's keep going."

Calloway had stopped struggling. Teague tried to get him to talk so he could assess the severity of his head injuries. "Look, it's over," the paramedic said. "There's no need to fight us. No one here is going to hurt you. Can you tell me your name? Do you know where you are?"

There was no answer, but Calloway seemed to be thinking. His eyes were focused and they tracked in the same direction. Pools of blood covered the floor and soaked through Calloway's once-blue shirt. Teague didn't know how much blood the man had lost and decided to begin replenishing body fluid intravenously.

The paramedic took a plastic container of clear saline liquid from his kit bag and prepared to inject a needle into a vein in Calloway's left arm. Calloway covered his arm with his right hand, however, preventing the paramedic from starting the IV.

"No needles," he said angrily. "I won't have you sticking me with no needles!"

"OK," Teague replied, placing a plastic cover back over the hypodermic needle. "But tell me this. Why? Why'd you do it?"

After a moment Calloway answered calmly and clearly.

"I'm not sure. . . . I guess I just went crazy."

Once Jim Tucker, Andy Peterson, and Auburn Calloway were safely off the airplane, David Sanders began to realize the crisis was finally over.

He walked forward to the cockpit of the DC-10 to make sure the jet had been properly shut down. That would ensure that the final thirty minutes of audiotape on the cockpit voice recorder were preserved. He reached below the throttles to the three engine start switches and made sure the supply of fuel to the plane's herculean turbojets was blocked.

David's jaw felt numb. He had a couple of deep puncture wounds on his right arm from the tip of Calloway's speargun, his right ear was dangling, and there were six open gashes in his head that would require stitches. But Sanders couldn't recall ever being more exhilarated.

Standing at the open door of the silenced jet, breathing in the cool afternoon air, the captain had a feeling of triumph such as he had never known. He and his crew had used their own courage, determination, and teamwork to overcome a violent, unprecedented emergency situation. He hadn't known Peterson very well or Tucker at all before the flight. But he was as proud of them, and as grateful to them, as any person could be.

To use one of his daughter Lauren's favorite words, together they had been *awesome*.

Sanders watched as Peterson's ambulance departed, sirens wailing. Tucker and Calloway were being put in two separate vehicles, and Calloway's wrists were still shackled. Good.

"Come on," a paramedic on board the plane urged Sanders. "You need to get to the hospital, too."

Sanders said he'd go in just a minute.

He went back to the cockpit to retrieve his reading glasses. After a few seconds of searching, he found the spectacles on the far left side of the aircraft next to the captain's seat. A hammer blow had bent the frames severely. But the lenses were undamaged. He folded the glasses and tucked them into his shirt pocket.

Next, Sanders realized his throat was parched. Dried blood coated the inside of his nose and mouth. The captain retrieved a large bottle of Crystal Geyser water from an ice chest in the galley area. Despite the tumultuous events aboard the plane, the red ice-filled cooler was still in its proper place.

Sanders walked to the emergency slide on the side of the aircraft. He tossed the water bottle onto the inflated yellow slide and watched it tumble to the bottom where a fireman retrieved it. Seconds later, he followed the water bottle, feet first, the way all crew members practice on life-size cockpit mockups of emergency slides.

The captain rode to the hospital in the same ambulance as Tucker. Sanders sat next to the tall copilot who lay motionless on the stretcher. Clear intravenous fluid was draining into Tucker's left arm. He was in and out of consciousness, his bloody uniform cut away by paramedics searching for hidden injuries. Tucker was draped in a white sheet, a tranquil, peaceful look on his face.

Sanders hadn't known the extent of Tucker's injuries until now.

The paramedics' unmistakable expressions of concern and their urgent mannerisms told Sanders that Tucker was gravely wounded. And then the sense of victory that Sanders had savored so recently suddenly seemed like a distant, faded memory.

In another ambulance, paramedic David Teague sat at Auburn Calloway's head and tried to assess his wounds. The patient's clothes were saturated with blood, and Teague wasn't sure where it was coming from.

The handcuffs were still on, and Teague pulled Calloway's ripped and torn shirt down over his hands. He was tied to a stretcher by a restraint that had been pulled across his midsection, and covered with a sheet. Two paramedics and a fireman sat beside Calloway while the ambulance raced toward the downtown hospitals.

Teague washed the blood from Calloway's forehead and monitored his vital signs. His heartbeat was strong and steady, and his blood pressure, though elevated, was not dangerously high. Teague examined the most prominent wounds on Calloway's forehead. The flesh was ripped and swollen, and the bleeding around his face wouldn't stop.

"Watch his hands," the fireman on the left side of the ambulance cautioned. "He's trying to loosen the restraints."

Underneath the sheet, Calloway had unfastened the belt around his midsection. Suddenly, he tried to jump off the stretcher. Teague grabbed the patient's head and pushed down on his chest. The fireman sat down on Calloway's thrashing legs, pinning them.

The paramedics pulled the sheet off Calloway, then tightened the strap around his belly and put another around his legs.

"Don't fight us," Teague said. "It's all over."

PART THREE

"DELIVER US FROM EVIL"

▼

▼

▼

Flight engineer Andy Peterson was the first to arrive at The Regional Medical Center.

The public hospital known as The Med specializes in emergency trauma care, and its double doors opened automatically as paramedics wheeled Peterson inside. His ambulance was the first to leave the airport, and Peterson was awake and alert when he entered the hospital.

Paramedics had begun replacing lost blood with intravenous fluids during the ten-minute ride downtown. But Peterson's face was blanched and expressionless, and his pupils were dilated. Peterson definitely had a concussion, but he knew his name and he knew he was in a hospital in Memphis. He also could move all his fingers and toes. These extremely positive signs had been discovered during the ambulance trip. Paramedics wheeled Peterson into the "shock trauma" center, where the staff began blood transfusions and stapled closed the wounds on his scalp. A few minutes later, they moved him to a nearby room for a CAT scan.

The CAT scanner, like a giant white halo, encircled Peterson's body as he lay on a flat metal table. The imaging machine whirled around Peterson's head. A few minutes later, sharp pictures showed doctors that the flight engineer's brain was in astonishingly good condition. The images showed several fractures in Peterson's skull, but the cracked bones were at the surface and had not penetrated his brain. There was no internal hemorrhaging and, despite the concussion, Peterson's brain seemed to function normally.

Auburn Calloway arrived at the hospital next.

He was awake, and his heart rate, blood pressure, and breathing were steady. But Calloway was still bleeding from several head wounds, and he didn't respond to the medical staff's questions. Doctors and nurses couldn't tell if Calloway was reluctant or unable to speak. But their primary interest was making sure the patient's vital signs remained stable. There would be plenty of time for talk later.

Calloway's shirt had been cut away during the ambulance ride by paramedics searching for hidden wounds. His wrists were still bound by handcuffs.

Technicians moved him into the CAT-scan room right behind Peterson. There was only one CAT-scan machine at the hospital, and it was needed to assess the severity of both men's wounds. Neither one of the injured pilots seemed to notice the other's presence in the small room, however. And the medical personnel didn't treat them any differently. Their job was to heal patients, and it wasn't supposed to matter that one was a criminal suspect and the other was a victim.

When technicians finished with Peterson, he was transported on a gurney to the intensive-care ward while Calloway went under the CAT scanner. Calloway flinched as the noisy machine screeched and whirled around him. His movement blurred the film images and rendered them useless. The technicians weren't sure if Calloway could understand their instructions, but they told him that if he didn't lie still and cooperate, they would sedate him. Anesthesia was an unpleasant experience, they warned. They would inject liquid sedatives, then put a breathing tube down his throat. It would be better for everyone if Calloway stayed completely still for a few minutes and allowed the machine to take clear pictures.

Calloway did not acknowledge their instructions, but the next CAT scan produced a set of marvelously precise images. They showed that Calloway's skull had been fractured in two places: the left side of his forehead and the top of his cranium. The skin was torn in both areas, and there was significant swelling, especially on Calloway's forehead, where a lump the size of a goose egg had formed. But the CAT scan showed that Calloway's brain itself was remarkably intact, with little or no internal bleeding. And the fractures had not splintered the skull or driven broken bones into the fragile organ.

Calloway might elect to have cosmetic surgery in the future to repair the scars, but he had no life-threatening injuries, and there was no need for neurosurgeons to operate immediately.

After the CAT scans were finished, Calloway was transported to the hospital's prison ward. The green-painted ward was identical to any other hospital room, but the door to the hallway was always open, and a security guard was posted there around the clock. A nurse there cleaned and dressed Calloway's wounds and removed his handcuffs.

Calloway had said nothing since entering the hospital. But he spoke to the nurse as she bandaged his head. "I can't feel the left side of my body," he said softly, quietly. "I'm paralyzed. It's like I had a stroke."

The nurse was skeptical. She had been treating patients with head injuries for more than twenty years, and never had a patient told her calmly and coherently that he or she had had a stroke. Such patients usually were frightened and disoriented; if they spoke at all, their words were slurred and incomprehensible.

The nurse silently walked toward the foot of Calloway's bed. She lifted the sheet that exposed his bare feet, then brushed her index finger against the soles of his feet. The light touch of her long fingernail tickled. Calloway's toes involuntarily curled downward each time the nurse grazed the bottoms of his feet. His reflexes were fine, she concluded. The nurse didn't say anything to Calloway as she returned to bandaging his head.

"I can't feel the left side of my body," he insisted. "I can't."

There was another, cruder method to see if a patient was faking paralysis. The nurse picked up Calloway's left hand and soothingly rubbed his arm. "Can you feel this?" she asked, gently patting the back of his left hand while lifting his arm off the bed.

"No," he answered, "not at all."

The nurse pinched the fleshy underside of Calloway's forearm as she lifted the limb even higher. "Nope," Calloway said again nonchalantly. "I still can't feel a thing."

By this time, the nurse had extended Calloway's arm until it was nearly vertical. The patient lay on his back, with the left arm outstretched, palm turned inward across his body. Suddenly, the nurse let go of Calloway's muscular limb.

She let it fall.

If a patient truly was paralyzed, the palm of his falling hand would smack him in the face. If not, his reflexes would take over and the patient's arm would land delicately by his side. The nurse watched Calloway's hand miss his face and collapse onto the bed.

"See?" Calloway offered. "I can't even hold my arm up."

"I understand," the nurse replied knowingly. "I'll make sure the doctors are aware of your condition."

Jim Tucker and David Sanders were in the last ambulance to arrive at the hospital. Paramedics had bandaged their wounds and assessed their injuries on the way to The Med. Sanders was in full command of his faculties. His answers to questions were clear and precise, and he could walk without assistance.

But Tucker's medical state was worrisome. He was barely conscious. His words were garbled, and he was unable to move the right side of his body. When he came down from the airplane on the emergency slide, his right arm had trailed uselessly behind him. Paramedics thought the short trip down the slide might have dislocated Tucker's right shoulder—it was twisted at such an extreme angle. But orthopedic injuries were the least of their concerns.

When they shone a light in Tucker's eyes, the dilated pupil on his right side didn't respond. And when they looked at the wound on the left side of his head, they saw a deep crater. The hammer blow had driven bone fragments deep into his brain. A neurological injury of this kind could cause irreparable damage, even death.

The paramedics knew, too, that some head injuries were worse than fatal. The neuro intensive-care ward on the third floor of The Med was a repository for some of the region's hardest, most tragic cases. Drive-by shootings, bungled suicides, car and motorcycle accidents—they all sent victims to the third-floor "vegetable patch." Many of the patients there were in irreversible comas, and they would never emerge from their states of suspended animation. And despite the best efforts of the doctors and nurses, many of the patients on the third floor never walked out alive.

The paramedics had radioed ahead to the hospital to let doctors know the copilot would likely need emergency surgery. From the radio descriptions of Tucker's condition that the hospital received, doctors worried that there might not even be time for a CAT scan. They had to be ready to operate immediately—without the road map that a CAT would have provided.

Time was of the essence, and for Jim Tucker, time seemed to be running out.

"IS IT JIM?"

APRIL 7
4:40 P.M.

The kids were changing into their soccer uniforms and Becky Tucker was preparing to drive them to practice when the phone rang.

It was Patty Ruleman, a friend who was also the wife of a FedEx pilot. Becky and Patty had known each other for years due to their husband's friendship and similar career paths. Both men had flown for People Express before being hired at FedEx in 1984.

"Hey, what are you doing?" Patty asked casually.

"Well, I'm kind of on my way out the door," Becky said apologetically. "I've got to get the kids to soccer practice, and then . . ."

"Where's Jim?" Patty asked, quickly cutting to the point.

"He's flying an out-and-back to San Jose," Becky said, a little surprised that Patty wanted to know. Usually, when Patty called, she and Becky talked about their kids, school, household projects— not their husband's flying schedules.

"Are you sure Jim's going to San Jose? Not San Juan or San Diego or someplace like that?" Patty wanted to know.

"Yeah, it's San Jose," Becky said, a little taken aback by her friend's rapid-fire questions. "I'm sure it's San Jose because he said it was close to San Francisco, and he's going to bring back some sourdough bread. What's going on?"

There was an uncomfortable silence on the other end of the line, and that, too, was unusual. Patty was one of the most glib, talkative people that Becky had ever known. It was disquieting to find her at a loss for words.

"Look, don't go to soccer practice right now," Patty advised. "I mean, don't go anywhere. I've got to make a quick phone call, and then I'll get right back to you. But stay right there. OK?"

"OK," Becky agreed, slightly bewildered by the conversation as she hung up.

Maybe Patty had heard from her husband, Steve Ruleman, that the weather in San Jose was bad. Maybe he had told her that Jim was likely to be stuck there for a day or two instead of coming home tonight. But the unsettled tone of Patty's voice and her pressing questions about Jim's whereabouts were alarming. In all the time they had known each other, Becky had never heard Patty sound so concerned or evasive.

Becky began sweeping the kitchen floor as she waited for Patty to call back. But in the spotless kitchen of her spacious home, Becky was suddenly overwhelmed by a crushing, claustrophobic sensation that her world was caving in. She picked up the portable phone, went into the living room, and turned on the television. The local CBS affiliate had broken into its normal programming to announce that FedEx Flight 705 had landed in Memphis after a hijacking attempt, and that all the occupants were on their way to local hospitals. But the reporters didn't know the pilots' names or their medical conditions.

Then the phone rang again.

"Patty, what the hell's going on?" Becky almost shouted into the receiver.

Patty's husband was at the FedEx hub, and he had heard that Jim was part of the crew on Flight 705. He had asked his wife to confirm the information with Becky and be ready to help her.

"Stay right where you are," Patty said firmly. "I'm coming to get you right now."

All three of Becky's kids heard their mother on the phone, and they hurried downstairs from their bedrooms. "Go back upstairs and hold hands," she ordered. "Pray for your daddy and the other pilots. They need help."

But thirteen-year-old Morgan hesitated. "What's the matter?" he asked. "I'm big enough. You can tell me."

Becky didn't want to get into a long discussion, but she shared what little she knew.

"It sounds like something happened on the airplane and Daddy's been hurt," she said. "We all need to pray for him. Now, I'm getting ready to go to the hospital to see him. I'm going to give you my beeper, the key to the front door, and some money so you can look out for Andy and Rachael while I'm gone. Will you do that?"

Morgan nodded and ran upstairs while Becky flipped back and forth between local news broadcasts. She turned the volume down low so the children wouldn't be able to hear. All the stations had cut into their normal programming, and they were showing the same pictures of a DC-10 stopped on the runway at Memphis International Airport and glimpses of injured pilots exiting ambulances at The Med.

Becky got back on the telephone and started calling neighbors. She had to find someone to stay with the kids while she was at the hospital downtown. But none of them answered. They were all running errands, just as she had planned to be doing. Finally, she contacted Jani Hayes, the wife of another FedEx pilot. Jani lived in Collierville, too, and their children were about the same age.

"Can you get my kids and keep them tonight?" Becky wanted to know.

"Is it Jim?" Jani asked. She was watching TV, too.

"Yes."

"I'll be there in five minutes."

"AN UNLIKELY HERO"

APRIL 7

5:02 P.M.

Susan Peterson was heating fish sticks in the oven and carrots and English peas were boiling on the stove for dinner when the telephone rang.

"Hello, this is Neil Lipe," the resolute voice began. "Do you know who I am?"

It took her a second, but sure, Susan remembered Neil. He and Andy were hired the same day at FedEx. They went through flight-training classes together, learning how to become flight engineers on Boeing 727s. Neil and Andy were both native Mississippians, about the same age, and devout Christians.

"I'm not supposed to call you," Neil said in a solemn tone. "I'm out at the FedEx hub, and there's been a really unusual event. I don't know if anyone has informed you about it yet. But you have to know that there was an attempted hijacking on Andy's plane today—and everyone is safe on the ground in Memphis. That's about all I know right now."

Strangely, the news didn't alarm Susan. She regarded it as almost comical.

"A hijacking? So did Andy knock the gun out of the bad guy's

hand and tie him up?" she quipped. To her, Andy seemed an unlikely hero. Besides, Susan thought, no FedEx officials had called. If
anything serious had happened to Andy, surely the company would
have notified her promptly. Maybe Neil had misunderstood and
some crackpot had phoned in a bomb threat. Maybe Andy's plane
had returned to Memphis as a precaution. Heck, the plane couldn't
have gone far. It was scheduled to leave about 3:00 P.M., and now,
two hours later, another pilot was telling her it already was back on
the ground in Memphis.

"I appreciate the call, Neil, I really do," Susan said. "I can't wait
for Andy to fill me in on the details. Is he being interviewed by the
police now, or the FBI? Is he still at the airport?"

"I honestly don't know where Andy is right now," Neil answered. "But I want you to know he's back on the ground in Memphis and the situation is under control. That's about all I know for
sure."

He gave Susan the telephone number for the FedEx flight operations department and urged her to call and ask for a manager. "I'll
call you back if I can get any additional information about Andy," he
said. "Please let me know if there's anything else I can do."

Susan thanked Neil for calling and said good-bye. As soon as
she put the phone down, it rang again.

"Hi, Susan, this is John Wilcoxon," said a neighbor and fellow
FedEx employee. "I just heard about the hijacking on TV. Pretty
wild. Is Andy around? I wonder if he knows anything about it."

Susan chuckled.

"I imagine he does know something about it," she replied play-
fully. "You know, Andy was on that flight. He was part of the crew!"

Susan was still treating news of the hijacking like a joke. The
plane took off and then it landed. It was no big deal, and everyone
was safe on the ground, right? But Wilcoxon went silent when Susan
said Andy was on the plane. And his silence alarmed her.

"Oh, Susan, I'm so sorry," Wilcoxon finally stammered. "My
God, I didn't know."

The tone of Wilcoxon's voice scared Susan. She suddenly realized the situation had to be much more serious than she had assumed. She hung up and turned on the small black and white television perched on the kitchen counter. She studied its sharp picture as she continued preparing dinner.

The local news stations were showing the massive FedEx DC-10 stopped on the runway at Memphis International Airport. An inflated emergency slide stretched from the right passenger door to the ground. Brief video snippets showed the bloody FedEx pilots being whisked on stretchers from ambulances into The Med.

According to the news broadcasts, two of the unnamed pilots were in critical condition.

The phone rang again. This time it was Ed Bradley, a FedEx flight operations manager. Somberly, he told Susan what she had already learned, that Andy had been injured at work. He also told her that FedEx was sending a company security guard to pick her up at home and drive her to the hospital.

"Well, what's Andy's condition?" Susan asked. "Is he going to be OK? How bad is he hurt?"

"I can't tell you that," Bradley replied. "Please. Just give me directions to your house, and I'll send security to pick you up."

Susan began reciting the directions. From the airport, get on Interstate 55 south toward Olive Branch. Get off on Highway 305, the third exit and . . . suddenly, she changed her mind.

"Listen, I appreciate the offer," Susan said. "I'll get a ride to the hospital myself." Then, calmly but firmly, she repeated the question about her husband's condition. Was Andy OK or not? The news broadcasts were saying two pilots were critically injured. Was her husband one of them?

"I can't tell you that," Bradley replied.

Susan wondered if the terse response meant Bradley really didn't know how badly Andy was hurt—or he knew but wouldn't say.

"I'm sure the medical personnel will be able to give you much more accurate information than I can," Bradley added. "We want to assist you in every way possible. Are you sure you wouldn't like a ride to the hospital? We can arrange that for you. It's no trouble at all."

"I'm sure," she said. "Thanks anyway."

Susan felt deeply frightened, yet at the same time strangely calm and at peace with her belief that God would guide her family through the ordeal. She was certain He would take care of her and her family no matter what. She called her minister, Richard Rieves, and asked for a ride to the hospital. She told him that Andy had been injured in a hijacking, and immediately, the pastor said he was on his way.

Rieves was the assistant pastor at River Oaks Presbyterian Church, but he planned to open a church in Olive Branch the following year, and Andy and Susan were to be founding members. Rieves and his wife, Rachel, were about the same age as Andy and Susan, and they had three young children, too. The families had become good friends during four years being active in the same church.

Next, Susan called her mother in Montgomery and asked her to call Andy's relatives and tell them about the attempted hijacking. Susan gave her mother the telephone numbers of Andy's parents in Goodman and his sister, Sandy, in Clarksdale, Mississippi.

"I'm doing OK," Susan told her mom. "But I may not be able to hold it together if I have to tell Andy's parents myself. They're strong people—but Andy means everything to them."

Susan took the unfinished fish sticks out of the oven and turned off the stove. All three children were seated at the square wooden table in the kitchen. They had been there the entire time she was on the telephone. Susan swept the kids into her arms and moved them to the living room.

They sat on the rug, and Susan held the squirming Will in her arms. The toddler with the unruly blond curls reached and tugged at everything he could get his hands on. Anna, the middle child, was silent and compliant. She studied her mother with searching brown eyes.

"We need to pray for your daddy," Susan began, outwardly calm, but her voice beginning to crack. "Daddy's been hurt. I don't know how bad yet. Mommy is going to the hospital to check on him soon."

Mary Margaret, at seven, the oldest of the three children, was alarmed by the tension in her mother's voice. "Is he going to die?" the girl asked.

Susan looked directly into Mary Margaret's pale-blue eyes. Susan didn't want to scare the children, but she couldn't mislead them, either. "I don't know, sweetheart," she answered honestly. "It's too soon for me to know that right now."

They sat in a circle on the beige carpet and began to pray.

"DRIVE SLOWLY DOWNTOWN"

APRIL 7

5:20 P.M.

Susan Sanders was preparing dinner for daughter, Lauren, when Kelly Roberts called saying she wanted to confirm their plans for the next morning.

Was 9:00 A.M. too early to come by? Which antiques stores did they intend to visit first?

It seemed to Susan a perfectly ordinary conversation until her friend, also the wife of a FedEx pilot, asked about David Sanders. He was on reserve today, right? Did he get called out on a trip? What was his destination?

"He was flying to California," Susan said. "In fact, I'm sure he said he was going to San Jose. He'll be back sometime after midnight. Why?" Roberts told her there was no real reason for the questions. Just curious. Oh, well. Got to go. Bye.

Susan went back to fixing dinner. She had made turkey soup during the morning, and tonight it would be perfect. That, with a loaf of fresh-baked bread from their countertop bread machine, would be a light but healthful meal. She and Lauren weren't big eaters, anyway.

The phone rang again.

It was David. That was odd, Susan thought. He must have gotten bumped from his flight. Flight managers occasionally replace regular crews with little or no notice if the managers need to operate a flight to remain current. It's a boon for the regular crew because they get paid the same whether they make the trip or not.

"Susan, is Lauren with you?" he asked.

"Sure, she's right across the counter."

"Good," he said, sounding unusually relieved at that small bit of information. "I'd like both of you to get in the car and drive, slowly, downtown."

Great, Susan thought. He's going to take us out to a fancy dinner at one of the restaurants by the Mississippi River. Maybe we could go to that French place, Paulette's. Maybe the other crew members would join them.

"I want you to know that I'm fine," David continued. "But I've got some cuts and bruises. There was an incident on the airplane today, and I'm at the hospital. I'm in the emergency room at The Med."

Susan was stunned. An incident? Did the plane crash or make a forced landing? Was anyone killed?

"I'll tell you all about it when you get here," David promised. "There are probably going to be some TV cameras at the hospital. Don't answer any questions, don't tell them who you are, don't say anything. Just come inside and someone from FedEx will meet you. But take your time and drive carefully. Everything is OK."

Susan told Lauren to turn on the television a few feet away in the living room. All three of the local stations were devoting huge sections of their broadcasts to the FedEx hijacking story. It was the first they had heard that a hijacking had been attempted on the plane her husband was flying. How strange that FedEx would be the target.

From the sound of his voice, Susan could tell her husband was his normal unflappable self. The news reports said two of the pilots were in critical condition. She was sorry for them and their families but relieved that David sounded all right.

Susan dialed Kelly Roberts's telephone number.

"You knew, didn't you?" Susan began.

"Yes," she confessed. "When you said David was flying to San Jose, that's when I knew."

"Well, David just called," Susan said, "He sounds fine. Lauren and I are on our way downtown to meet him."

"FADING FAST"

APRIL 7
5:22 P.M.

Patty Ruleman, a lifelong Memphis resident and former registered nurse, drove down back roads and side streets on the way to The Med. Becky Tucker had brought a telephone book from her house, and she looked up the hospital's patient-information telephone number, then dialed the cellular phone in Patty's car.

"I'm Jim Tucker's wife," she explained to a receptionist, then to an emergency room doctor. "He's one of the FedEx pilots that was just brought there. I'm on the way to the hospital right now, but I need to know how he's doing."

The doctor paused for a moment. What was her husband's name again?

"Tucker," she said. "Jim Tucker, the copilot."

"You're talking about the big guy, right?" the doctor asked.

"Yes! He's real tall. How's he doing? Is he still alive?"

"Yeah, he's alive and his condition is stable right now," the doctor answered. "We're getting him ready for surgery, and he's going to be on his way in a few minutes. But we'll try to wait until you get here before we start."

Patty whipped her Toyota Camry into a parking lot reserved for doctors at The Med, then took Becky on a shortcut to the emergency room. FedEx officials had cordoned off a wide area at the front entrance, and the two women marched right by it. An elderly hospital chaplain spotted them, and he silently accompanied the two women to the emergency room.

When they got there, Becky asked a nurse in hospital scrubs where she could find Jim Tucker, the wounded pilot.

"Follow me," the nurse directed. "He's fading pretty fast, and he may not recognize you. He's going into surgery soon, so you won't have much time with him."

Becky spotted her husband wrapped in green sheets on a gurney. His head was bandaged and his clothes were cut away, and he was caked from head to foot in crusty blood. Dry, brownish splotches covered his face, chest, and arms, and blood stuck underneath his fingernails.

"I'm here, Jim," Becky said, taking his hand. "I'm right here."

Jim stirred with recognition at the sound of her voice and opened his eyes. But the normally white portions around each iris were the color of garish lipstick from internal bleeding. Becky put her face directly in front of her husband, but she couldn't tell if he saw her. "You're going to be OK," she told him, trying to sound confident. "Hang in there."

Becky started to quietly recite the Lord's Prayer in her husband's ear.

"Our Father who art in heaven, hallowed be thy name. Thy kingdom come, thy will be done, on earth as it is heaven. Give us this day our daily bread. And forgive our debts as we forgive our debtors. And lead us not into temptation, but deliver us from evil: For thine is the kingdom and the power and the glory, for ever. . . ."

"We're out of time," a nurse told Becky sympathetically. "We've got to get going."

A team of nurses and technicians pushed Jim's gurney forward, through the double doors that led to the surgical suite. Another nurse stayed back to talk to Becky, but the nurse could provide no assurances other than that the medical team would do the best they could. Jim's brain appeared to have been severely injured. Neurosurgery was risky, but in Jim's case, less so than allowing time to slip away without medical intervention. It was possible that Jim could die on the operating table. If he lived, he might never be the same.

"This is going to take awhile," the nurse cautioned. "He could be in surgery for three or four hours or more. How quickly it goes will be depend on what we find. Try to be patient and stay calm."

APRIL 7

5:25 P.M.

The telephone at Andy and Susan Peterson's home started ringing constantly.

Friends, neighbors, Andy's coworkers—all of them were offering help and trying to learn more about the attempted hijacking. But none of the callers seemed to have any new information. They had seen or heard the news on CNN, local television, and national radio. Soon it would be on the network news, too.

Where was the pastor, Richard Rieves? Susan had called more than thirty minutes ago, and she was growing more anxious all the time. Why hadn't he arrived yet? From his home in east Memphis, he should have been able to cover the distance to her house in twenty minutes or less. To make matters worse, Richard's wife kept calling to ask if he'd arrived yet. She had learned from a church member who was a resident physician at The Med, that Andy was in bad shape, and wanted to tell Richard so that he could prepare Susan. But at the same time she didn't want to alarm Susan.

Neighbors began showing up at the house unannounced and volunteered to baby-sit for the children. Susan was giving instructions to one of them when a Ford Taurus pulled into the driveway. It was Richard. Susan kissed the kids, grabbed a jacket, and jumped into the car.

Richard immediately apologized for the delay.

"Traffic was a mess," he said. "My car was about out of gas. Then I had to wait for what must have been the world's longest and slowest freight train. It must've been two miles long."

"That's all right," she said. "I appreciate your coming. Rachel called. Do you want to talk to her before we leave?"

Richard declined in order to get Susan to the hospital as quickly as possible.

"Do you want to listen to the radio on the way?" Richard asked.

Susan decided to wait and learn the extent of Andy's injuries when they arrived at the hospital in thirty minutes or so. Richard expected Susan to be emotional, and he was surprised by her composed, factual analysis.

"The news reports have been saying two pilots were critically injured in an attempted hijacking," she said. "I hate to be a pessimist, but one of them is probably Andy. As the flight engineer, he's the first one a hijacker walking into the cockpit would encounter. And since the plane landed safely, the captain and the copilot were probably flying. So chances are Andy's hurt pretty bad.

"Plus," she continued, "I know Andy. He's so observant. He notices everything! If someone was acting weird, or if something wasn't right about some of the passengers, he'd recognize it before anyone else. If a hijacker came in the cockpit, Andy would try to do something about it right away. It's his nature."

Richard drove faster than the fifty-five-mile-an-hour speed limit on the way to the medical center. Yet each time a car passed them, Susan had to suppress the urge to slam her foot against the gas pedal. "Come on, Richard!" she wanted to scream. "Punch it!"

It was almost 7:00 P.M. when they pulled up to the emergency room entrance at the hospital. An elder from their church was waiting there along with Mark Boorsma, the resident physician and church member whom Richard's wife had spoken with.

The doctor was wearing a white laboratory coat, and he smiled when he saw Susan.

"Guess who I just talked to," the doctor asked her.

"Andy?"

"That's right," he said reassuringly. "Let me take you to him."

"A CADILLAC WITHOUT POWER STEERING"

APRIL 7

6:42 P.M.

Close observers could see the DC-10 was damaged even before FedEx ground workers towed it to the company's maintenance hangar.

A cleaning crew already was engaged in the macabre task of washing blood off the cockpit instruments, walls, ceiling, and floor as the airplane moved slowly toward Hangar 10, the maintenance facility next to the sprawling FedEx package-sorting hub. An FBI photographer had been on board to document the crime scene, and agents had finished collecting evidence.

All the freight on the aircraft had been unloaded, and the cargo containers were in the process of being moved onto three smaller Boeing 727s for the trip to San Jose. Every package that had been aboard Flight 705 would arrive at its destination on time.

Now that the aerial crisis was over, it was time for company managers and mechanics to assess the condition of the DC-10 itself. As a practical matter, the company needed to return the wide-body jet to service as soon as possible. Also, the quicker the plane could get back in the air, the easier it would be to downplay how close the company had come to disaster. The entire FedEx hub had almost been obliterated by a single, disgruntled employee, and managers didn't want to discuss "what if" scenarios.

"The plane's perfectly airworthy," FedEx spokesmen hoped to be able to tell reporters soon. "We looked it over, gave it an oil change and a lube job, and put it back in revenue service. No big deal."

If pressed, they could say they had made some precautionary repairs to an already airworthy plane.

Reality, though, was more complicated.

Jimmy Price, an off-duty FedEx DC-10 captain, stood on the ramp with a group of aircraft mechanics and scrutinized the mammoth plane as a tug driver pushed it tail first into the empty hangar. The tip of the gargantuan plane's rudder barely cleared the top of the sliding door's frames.

As the wide-body jet rolled slowly by, onlookers saw a number of airframe problems or "discrepancies." Jagged pieces of torn sheet metal were exposed on the tips of the plane's seventy-one-foot-wide horizontal tail where a pair of three-foot-long counterweights had been ripped from the tips of the elevator. The two hundred-pound weights made from dense depleted uranium had apparently been shorn from the airplane in flight.

Such damage was incredibly rare, maybe even unprecedented for an aircraft that landed safely. The observers knew the damage to the tail could only have been caused by extreme circumstances, such as the plane far exceeding its maximum design speed.

The counterweights are designed to lighten elevator forces and make it easier for pilots to adjust the plane's pitch in flight. Even though the elevators are hydraulically boosted, the absence of counterweights would make the control forces abnormally heavy—especially at high speeds. The ailerons, which control the plane's roll, would be normal. But pilots would have to pull and push mightily on the yoke to alter the plane's pitch without the counterweights. The control columns would feel like the steering wheel on a Cadillac without power-steering fluid.

As the plane moved deeper into the hangar, other problems emerged.

Fuel from ruptured wing tanks dripped steadily onto the gray-painted floor. DC-10s have "wet wings," meaning fuel is stored in metal compartments inside. The overweight landing or abnormally heavy acceleration or G forces apparently had sent tons of fuel sloshing through the tanks. And the extraordinary pressures from the shifting liquid appeared to have pulled apart metal borders inside the wings, which now dripped like wet sponges.

The two engines mounted on pylons underneath the wings were

intact. But several metal panels on each of the two cowlings that enclose the engines were gone. The missing round six-inch metal panels wouldn't cause any aerodynamic problems for the airplane in flight. Mechanics pulled the panels off regularly to inspect the engines and check oil levels. There had even been a few cases in which planes had flown entire trips without the crews ever noticing the panels had been removed. Price and the mechanics suspected that the panels on this plane had blown away in flight—further confirmation that the DC-10 had been subjected to extraordinary stress.

The DC-10's brakes would have to be replaced, along with all twelve tires. The overweight plane had been brought to a rapid stop, and most of the tires had cord showing. The landing gear looked fine, though. So did most of the control surfaces. There were no major hydraulic leaks.

As the plane moved into the hangar, several FedEx managers marked the damaged items on clipboards. They called in an extra crew of mechanics to examine every inch of the plane. The inspection had to be done thoroughly, quickly, and quietly. It would mean less paperwork and fewer headaches for everyone involved.

The leaky fuel cells could be patched in a hurry. Once FedEx workers drained the massive fuel tanks, mechanics could crawl inside to locate and replace any popped rivets or torn sheet metal. The missing access panels, too, could be easily replaced. There was a whole stack of spare panels in the maintenance shop. And installing new wheels and brakes was a laborious but relatively simple task.

The counterweights would be a challenge, however. Those don't normally need to be replaced as a part of regular maintenance. Where could extra counterweights be found? And if they were located, could FedEx maintenance crews install them? Did the job require any special tools? What sorts of inspections were required? No one seemed to know the answers right away.

"Hey, just forget about the counterweights for a minute," one of the mechanics advised, staring intently at the tail. Just looking at the elevator—the movable portion of the horizontal tail—the mechanic could see that it was warped and deformed. In addition to having the counterweights pulled off, the hinged metal surface that controls the plane's pitch had been twisted. None of the mechanics had ever seen anything like it. But the more they looked, the more obvious the damage became.

"I'll call McDonnell Douglas right now and see if we can get a new elevator sent today," a FedEx manager volunteered. "If we have to, we can get some of their specialists to come here and help us install it. We can probably change the elevator in a day or two. But if anyone asks, all we're doing here is routine maintenance. Does everyone understand that?"

"A BAD HAIR DAY"

APRIL 7
6:45 P.M.

Susan Peterson hurried into The Med with Mark Boorsma, the doctor from her church, and Richard Rieves.

The trio came through a narrow brick courtyard where ambulances brought sick and injured patients. A pair of wide double doors automatically parted as they strode into the building where a pair of Elvis paintings looked down from the wall. The late singer's estate was a major hospital donor, and the state-of-the-art trauma center was named for Memphis's favorite son.

Boorsma guided Susan past the two-bed shock trauma room, where the most critically injured patients are treated. They swept through a series of corridors on the ground floor and finally arrived at the main trauma center.

Except for all the medical equipment, the place was like a FedEx office building. There were pilots in uniform, managers wearing suits with purple ID cards on their lapels, and company security personnel everywhere. They seemed to far outnumber the doctors and nurses.

Boorsma had spoken with the other doctors about Andy, and he brought Susan up to date on her husband's medical condition.

"He was attacked with a hammer and suffered some pretty severe head injuries," the doctor said. "Andy lost a lot of blood, but the bleeding has stopped and the blood is being replaced.

"The first priority for the emergency room doctors was to stop the bleeding and assess what, if any, brain damage Andy suffered. So they stapled the wounds closed to stop the bleeding. It worked. They also did a CAT scan of Andy's head, and that's what gave us the really good news. It's almost miraculous, but there was no internal bleeding. It looks now like there won't be any permanent brain damage."

Susan closed her eyes and Boorsma could see her lips move.

"Thank God," she said silently, over and over again, her hands clasped in prayer.

"Now, he's not quite out of the woods yet," Boorsma cautioned. "The next twenty-four hours will be extremely important. They'll keep him under close observation—he'll probably spend the night in intensive care. Don't let the fact that he's in intensive care scare you. That just means they're going to be watching him especially close to make sure he doesn't have any complications. Tomorrow, if everything goes all right, he could be moved to a regular hospital room."

Andy was being treated when Susan arrived, and the nurses told her to wait outside until the doctors were finished. She stood in a hallway with Boorsma and Rieves. But when the FedEx pilots, managers, and employees learned that Susan was Andy's wife, several related stories of her husband's bravery and good humor in dealing with his injuries.

"He's awake and alert," one pilot said.

"He was cracking jokes while they were sewing him up," another added.

Why, Susan wondered, if all these strangers had been allowed to talk to her husband, was she being prevented from seeing him? An Air Line Pilots Association representative gave Susan his business card and let her know that members had volunteered to help out by mowing the lawn, bringing meals and groceries, looking after the kids, anything.

"I've just been to see Andy," he said. "They assure me he's going to be OK."

A FedEx manager made similar offers. Also, FedEx security personnel were on the way to Olive Branch to wait outside their home and keep reporters or unwanted visitors away. If the union pilots were bothering her, managers assured her they could get rid of them, too.

Susan's frustration grew. She wanted to be polite. But she had been in the hospital for almost an hour, and everyone, it seemed, had been allowed to see Andy except for her. Her patience was at an end.

"When can I go see him?" she pleaded. "Please don't tell me to wait any longer."

"They're cleaning him up for you," she said. "They're almost done. He knows you're here."

"Look. Andy was there in the delivery room with me when all three of our children were born. He did fine. Now, I don't like the sight of blood, but I can take it. I want to see him, please."

Finally, Boorsma got clearance to enter the trauma center's overflow room where doctors were still working on Andy. Susan strode into the windowless rectangular room with a dozen beds placed against the walls—only a few of them occupied.

Boorsma and Rieves were close behind her.

Susan had expected Andy to look bad, but when she saw her husband propped up in a sitting position on a hospital gurney, she barely recognized him. His face was the size and shape of a basketball, his cheeks and chin merged in shapeless swelling, and his skin was as white as talcum powder. Deep purple rings of pooled blood hung in puffy semicircles around his eyes.

Worst of all, Andy's head was shaved except for a thin strip of blond hair on top, which was stained red. Jagged cuts, indentations, black silk sutures, and thick metal staples held the pale flesh on the sides of his head together.

"Honey, I'm having a bad hair day," the pilot offered, forcing himself to smile about his crimson mohawk. Rieves put his arm around Susan to catch her if she fainted.

Susan didn't flinch. She stared softly at her husband, then came to the side of the bed and took his hand. It felt cold to the touch. There were black-and-blue bite marks up and down his forearms. A long red gash snaked its way from the inside of his right elbow across his biceps, where the point of Calloway's spear had sliced into him. An intravenous tube dripped saline solution into a vein in his left arm.

She kissed him on the cheek, then pressed the back of her hand gently against his swollen face.

"Yeah, Andy, you are having a bad hair day," she said. "But right now I'm just glad you're alive. That's all that matters. You're alive and you're going to be OK."

Susan bent down and gingerly hugged him.

Even though the thermostat in the hospital room was turned up high, and Andy's legs and waist were covered with sheets and blankets, he shivered.

"Are you cold, sweetheart?" Susan asked.

"Kind of."

The adrenaline was wearing off. Andy was feeling more and more pain, although he did his best not to show it. The shivers, Boorsma explained, were a normal part of the body's reaction to shock.

"Can you tell me what happened on the plane, Andy?" Susan asked. "Do you remember anything?"

He nodded, looking suddenly exhausted.

"A guy hit me in the head with a hammer," he explained. "He bit me, too."

Andy raised his left arm slightly, showing Susan a series of bite marks that made the appendage look like a half-eaten piece of corn on the cob. Andy rested his head back against the pillows and grinned, his white teeth showing.

"But don't you worry," he added. "I bit him, too."

As Susan began to realize her husband would be all right, the tension that had built so quickly during the last two hours receded at once. Tears welled up in her eyes, then streamed down her cheeks. Richard called the people in the room to circle around Andy, and they held hands and prayed.

"Thank you, God, for sparing Andy's life today." he began. "Thank you for allowing him to remain with his family and friends who need him. . . ."

A few minutes later, the nurses asked Susan and the others to leave. Visiting hours were over, and they were transferring Andy to another part of the intensive-care ward for the night. "Visiting hours begin tomorrow morning at nine," a nurse told Susan. "You can come back then."

Susan was worried that there might be an emergency during the night and that no one would let her know. Her husband could have died during the three and a half hours that had passed from the time the plane landed until she had arrived at the hospital. If he passed away alone during the night, she would never forgive herself for failing to be by his side.

But the hospital staff insisted that she leave.

Get some rest and come back in the morning, they told her. If anything happened during the night, good or bad, the nurses promised to call.

APRIL 7

11:00 P.M.

Doctors wanted David Sanders to spend the night at The Med: He had a concussion, there was a risk of infection from many deep cuts and lacerations, and there could be internal bleeding. But the DC-10 captain flatly refused.

"Thanks for your concern," he told them, "but I'm going home. It'll be better for my family and it'll be better for me. Really."

At 11:00 P.M. he left the hospital with Susan and Lauren in Susan's white 1986 Oldsmobile sedan. A FedEx security guard drove, and another followed in a company car. They arrived home close to midnight, leaving the guards to spend the night in a FedEx car on the long, unpaved driveway that led from the winding street to their mobile home and as-yet-undeveloped lot.

Susan placed several logs in the fireplace, lit the kindling with a long wooden match, and put a pot of water on the stove for tea. Her husband had been through a harrowing ordeal, but now he was home safely, and she sought to reassure him.

David tried to relax, but his mind still raced. He wondered if Jim Tucker and Andy Peterson would live through the night. Would they suffer permanent brain damage? What about Auburn Calloway? Why had he attacked the crew? What was he trying to accomplish?

David and Susan had talked briefly with Jim and Andy and met their wives at the hospital. But the three men hadn't known each other prior to boarding the DC-10, and each of the families had been overwhelmed dealing with its separate situation.

David sat on the couch drinking decaffeinated tea while the heat of the crackling fire warmed the room. As the night wore on and the adrenaline receded, David began to feel his injuries. He had an excruciating headache, and the stitches and cuts made it almost impossible for him to rest his head on a pillow. There were a dozen sutures in his right ear, and the muscles in his jaw were sore. He took a few pain pills. The doctors warned the medication would make him drowsy, but David stayed wide awake despite the soothing environment Susan had created.

They went to bed but couldn't sleep. As the low rays of sunlight crept through the windows, David got up and took a walk around their property. Eventually, the rising sun sparkled on the lake to the southwest, and songbirds in the blossoming trees were engaged in their morning havoc. The hilltop where they would build their future home still beckoned, but the events of the previous day made everything seem different, and less certain.

When he returned to the mobile home, Susan was in the kitchen.

"You hungry?" she asked. "I can make breakfast."

David shook his head. No appetite at all.

Lauren was sound asleep in her room.

"I can't eat either," Susan said. "What do you want to do?"

"I'd like to go back to The Med and check on Jim and Andy."

"Yeah," Susan said. "Let's go."

BEAUTY REST

APRIL 7

11:15 P.M.

Susan Peterson checked into the Hampton Inn on Union Avenue, a few blocks from The Med.

It was a cool, starry night. In about seven hours, morning sunlight would pour through the hotel window. Susan tried to sleep but it was useless.

She called home to check on the kids. She prayed. She called her parents in Montgomery. She called the hospital every hour for an update from the nurses on duty. Every time she closed her eyes, she saw her husband's ghastly wounds. He had been in a fight for his life, and she couldn't imagine what that must have been like. Why would anyone want to harm Andy or, by extension, her or their three children?

At 5:00 A.M., she dialed the direct number to the intensive-care nursing station for the fifth time.

"How's he doing?" Susan began. "Is he awake yet? Can you tell?"

Two narrow slits showed the nurses that Andy's swollen eyes were indeed open. "Is that Susan?" the patient asked, raising his voice so that the nurse on the telephone twenty feet away could hear him. "If that's Susan, don't hang up. I'd like to talk to her."

Andy struggled to get out of bed, but another nurse hurried over to stop him.

"If you promise to stay in bed, we'll wheel you over to the phone," a nurse offered. "We've told your wife a hundred times you're doing just fine. But I get the feeling she'll only believe it if she hears it from you."

"Y'all know Susan pretty well," Andy chuckled. "Are you sure you met her for the first time yesterday?"

"We're sure," the nurse laughed as she pushed Andy's bed

toward the telephone. Another walked beside them carrying the apparatus that held the bottle of intravenous fluid connected to Andy's arm. The long telephone cord stretched down to Andy's bed, and because the wounds on the left side of his head were still fresh, a nurse held the receiver a few inches from his right ear.

"Hey, Susan. It's Andy."

"You don't need to introduce yourself," she said sweetly. "You might look a little different, but your voice still sounds the same."

"That's good, I guess." Andy's throat was dry, and he wasn't sure how long he could talk.

"Susan, I want to let you know that they're taking real good care of me here. I don't think there's anything to worry about," he said earnestly. "Say, you're coming to see me today, aren't you?"

"Are you kidding? Of course I'm coming to see you. I'd be there right now if they'd let me."

"That's great," he went on. "We may not want to bring the kids right away. The way I look now, I'd probably give them a fright."

Susan started to laugh, but sobs came out instead. Once she started crying, she couldn't stop. Each time she began to say something, the cries became louder. She cupped her hand over the telephone mouthpiece, but Andy and all the nurses around him could hear her wails. Andy pretended not to notice.

"You know, I'd better get my beauty rest," he quipped. "I want you to do the same. I'll see you when you get here. I love you, Susan."

It didn't seem possible, but when Susan Peterson arrived at The Med the morning after the attack, there were even more FedEx people than the previous evening.

The Air Line Pilots Association was keeping a twenty-four-hour vigil at the hospital, and company managers were there, too. The place was full of purple FedEx ID badges.

"Andy's getting some color back in his cheeks," one of the pilots told Susan when she arrived at the intensive-care unit. "He's awake and alert."

"You've been to see him?" she asked. "They told me visiting hours don't start until nine."

"Oh, we've been in there most of the morning," the pilot replied. "He seems like he's in real good spirits. The doctors said the second CAT scan went real well, too. Your husband is one hard-headed hombre."

Susan simmered inside. She knew that Andy was too nice to tell anyone who came to see him to go away. He was probably exhausted and in pain. But instead of saving his energy for healing, he was entertaining a bunch of acquaintances from work. They probably wanted him to recite details of the attack so they could gossip about it in the crew room during hub turns.

But when she wanted to see him, the nurses told her sternly that visiting hours began at 9:00 A.M.

FedEx had set up a private waiting room for families of the three Flight 705 pilots. Susan entered and glanced at her watch. It was five minutes until nine. Two men, a FedEx manager and a pilots' union leader, introduced themselves and offered their assistance.

Susan had been as patient as she knew how to be. Now she decided it was time for her to take charge.

"How about getting me a diet Coke?" Susan asked, wanting to get rid of them.

The union member promptly left to retrieve the beverage.

Then Susan addressed the FedEx manager. "There's something else I'd like you to do for me," she began.

"Sure thing," he said, standing almost at attention. "Just name it."

Susan leveled her determined blue eyes at the stocky manager. He was about her height, maybe ten years older. She spoke softly, but her clipped, authoritative tone left no room for misinterpretation. "I don't want anyone who's not a doctor or a nurse visiting Andy today," she instructed. "He's tired and he needs rest. He doesn't need to talk to anyone right now. OK?"

"Sure thing, Mrs. Peterson," he said. "I'll take care of it."

The burly FedEx manager started to walk away, but Susan stopped him. "And when you're done," she added, "I want you to stand by the door to his room. Keep everyone who doesn't work here out. Let them know we sincerely appreciate their concern, but right now Andy has other priorities. OK?"

"Yes, ma'am."

David and Susan Sanders went to Andy Peterson's hospital room and Andy motioned for them to come in.

The four talked about the things they had done to pass the sleepless night. But when David queried Andy about the events on the plane the previous day, the flight engineer recalled only scant details of the attack. His memory of the event itself was fragmented. He remembered bits and pieces of the protracted struggle aboard the airplane, but large gaps of time, for him, had vanished.

David was anxious to compare his recollections with Andy's. David asked what Andy and Jim Tucker had been doing at certain moments while he was in the cockpit. What did Auburn Calloway do? What did he say? How was his demeanor?

"I'm sorry," Andy apologized. "I'm just drawing a blank. Maybe it'll come to me later."

Susan Sanders smiled at Andy sympathetically. During the previous night, she had heard her husband recount his version of the struggle on the plane, and she thanked Andy for all he had done. David had said the humble, tenacious flight engineer was invaluable in defeating Calloway.

"I kind of remember," Andy smiled, "but just vaguely."

"Well, I want you to know that you were magnificent," David added emphatically. "You saved my life, and Jim's, too. That guy was trying to kill all of us."

Jim Tucker, they learned, had undergone delicate surgery. Yesterday, doctors removed splintered bone fragments and a blood clot the size of a walnut from Jim's brain. He still hadn't awakened.

David and Susan Sanders went into the waiting room that FedEx had reserved for family and friends of the injured pilots. The place was filled with company managers and off-duty pilots. They congratulated David for landing the jet safely, but everyone's mood was tempered by concern for Jim. His life was in jeopardy. And if he lived, there was a real chance he could remain in a permanent vegetative state or lose massive portions of his memory and cognitive ability.

Becky Tucker was there in the waiting room. She was on the phone much of the time, making arrangements with her family, friends, neighbors, and FedEx managers. She received periodic updates on her husband's condition from doctors and nurses.

David greeted her and told her how vital her husband had been to the crew's survival.

"If not for Jim, I don't know what we would have done," he said. "If not for Jim, we could not have lived. Of that, I'm absolutely certain."

Becky thanked the captain for his kind words. But she couldn't help applying them to her own family's future: "If not for Jim, I don't know what we'll do. . . . If not for Jim, we cannot go on." Of that, she was equally sure.

Becky explained that Jim was likely to wake up soon. The operation had gone as well as could be expected. Jim had been put under a general anesthetic, so he would be groggy when he woke up, and it would likely be another day or two before doctors could begin to assess the results.

David and Susan sat down and resolved to wait as long as Becky wanted them to stay. As far as the doctors could tell, the surgery had accomplished its purpose. The blood clot was gone with little apparent damage to the surrounding portion of his brain.

The doctors warned against too much optimism, however. The immediate danger was over, but the results from these kinds of surgeries could be unpredictable. The copilot was awakening, though, and he wanted to see Becky.

She asked David and Susan to come along.

The fog of anesthesia was still thick, but Jim reached out and took Becky's hand as soon as he saw her. He was gaunt and pale, his head was completely shaved, and his scalp was laced together like a football with scores of thick, rough stitches. His face was scratched and bruised, but not as swollen or discolored as Andy's.

When Jim saw David Sanders, he tried to speak but his voice was a faint whisper. He tried to sit up but couldn't move. David had to bend down and put his ear a few inches from Jim's mouth in order to hear him.

The copilot's throat was dry, and his words came out in a raspy whisper. "He was so sneaky," Jim said, his voice barely audible. "In the back of the plane . . . He was so sneaky."

David looked into Jim's glassy, red eyes.

"Yes," the captain said. "You're talking about the attacker. He kept trying to trick us, too. He kept trying to fool us. Did he do that to you?"

Jim nodded weakly.

"He said he would stop," the copilot said slowly. "I didn't want to fight. . . . He was so sneaky."

"ON MY WAY"

APRIL 8

4:00 P.M.

Angelique Michelle Calloway visited her estranged brother in the prison ward at The Med.

Large, with broad shoulders, Angelique wore thick makeup. She and her brother hadn't seen each other for years. When Auburn was in the Navy in San Diego, Angelique had gone to visit him and try to improve their relationship. But they didn't get along, even then. Angelique had tried to reach out to Auburn when his daughter, Keelah, was born, but to no avail.

Now Angelique was a reading teacher in Centreville, Virginia. She had flown to Memphis immediately when Auburn's ex-wife, Patricia, told her that he had been injured. In the Memphis airport, she saw the Memphis newspaper had several stories about the attempted hijacking of the FedEx DC-10. The banner headline screamed FEDEX CREW BEATS ATTACKER: LANDS JET.

But Angelique knew her brother, and she didn't believe the newspaper. He could be moody and withdrawn at times—but hijacking a jet? Come on. He was too smart for that. Angelique took a taxi from the airport to the downtown hospital. She had to sign in with a security guard who escorted her to the door of the prison ward and allowed her to enter the green room alone.

Auburn lay on a hospital bed. His head was covered in gauze bandages, but his eyes were clear, and she saw an immediate look of recognition in his face.

"Oh, Auburn," she said. "Look what they've done to you!"

Even through the bandages, Angelique could see a swollen knot on his forehead. The bandages were coated with antibacterial ointment to keep the deep cuts on his scalp from becoming infected. Auburn swallowed deeply and tried to clear his throat. Wasn't anyone paying attention to him? Angelique wondered.

"Why did they do this to you?" she asked. "What happened?"

Auburn rolled his eyes. He said in a scratchy voice that he couldn't get into the details. He wanted to know about the kids. Tomorrow was Burney's birthday. Were the kids OK? Were they going to visit him?

Angelique said his ex-wife was on the way to Memphis already. FedEx was trying to treat the families of all the injured pilots equally, so the company bought Patricia an airline ticket from San Diego. She planned to visit him at the hospital later today.

To Angelique, her brother seemed like the same intense, brooding person she had grown up with. Their childhood was filled with torment and sadness. Their parents argued and fought. Young Auburn had tried to stand between his arguing parents to protect his mother, but the boy's efforts were futile. When Auburn and Angelique were teens, their mother, a teacher, was hospitalized with paranoid schizophrenia. She accused her husband of plotting against her and told the children of her many suspicions.

Their father began spending more and more time away from the house. Three years after their mother's first hospitalization, she was committed to a sanitarium full-time. After that, their father was an occasional visitor at the house.

Auburn sought refuge in education. He was a quick study at science and mathematics and a member of the chess and debate clubs. He had a powerful physique and tremendous stamina, and coaches often tried to recruit him to participate in sports. But Auburn was contemplative and individualistic and had little interest in team activities.

Even now, when Angelique looked into her brother's soft brown eyes tinged with bright flecks of yellow, he seemed distant, deep in thought. She sat down in the chair next to his bed and touched his forearm. It was nicked and scratched, and the knuckles on his hands were raw and sore. The two siblings were silent for several minutes.

Finally, Auburn spoke.

"There's something I want you to do for me," he said solemnly. "I don't want to argue about it. I don't want you to question me about it. There's something that needs to be done. Will you do it?"

Angelique nodded eagerly.

"Sure, baby. Sure," she said. "Anything."

"OK," he said. "Take this pillow out from under my head and smother me with it. Do it quietly. I promise not to resist."

Angelique couldn't believe her ears.

"No, Auburn, I can't," she said. "Whatever you're worried about, it's not that bad. You'll be OK. Anything you need, we'll get it for you. You aren't guilty of anything. You won't go to jail."

Auburn tried again. Maybe if Angelique didn't have to actively participate in his death, maybe if she didn't have to be there, perhaps then she could be useful.

"OK, then," Auburn said after a long pause. "There's something else."

Angelique nodded again. But this time, she was more tentative.

"My life needs to end very soon," he said, keeping his voice low so that the guard outside couldn't hear him. "I can't get into the reasons. . . . I need you to get me some cyanide, some strong depressants. Now, get me the tools I need to send me on my way."

"THAT LITTLE VOICE"

APRIL 8

4:30 P.M.

Jim Tucker awakened slowly and partially from his first long rest after surgery.

His eyes were open and could see. But the images didn't seem to register. He tried to shake out the cobwebs, but the mental fog was too thick. Maybe the lingering effects of the anesthesia were keeping him locked in this groggy postoperative dream state. There was no way to tell.

Jim recognized Becky. She was right there beside his bed.

He tried to reach out to her with his right arm, but the limb was unresponsive. The arm stayed immobile beside him. He tried to speak, but words came out in incomplete, disorganized jumbles. Becky patted his shoulder and gazed down at him as if to say it was all right to remain silent. She understood.

Becky had been warned that Jim would probably be exhausted after the brain surgery. There had been persistent bleeding within the sensitive organ, and the doctors tried to staunch it. But although they had successfully removed a blood clot, there was no reliable way for the doctors to immediately determine the copilot's chances for recovery.

Jim's brain had been severely injured. Surgery had traumatized it again. The delicate organ was bound to swell, and the swelling put pressure on areas that control memory, vision, motor skills—everything. The blood clot had raised the pressure in Jim's brain to dangerous levels, and now it was gone. But there was a chance another could form in the same place. All that his family, the medical staff, and the other pilots could do was wait and hope.

Doctors and nurses returned to Jim's hospital room, and they pestered him with the same annoying questions they always asked. "How many fingers am I holding up? What's your name? Who's the president of the United States?" They pinched him on the left arm and the right arm, the left foot and the right foot.

"Wiggle your toes," someone in a surgeon's gown commanded sternly.

Jim did his best to comply. He wasn't absolutely certain his answers were correct or his responses satisfactory. His feeble replies lacked conviction. But he really wasn't sure he cared about the answers, or the questions, or the questioners.

A strange sense of detachment engulfed him. The constant banter that had always filled his mind wasn't there anymore. That little voice, that Jiminy Cricket conscience, was silent. And there was a desert of absolute nothingness in its place. He recognized voices. He saw people he knew. But the visual cues were accompanied by none of the usual emotions.

He didn't feel happy or sad, frightened or angry. The invisible wellspring of ideas, that boundless source of creativity and vitality that had always supplied him with thoughts, dreams, and visions, was simply gone. Jim was barely existing.

His vision was fine, but the flickering pictures he saw didn't stick. When he closed his eyes, there was only blackness. He had no imagination. His ability to empathize with other people, one of the strongest aspects of his personality, was gone.

Was he supposed to be glad that Becky was in the room? Was he supposed to feel comforted by her soft green eyes looking down on him? Did the doctors and nurses give him confidence? He couldn't even formulate the questions.

Jim was numbed by an apathy such as he had never experienced or imagined.

On top of that, his body seemed incapable of doing what he asked of it. Little things, like turning his head, swallowing, or moving an arm or leg, required more energy and coordination than he possessed. There was no freedom of thought or movement. He was stuck in limbo, merely passing time inside the frame of what used to be Jim Tucker.

And time itself had lost meaning. It was dark outside the hospital window, but that meant nothing to him. Had he been in the hospital an hour, a day, a week? Units of measure were just interchangeable words, abstract concepts. A minute seemed no different from a day.

After a while—Jim had no idea how long—the doctors and nurses disappeared. He just looked up, and they were gone. Becky was still in the room. She kept telling him to rest, to go to sleep. Her voice was soothing and beautiful. The room was dim, the lights turned low.

But Jim resisted the temptation of sleep. If he closed his eyes, he wasn't sure he would ever wake up. In Jim's mind, sleep and death were indistinguishable. Did that make any sense? Was it logical?

Jim was beyond knowing. And he was nearly beyond caring.

APRIL 8
5:00 P.M.

The parade to David and Susan Sanders's mobile home began the afternoon following the attack.

The first arrival delivered a succulent honey-baked ham. Other visitors brought lasagna, an eggplant casserole, pasta salad, two apple pies and a peach cobbler—and an entire cooler of Molson beer on ice. FedEx managers dropped off several giant "get well" cards signed by hundreds of employees. Company couriers began stopping by to hand over bundles of cards and letters sent via overnight delivery.

The phone rang almost constantly. Callers expressed congratulations, sympathy, and best wishes all at once. And the fax machine in David's tiny office was bombarded with so many messages that it twice ran out of paper. Susan went to work in the kitchen. Her first task was finding room for all the sumptuous food the guests had brought. And even though David hadn't slept at all the previous night, he cheerfully welcomed unannounced visitors throughout the evening.

Most of the guests were FedEx pilots and spouses insatiably curious about the incident itself. They wanted solid information to help them reconstruct the entire episode in their own minds. David was happy to oblige. There are few things pilots enjoy as much as good flying stories—and telling them can be as instructive as listening to them. David spared none of the details. He recounted the story vividly and often. And he emphasized the more surreal aspects—like the moment he realized his jaw had been knocked out of alignment.

"I couldn't figure out why my teeth didn't fit together," he laughed, extending his lower teeth like a barracuda. "Having a dislocated jaw makes it challenging to talk on the radio. And what are you supposed to say, anyway? Hey, center, this is the captain of FedEx Flight seven-oh-five, and I have an underbite?"

The atmosphere at the Sanders home was animated and emotionally charged. Visitors stayed late into the evening. Kathy Morton, the DC-10 copilot who had been bumped from Flight 705 when her trip went overtime, was among the guests. She apologized for endangering the replacement crew, but David would hear none of it.

"This may sound strange," he said in a reflective moment, "but I'm glad I was on that plane with Jim Tucker and Andy Peterson." The captain's voice trailed off and his eyes became moist. David spoke about the other pilots in reverential terms. Perhaps God had *chosen* them to be part of the crew.

Morton thanked the captain. But she said she knew Auburn Calloway. She had flown with him all week. Maybe she could have calmed him down or talked him out of the attack. Maybe her presence would have prevented this whole tragic series of events.

David disagreed.

"He was going to do what he was going to do," the captain insisted. "If Auburn Calloway had been the flight engineer on that plane, he would have succeeded."

Susan could tell the guests were lifting her husband's spirits. The more he told the story of what transpired on the airplane, the more comfortable he seemed to become with the horror and absurdity of it. Finally, around midnight, the last of the guests had gone, and the food was neatly and tightly packed into a refrigerator that had been designed to hold far less. David hadn't eaten any of it. He went to bed, but for the second straight night, David couldn't sleep. The wounds on the right side of his head were tender, his ribs ached, and his jaw was sore. It seemed as though half his muscles had been pulled or torn, and his entire body felt like a giant cramp. The pain medicine seemed entirely ineffective.

Around 3:00 A.M., David went to his office and began reading the faxes that had piled up in the paper tray and spilled onto the floor. Most of them were from well-wishers, but others came from people who had known Auburn Calloway or had flown with him at FedEx or in the Navy. A former Navy pilot said Calloway nearly caused an S-3 to crash when, seconds after a night catapult launch, he mistakenly raised the flaps when he meant to retract the plane's landing gear. He told how Calloway accused the Navy and his shipmates of racism and constantly kept a journal of all the perceived racial slights he encountered—from an enlisted man whistling "Dixie" while mopping a corridor to an officer selecting the movie *Song of the South* for entertainment.

Another fax contained a letter of reprimand that a FedEx captain had written about Calloway. The letter criticized the flight engineer as a "disruptive influence" in the cockpit who sought to create animosity and dissension where none existed. Others told how Calloway had been dismissed from previous jobs at Flying Tigers and Gulf Air.

But the most interesting fax anonymously informed David that Calloway had been scheduled to face a disciplinary hearing at FedEx on April 8. All that was news to David. He planned to pass the information along to the other pilots the next time he saw them.

"ANOTHER FAMILY"

APRIL 10

7:00 P.M.

For Susan Peterson, the best thing about moving Andy from intensive care to a private hospital room was that she could spend nights with him.

Andy was transported upstairs and through a long series of corridors to a bright, sunny room large enough for a second bed so Susan could sleep there at night. They also got their own telephone and bathroom, but for what it cost, Andy quipped, the hospital room ought to have some fancy amenities. For the same price, they could go a few blocks to The Peabody, the five-star hotel where they began their honeymoon twelve years ago.

Andy's wounds still looked frightful. The crucial first twenty-four-hour period following the injuries had passed without complications, however, and Andy had been upgraded to fair condition from critical. Doctors and nurses made sure his wounds weren't becoming infected, but planned no invasive procedures.

Hundreds of cards and letters had poured in, mostly from other FedEx employees around the world. Susan read them to her husband. Some made them chuckle, and others brought tears to their eyes. So many flowers arrived each day that Susan began giving them to the hospital staff to redistribute among patients in other rooms.

On Andy's fourth night in the hospital, Frederick W. Smith, the founder, chairman, and president of FedEx, came to visit. He was on a business trip at the time of the attack and refused to comment on it publicly. But he was in Washington the next day, and a reporter from the Associated Press saw Smith and asked him about the attempted hijacking.

At the time, Smith said Calloway was trying to kill himself when he attempted to seize control of Flight 705. "It was clear the guy was trying to commit suicide," Smith said. "The guy just went berserk."

But when the charismatic FedEx leader saw Andy, he seemed stunned by the seriousness of the wounds he had suffered. Smith had spoken to David Sanders by phone, and he met briefly with Jim and Becky Tucker. Usually talkative and at ease with FedEx employees, the chairman was uncharacteristically quiet.

After a brief introduction, Andy spoke first.

"I'd like you to know, Mr. Smith, that Jim and David did an excellent job flying the airplane," he said. "They were outstanding."

Smith nodded vigorously. He customarily wore perfectly tailored dark business suits and pressed, starched white shirts. But it was Sunday night, he had just returned from a weekend with his family at their condominium in Destin, Florida, and the tanned chief executive was dressed in a pink golf shirt. Concerned about looking too casual, Smith borrowed a blue blazer, the kind worn by FedEx security guards. But the inexpensive garment was clearly too wide in the body and too short in the arms.

"McDonnell Douglas sure builds some fine airplanes, don't they?" Smith teased, his dark eyes shining. "You guys definitely proved those DC-tens are built strong. That's one of the reasons we decided to buy so many of the darn things in the first place."

Smith, a combat veteran in Vietnam, had learned through experience that levity could cheer up wounded men. He had seen more than his share of casualties during two tours in Southeast Asia that included some of the fiercest, most intense fighting of that long conflict.

In contrast to the death and injury that were so common in wartime, however, these wounds had been inflicted by a fellow aviator and FedEx employee. And unlike the young Marines Smith served with in Asia, these were grown men with wives, children, and houses in the suburbs. It didn't make their suffering any more tragic than the pain he had witnessed decades before. Yet it was different, unsettling and awkward.

Smith told Andy he had played a vital role in helping the crew survive the attack, and that he and 100,000 other FedEx employees were grateful to him. He reached down to shake Andy's hand and was encouraged by the flight engineer's firm, solid grip.

"I know you've got a wonderful family already," Smith said, glancing at Susan. "But I want you to know you're part of another family at FedEx. We take care of our own. If there's anything we can do for you, let us know. Whatever it is, we'll get it done. That's a promise."

Smith stood beside Andy's bed for several minutes. They talked about airplanes, and they talked about Mississippi. Andy was born in Goodman. Smith was born in Marks, a cotton-farming area in the flat delta a few miles south of Memphis.

A few minutes later, the CEO was gone, escorted by an entourage of security guards and aides—all wearing identical jackets.

"THE CORPSE ON DISPLAY"

APRIL 12
7:00 P.M.

The guests at Andy and Susan Peterson's home weren't quite sure how to act.

On the day Andy came home from the hospital, nine couples who knew the Petersons from their neighborhood, church, or FedEx gathered in the living room of the home in Olive Branch. Each of the guests had cooked meals, washed clothes, cut grass, gone grocery shopping, or run other errands for the Petersons in the tumultuous days after the attack. Now, to show their gratitude—and to make sure that Andy didn't have to wear himself out repeating his story over and over—the Petersons invited some of their closest friends to hear his firsthand account of the aerial ordeal.

As they filed into the Petersons' living room, the mood was somber and reserved. Men wore coats and ties, and the women dresses. To Susan, the gathering had the look and feel of a funeral visitation. Andy, the corpse on display, sat virtually motionless in his favorite overstuffed chair, his feet propped up on an ottoman. Portrait photographs of the Petersons' three children smiled down from the walls.

Pastor Richard Rieves and his wife, Rachel, had arrived early. Richard knew that Andy tired easily, and he had promised Susan that he would help break up the gathering after half an hour or so. Richard had forewarned each of the guests before they came.

The friends sat close together on the living-room couch and chairs. A few stood, and others sat on the carpet by the fireplace. After Richard led the group in a short prayer, he asked Andy to say a few words. The guests listened in rapt attention.

"First, I'd like to thank y'all for coming," Andy began. "Y'all have been a tremendous help to Susan and me, and we can't say how much we appreciate your efforts. These have been some trying times, and y'all have been there for us."

The swelling in Andy's head had receded somewhat. The open cuts on his scalp and forearms were covered with clear ointment. His eyes were still puffy, with semicircular pools of purple blood showing through his fair skin. Andy was as muscular and trim as ever. Yet the smallest movements—lifting his arms or turning his head—required great energy and planning. He moved like an old man.

"I'll start out by saying that I'm a little hazy about some of the details of what happened on the plane," he said. "The main thing that I do remember clearly was a flash of light, just brilliant white light like I had never seen before. Then, when the light faded, I could see a long tunnel. I felt myself being pulled through the tunnel. I didn't have any pain or any fear. It was almost like an out-of-body experience.

"They say that when you're drowning, you see your life flash before your eyes. That didn't happen to me. I just remember the light, then the tunnel."

Andy took a sip of water from a glass by his chair, then continued.

"When I got to the end of the tunnel, I had this very calm, very peaceful feeling, like I was floating. At first I was alone. Then our pastor, Billy Spink, appeared. He was dressed all in white.

"I asked him, 'Where is Richard Rieves? Why isn't he here?' "

Susan grimaced. She recognized Andy's offbeat sense of humor and knew he was joking.

"Billy said Richard was still an assistant pastor, still an apprentice," Andy continued, a wry smile crossing his lips. "He told me, 'When Richard gets to be a full pastor and has his own church, then we'll trust him with big jobs.' "

That was the punch line.

But the room was completely silent. No one seemed to get Andy's joke. Or if they did, no one thought it was funny.

Finally, Richard chuckled. Then some of the others joined in. The laughter was infectious, and soon the whole group was in an uproar. Nervous chuckles were followed by belly laughs. Andy smiled, enjoying his own humor.

He wanted to show his friends that the attempted hijacking hadn't changed him. No one needed to treat him differently because of his injuries. He was still a regular guy. Someday, when the bandages were gone and the scars healed, they wouldn't know he had ever been hurt. Andy didn't want special attention.

When the noise died down, Andy went on with his story, his tone conversational and informal.

"The guy that hit me, I didn't know him," Andy said. "I'd never met him before we got on the airplane. I'd never flown with him. He didn't say anything to me before the flight. When he hit me, I

thought it was with his fist. I didn't see that he had a hammer until
later. And I didn't know I'd been hurt until I saw all the blood.

"After that, it was a matter of trying to get control of the situation," he said. "It wasn't easy, but with God's help, we finally succeeded. The other pilots were great. They did a great job of flying the airplane. I can't imagine what would have happened if we failed."

PART FOUR

''TO THE EDGE AND
BACK''

▼

▼

▼

"PAIN IS GOOD"

APRIL 13

1:00 P.M.

After several days at The Med, Jim Tucker moved across the street to Baptist Memorial Hospital to begin physical and cognitive therapy.

The copilot's memory was coming back in shreds and patches, but there were tremendous gaps. He could count to ten in Spanish, but not English. He knew the days of the week only in French. He remembered that George Washington was the first president of the United States and Abraham Lincoln had freed the slaves. But he couldn't remember his children's birthdays.

Earlier in the week, his children had come into his hospital room one at a time. There, with Becky standing by, the kids struggled to keep their composure. Jim's head had been shaved, and black stitches that looked like heavy fishing line closed the long, curved incisions that doctors had cut during surgery. His eyes were bloodshot and his cheeks were pale and drawn.

Morgan tried to comfort his father, but the boy was stunned by the blank look in his dad's eyes. His father didn't seem to recognize him. Andy, the talkative one, had been told not to ask his father questions out of concern he might not be able to answer. When Andy entered the room, the boy stared at the walls and found it impossible to say anything. Rachael, too, had been unable to speak. She cried and shivered at the sight of the battered, fragile-looking shadow of the man who was her dad.

Jim was powerless to reassure them. The little voice inside him—that invisible energy source that constantly used to generate ideas, invent jokes, and interpret events—was mending very slowly. Jim was constantly in pain, and he tired easily. Fatigue overwhelmed him sometimes, and left him in a distant, almost vegetative state.

Jim was put in a ward with other physical therapy patients on the eighteenth floor of Baptist Memorial Hospital. Each room had an excellent view of the city from large north- or south-facing windows. Patients had their own bathrooms and showers, and guests could spend the night.

True to his nature, Jim wanted to get started with the physical therapy right away. Confinement, inactivity, and boredom had always bothered him more than physical discomfort. He knew he had been seriously injured and that some of the damage might be permanent. But he had to know exactly where he stood and how much harm had been done. Once Jim knew the unvarnished truth, he could set realistic goals and lay out a schedule for his recovery. He would do his best to meet or exceed each goal. With Becky's encouragement, he was ready to start.

One of the first exercises looked simple. Therapists put an inflated rubber beach ball in the center of the floor and instructed Jim to lie on it. He was supposed to put his chest on the ball, then roll it left and right, up and down, while maintaining his balance. Therapists would be standing by to catch him if he fell.

Jim moved forward and gingerly put his broad chest on the ball. Within seconds, the ball began to roll out from under him. Once he started to lose his balance, he tried to redistribute his weight, but the right side of his body failed to respond quickly enough. Inevitably, he slid off, and the therapists caught him again and again.

Each therapist was part cheerleader, part drill sergeant. They reminded Jim of the Marines who berated him during officer candidate school in the Navy. Pain is good, they used to chant. Extreme pain is extremely good.

Another task the therapists set up for Jim involved a line of small paper cones, which he was to rearrange with his right hand. But simply reaching out and grasping them was impossible at first. He watched his hand move in the direction of the cones, but it didn't respond intuitively. The appendage was like a clumsy paw. He could direct it if he watched it and concentrated intently. But if he took his eyes off his right hand, he had no idea where it was, whether his fingers were open or closed in a fist. He couldn't pick up a pen or write his name. The frustration was almost unbearable, but Jim had promised the therapists at the outset that he would cooperate with them fully and trust them completely.

"I'll do anything you tell me to do if it'll help me get better," he had said. "I'll do absolutely anything and everything."

They had Jim walk between two parallel bars, encouraging him to use the narrow wooden rails to keep from falling. Jim could feel his right leg, but he had to concentrate in order to move it. And concentrating exhausted him. Therapists then set the bars on a slight incline to make Jim walk uphill. He tried, but it was impossible. Even the smallest stairs were insurmountable.

Jim saw anger and despair in the faces of wheelchair-bound stroke victims who shared the eighteenth floor with him. He shared their rage, too. But the therapists warned him not to succumb to it and to understand that progress, if it was to be made at all, would come in tiny increments. There would be setbacks along the way. He had to expect them. He had to deal with them constructively.

Becky vowed that she would never let Jim see her cry about his injuries. She had to be strong and supportive. When she needed to cry, she would do it alone. She would cheer on his progress when she saw it, no matter how small the improvement or how glacial the pace.

Jim needed her at the hospital, but the kids needed her at home. She spent many nights at the hospital with Jim; then she would drive home to greet the kids when they came home from school each afternoon. She tried to keep their lives as normal as possible during the hours she was home. Then she would return to the hospital in the evenings.

Jim's mother, Evelyn, and his father, Jim, came to Memphis the day after the attack. Evelyn became acutely aware that her son, who had always been able to crunch numbers quickly and solve complicated mathematical problems in his head, was now having problems remembering basic multiplication tables.

"What's five times five?" she quizzed.

"I don't know."

"What's six times six?"

Jim was exasperated.

Evelyn went down to the store in the hospital lobby and bought a steno book and a pen. She returned to her son's room and wrote out multiplication tables from one to twelve—just as she had done when he was in grade school in Florida thirty-three years before.

Jim had learned the multiplication tables once, she reasoned. He could do so again.

Evelyn, a retired librarian, handed the steno book to her son. Its blue-lined pages were covered with a neatly printed grid of lines and numbers.

"Let's start again," she said undaunted, cheerfully settling into a seat at the foot of his bed. "Look at the book if you have to. Now, what's four times four?"

"HIS CONSTANT ADVOCATE"

APRIL 16

10:00 P.M.

Jim Tucker lay awake in his hospital bed with a throbbing headache.

It was his ninth night in the hospital, and he had been making steady progress in rehabilitation. All the therapists told him so. But there still were profound gaps in his memory, a lack of physical coordination, and involuntary alterations in his thinking patterns that both frightened and confounded him.

Jim could recount obscure radio frequencies for control towers and navigational beacons at Memphis International Airport and around the country, but he couldn't remember his telephone number. He could recite the Lord's Prayer from beginning to end, but it was a struggle. It had taken him days to relearn the passage he had known by heart since boyhood.

Earlier in the day, Jim had eaten lunch with Becky in a sunny outdoor courtyard. The fresh air and sunshine had aroused his senses. But the headache had started a few hours later, and now Jim felt generally miserable.

Becky was snoozing on a cot next to Jim's elevated hospital bed. She was his constant advocate. If there was anything Jim wanted, no matter how trivial, she would make sure he got it. If Jim needed to see a nurse, he didn't have to press a buzzer and wait for one to arrive. Becky would venture out into the hallways and bring one back.

Becky had been meek and quiet during the first few times she came to the hospital. Now she had a mission, and the staff quickly learned that it was easier to comply with her polite but forceful requests than argue or protest. She was persistent, she didn't take no for an answer, and she refused to be ignored.

Jim rubbed his forehead.

Maybe he should take some more aspirin or Tylenol or something. He felt as if his head was about to crack like sheets of ice in the spring. He reached toward a lamp at the side of his bed. When he turned his head, he felt moisture where the back of his head had been resting on the pillow.

"Hey," Jim said, awakening Becky. "Would you come over here and take a look at something for me?"

Becky rolled to her feet in a single motion and walked half asleep to the other side of the room. She clicked the lamp on.

"Oh, my," she gasped.

"What?" Jim asked. "What is it?"

"I don't know, sweetheart, but I don't like it," she answered, suddenly wide awake. "I'd better go get somebody to take a look at this."

"What do you see?" Jim wanted to know. "Tell me."

Becky punched the button on the side of Jim's bed that automatically called for a nurse.

"Well, the stitches holding your wounds together look good," she began, trying to sound optimistic. "But your pillowcase is covered with blood and some sort of oozing, yellow gunk. And the skin looks red and kind of irritated and inflamed."

Jim began to shake his head in disbelief, but the slightest movement caused searing pain. "You think it's infected?" Jim asked.

"I'm afraid so, darling," she said. "I'm afraid so."

Becky quickly left the room to find a nurse. Minutes later, she returned with several nurses and a young physician, a neurosurgery resident, in tow. She marched them into the room and stood by the door as though she was guarding a group of prisoners.

The resident pulled on a pair of plastic gloves and shone a tiny flashlight at Jim's wounds. He examined the moist, bloody residue on the pillow. Clearly, something was infected. Maybe it was the outer wound. Maybe it was deeper. Of all the body's organs, brains are the most susceptible to contamination. Infections can spread rapidly with catastrophic results.

"OK," the youthful doctor began, "we're going to collect some cultures and send them to the lab for analysis. That way we'll know exactly what we're dealing with. It's Sunday night, so we're not going to get a definitive answer until tomorrow morning at the earliest. Usually, it takes less than twenty-four hours. But we're going to monitor this situation very closely."

"Aren't you going to let anyone else know about this?" Becky asked, not entirely confident in the young physician's judgment. "Shouldn't you check with someone else?"

"As a matter of fact, I will," the physician said, trying not to take offense. He had been through four years of college, four years of medical school, and three of the five years his neurosurgery residency would last. "I'm going to page Dr. Ray right now."

Dr. Morris Ray was the chief neurosurgeon at the Semmes-Murphey Clinic in Memphis, the largest private neurosurgery group in the country. At fifty-seven, Ray had been performing delicate brain and spinal cord operations more than half his life.

And Ray had a special rapport with pilots. He was a civilian flight instructor himself, and he had logged thousands of hours at the controls of a wide variety of private airplanes. He owned a bright red Pitts Special, a two-seat biplane, and used it each summer to compete in aerobatic flying contests.

For Ray, the strenuous, exacting pursuit of aerobatic flying was a welcome relief from the stress and tension of his job. Flying airplanes demanded his full concentration. Each forty-five-minute flight was crammed with loops, rolls, and spins. When Ray landed, he would discover that he hadn't thought about critical surgeries, budgets, staff meetings, or liability suits for the entire time he was airborne. Briefly substituting aerial concerns for the worries he faced on the ground broke the gnawing pressures of his job and refreshed him.

And Ray was convinced that in the long run, his patients benefited from his avocation, too.

"A MONA LISA SMILE"

APRIL 17

6:15 A.M.

Dr. Morris Ray strode into Jim Tucker's hospital room, all business.

The doctor normally took his Great Dane walking in nearby Overton Park each morning at sunrise. The outing with the ninety-pound, white-muzzled family pet had been a treasured ritual for almost ten years. Ray and Lady took a brisk, three-mile walk through the center-city park to the Egyptian gates of the city zoo and back to his Midtown home. But today the doctor skipped the park and its flowering trees and came straight to work. The previous night's call from the resident physician, informing him of Jim's infection, had alarmed the senior surgeon.

Ray wanted to identify the bacteria and start combating them immediately with antibiotic drugs. If the infection had entered the pilot's brain, Ray would have to operate. If that was the case, the sooner he got started, the better the chance for success.

An aggressive infection could kill a patient in less than a day.

"I understand you had a long night last night," the doctor began as he entered Jim's room. "Our first job this morning is going to be identifying the culprit. There are all kinds of bacteria, and we treat some of those nasty little bastards differently from others."

Ray studied his patient intently. Jim's eyes were clear and focused. But deep, dark rings were forming under them, probably from pain and a lack of sleep.

The doctor felt the strong, steady pulse on Jim's right wrist. Checking the pulse was more a habit than anything else. Ray knew it was important for doctors to physically touch their patients. He didn't pretend to understand why it helped them heal. But even with all the high-tech advancements in the medical field, sick people wanted to be touched. They needed physical contact, even if it was only the firm, comforting feel of Ray's large hands on their wrists and arms.

At six feet two inches tall, Ray towered over the hospital bed. His unruly hair was turning salt-and-pepper gray, and the close-cropped beard he had recently grown was streaked with white. His glimmering brown eyes usually were mischievous and playful. But when dealing with patients, they could become distant and inscrutable.

If Ray was concerned, he didn't want his patients to know it. The poker face he automatically took on was one method of shielding them. His eyes hardened as he started to talk to Jim.

He explained that the hammer that had crashed into Jim's skull had likely driven germs into the bone, and maybe into his brain. Doctors had cleaned the wound and the exposed portion of Jim's skull during the first surgery, but bones are porous, and microscopic germs can become lodged inside tiny holes and crevices, then emerge days or weeks later to cause havoc.

When foreign objects enter sensitive organs, the body tries to contain them and prevent the infections from spreading. In the brain, infection can cause abscesses—localized collections of pus surrounded by inflamed tissue. The abscesses take up space and put pressure on other parts of the brain. As pressure builds, there is a tendency for abscesses to rupture, spreading germs throughout the brain with tremendous speed. Doctors can try to remove abscesses surgically, but they prefer to go after the infections with medication first.

If medication doesn't help right away, they operate.

Jim's condition was very serious, Ray said, arms crossed at his chest. He recommended aggressive treatment—probably a combination of antibiotic drugs and surgery. He already was in contact with doctors in the laboratory. Together, they would come up with a strategy. He warned Jim that it was all going to happen very fast.

Ray sat at the edge of Jim's bed. Another doctor long ago had taught Ray to sit down after entering a patient's room. Sitting gave patients the impression that the doctor was spending more time with them. For some reason, five leisurely minutes with a seated doctor seemed longer to frightened patients than ten minutes with the doctor nervously standing.

Ray tried not to seem rushed.

He looked at Becky, who had spent the night in the room with Jim. She was eating breakfast near the window. Patients and guests were offered bacon and eggs for breakfast each morning, and for cafeteria food, it was pretty good.

"You haven't had breakfast yet, have you?" the doctor asked Jim.

"Well, yeah," Jim answered. "Having something to eat usually helps my headache go away."

"OK," Ray said, trying to conceal his exasperation. "Don't eat or drink anything else. If we have to operate, you can't have anything in your stomach. Don't swallow anything unless I tell you. OK?"

Jim's breakfast meant Ray couldn't operate until noon at the earliest. In the meantime, he would send Jim for another CAT scan. If there was an abscess in his brain, the scan would show it. Then he could come up with a plan for combating it.

Neurosurgery had advanced light-years during Ray's career. Doctors had vastly improved tools and techniques. But at a very basic level, the brain was still a mystery. Removing a tumor, a blood clot, or an abscess could have unintended consequences and unpredictable side effects. Memory or vision loss, personality changes, hearing or speech difficulties could debilitate patients even after seemingly flawless surgical procedures.

Several hours later, the CAT scan images were complete. They clearly showed an abscess in the same general area where doctors had removed the blood clot more than a week ago. Ray wanted to start antibiotics immediately, then operate to make sure the infection couldn't spread. He planned to reopen the incisions that doctors had made during Jim's first surgery and remove the four-inch piece of skull they had cut in that original operation. But this time, instead of putting the oval-shaped bone flap back in his head at the end of the procedure, Ray proposed removing it permanently. The surgeon outlined his plan for Jim, explaining what he wanted to do in clear terms.

The important thing now was to stop the infection, Ray said. In all likelihood, that piece of bone was part of the problem. Tiny crevices in the bone were probably harboring bacteria that threatened to infect Jim's brain, now and in the future.

Without the bone flap, Jim could still continue his recovery. If, in a year or two, he wanted to replace the missing piece, doctors could insert a customized plate of hardened composite material that would be tailored to fit perfectly. That procedure was relatively simple. But whatever Jim decided, time was of the essence. They needed to move quickly.

"Heck, let's just leave the piece of bone out then," Jim decided with a casual flip of his wrist. "For now, let's concentrate on fighting the infection."

"Good, that's what we'll do," Ray said. "I think that's the right decision."

"But tell me something," Jim said. "Am I going to die? I mean, really. What are the chances?" He searched the doctor's face for any sign of an answer, but Ray's stern countenance was unreadable.

"We're not in the business of killing people," Ray said, unfazed by the query. "We're in the business of doing everything we can to help people."

"OK," Jim said, still searching for clues. "But if you were in my position, would you be worried? Would you be concerned?"

"Well," Ray said, cracking a slight Mona Lisa smile, "If there's any worrying to be done, please let me do it. I'm a professional worrier. It's my job. I get paid for it. I worry all the time—about everything."

The doctor patted Jim on the shoulder.

"Your job is getting better when this surgery is over," Ray said. "Save your strength, and use it to fight off that infection. If you do your job right, you'll make the rest of us look like geniuses. OK?"

"OK," Jim sighed, slightly frustrated at his inability to glean the hard statistical information he was looking for. "I'll try to make you look good."

"THEIR OWN TOUGHEST CRITICS"

Jim Tucker was in his hospital room recovering from his most recent surgery when ALPA officials told him he had a visitor.

Donald E. Hudson, M.D., a psychiatrist and the pilot union's top aeromedical adviser, had come to Memphis from Denver to see the Flight 705 crew. Hudson, a founder of ALPA's Critical Incident Response Team, made it a point to meet with pilots who had recently survived life-threatening episodes.

His team had been founded after an Aloha Airlines accident in which the top of a Boeing 737 peeled off in flight in 1989. Mimi Tompkins, the copilot on that plane, called Hudson a year later in emotional turmoil. Even though the terrifying incident she experienced was brief, and even though she was regarded as a hero for her role in landing the severely damaged jet, Tompkins continued to suffer flashbacks, anxiety attacks, and nightmares. Certain sounds triggered powerful memories and stark images that flooded over her like a tide. It was as though a tape recorder in her mind replayed the same events over and over—and she was powerless to stop it. She couldn't forget, and she couldn't block the incapacitating images and emotions.

Hudson determined Tompkins was suffering from post-traumatic stress disorder. He searched medical records and documented thirty-five more cases of airline pilots who had developed symptoms of the emotionally crippling condition since 1987. Of those, eighteen had been treated successfully and resumed their careers. Seventeen had not, and all of them had left the flying profession.

Hudson knew that psychological counseling had an 85 percent success rate against post-traumatic stress disorder if treatment began quickly. Symptoms usually started showing up between three and six months after the event, however, and once the symptoms started, psychological counseling was far less effective. Time was of the essence.

Hudson found the bright, flowery hospital room where Jim and Becky were staying. The psychiatrist also planned to meet with David and Susan Sanders, and Andy and Susan Peterson.

Jim still had difficulty talking and moving his right side, but his blue eyes were sharp and clear, and doctors said the surgery to remove the abscess from his brain appeared to have been a complete success.

Hudson was encouraged by the gifts and the hundreds of cards and letters of support the pilots had received. Peer support was invaluable to pilots recovering from stressful incidents, and it was rare. About 70 percent of all commercial-airline accidents contain some element of pilot error, and the individuals involved are often criticized, second-guessed, and mercilessly picked apart by other pilots. Hudson saw that the Flight 705 pilots would be spared the excessive Monday-morning quarterbacking from their peers. He was concerned, however, with the way each of the pilots would judge themselves. They were sure to be their own toughest critics.

Like Mimi Tompkins, the copilot of the Aloha Airlines flight, they would replay the incident in their own minds thousands and thousands of times. Those never-ending critiques, he surmised, were likely to be especially wrenching for David, the captain. His physical injuries were less severe then those of the other two Flight 705 pilots, and his memory of the event was crystal clear.

The fact that Sanders's physical wounds were comparatively light, Hudson knew, was a mixed blessing. The captain was fortunate to have avoided debilitating, life-threatening injuries. Yet his psychological burden was likely to be heavier.

"He's probably going to feel like a platoon sergeant whose squad got ambushed," Hudson warned the Tuckers. "He's going to have tremendous feelings of guilt—no matter how unjustified or irrational that may seem. Be aware of those feelings and respect them. They are real."

Hudson knew that Jim and Andy also would face tall obstacles on their long roads to recovery. They would likely have fantasies and imagine hundreds of things they might have done differently to improve the outcome. In their minds, they would want to see themselves making all the right moves, disarming Calloway and preventing injuries to themselves and their fellow pilots.

"Real memory and emotional memory are different," Hudson counseled. "What happened to each of you was like being mugged. When someone comes up and puts a gun to your wife's head, most people instinctively freeze. They're not Clint Eastwood, so they don't have the perfect heroic reactions all the time.

"No matter what the actual situation was on the plane, your emotional memory is going to play tricks on you. You'll have strong feelings of shame, that the accolades you receive aren't deserved. You'll feel like a deeply flawed human being, and that's going to bring all kinds of grief. But try to put it in perspective. The pilot culture demands perfection at all times and allows no room for doubts or second thoughts. You know that's unrealistic."

Hudson told Jim that he and the others pilots should be proud of what they had accomplished together. They had saved their lives, their aircraft, and an unknown number of people on the ground. Those facts were indisputable. The psychiatrist avoided talking about the effects the incident was likely to have on their families, however, or their jobs should they someday return to professional flying. Hudson hoped he would have a chance to talk with them about those subjects later.

For now, they were likely to find even the information he had given them discouraging. And from his experience with families of other pilots who had been involved in dangerous aviation incidents, Hudson knew that spouses and children suffered, too.

Some spouses develop "sight anxiety," and they become terrified when their pilots go away—no matter how briefly. Even on a trip to the corner store, the spouses feel they are saying good-bye for the last time. Suddenly, the world seems like a very lonely and dangerous place.

Other changes are more insidious.

Often, the pilot's personality changes after a life-threatening event or head injury. A spouse who had been drawn to a confident, self-assured airline captain is suddenly stuck with an indecisive person seemingly incapable of making independent decisions. The person they always thought of as a rock turns out to be clay.

Other pilots have the opposite reaction. They become thrill-seekers, trying to find something—anything—to duplicate the intense rush they got during their moments of jeopardy.

Hudson, himself a pilot and Air Force flight surgeon, also knew that most injured pilots are profoundly disappointed if and when they finally return to the cockpit. Far from the joyous feelings of freedom flying used to evoke, some survivors come to regard aviation as a dangerous, stressful occupation. No longer are they masters of their own destinies, in command of everything around them.

Instead, they realize they are fallible human beings subject to the vagaries of countless factors beyond their control.

"AN ABERRATION"

MAY 23

1:30 P.M.

Prosecutors expected Auburn Calloway's bond hearing to be a formality.

Government lawyers thought it would be easy to convince a federal magistrate to keep the former FedEx pilot in jail without bail until trial. Calloway was charged with attempted air piracy, a violent crime that carried a maximum sentence of life in prison. As a pilot, he was a risk to flee the country. Prosecutors believed they had a simple task in convincing the judge to keep him in jail.

U.S. Magistrate James Allen, a genteel-looking southerner with a smooth regional accent, silver hair, and gold-rimmed glasses, would decide whether to set bail or keep Calloway in prison until trial. Allen's history on the bench gave prosecutors reason for optimism. The magistrate had denied bail in previous high-profile cases. And in 1991, Allen organized a tribute dinner for Hickman Ewing, Jr., a law-and-order Republican who, at that time, had been the top federal prosecutor in West Tennessee for nine years.

John Fowlkes was the prosecutor in charge of the case. Tall, energetic, in his mid-forties, he had years of experience as a state prosecutor before joining the federal district attorney's staff. A slender African American with wide shoulders and light, freckled skin, Fowlkes wore round gold-rimmed glasses and conservative charcoal suits. He spoke in clipped, rapid phrases but chose words carefully and used them economically. On rare occasions when he did speak at length, he emphasized certain words with quick, chopping hand motions.

Fowlkes planned to call just one witness, Jennifer Eakin, an FBI agent in Memphis who had interviewed FedEx DC-10 captain David Sanders at The Med after the attack. She could talk about the prolonged, savage nature of the assault, the severe wounds inflicted on the crew, and the potential for a catastrophic crash if Calloway had succeeded in taking control of the plane.

The defense was led by Charles Ogletree, the Harvard Law School professor who had represented Anita Hill when she testified in Congress against U.S. Supreme Court nominee Clarence Thomas. Ogletree and Calloway had been friends since 1970 when they both were students at Stanford University. The defense asked the court to set bail, arguing that Calloway had never been in trouble with the law before. And Calloway had been severely injured aboard the FedEx plane on April 7. In his debilitated physical condition, the defense would assert, he couldn't possibly be a threat to anyone.

Angelique Calloway, the defendant's sister, would offer her house in Centreville, Virginia, as collateral to secure bail for her brother. A long string of witnesses, including Calloway's ex-wife, would testify that he was a dedicated family man and not prone to violence. Ogletree and his associates had told their client candidly before the hearing that there was little chance he would prevail, but the attorneys vowed to put up a spirited fight.

A group of television and newspaper photographers waited in the basement of the federal building in Memphis. The defendant, they knew, would enter through the underground parking garage, then ride an elevator to the federal magistrate's courtroom. For the media, it would be their first glimpse of the defendant since the day of the attack. And then their view had been limited to a few short glances as Calloway, barely conscious, was quickly moved from an ambulance to the trauma center at The Med.

Newspaper and television photographers plunked coins into the vending machines in the basement while they waited for the prisoner. Each photographer kept close track of the blinking lights that showed the positions of all four elevators in the federal building. Each time one of the elevators came to the basement, the photographers would jockey for position and aim their lenses at the door. Usually, the brown doors parted to reveal the surprised faces of government workers on their way to the basement cafeteria. The photographers had to be vigilant, though. They would have only one chance to see Calloway. If they missed it, they would have to deal with the wrath of angry editors and producers later.

When Calloway's entourage finally came through the elevator, Ogletree was the first through the doors. Reporters blurted out questions while the cameras rolled.

"Are you going for the insanity defense?" one asked.

"Is race going to be a factor at the trial?" another chimed in.

Ogletree smiled but said nothing.

Then two federal marshals, a man and a woman, entered the basement pushing an African-American man in a wheelchair. The photographers turned and took aim. Shutters clicked and strobes flashed, temporarily brightening the windowless hallway.

Auburn Calloway sat grimacing in the wheelchair, motionless. Eyes closed, face frozen in pain. His ankles were shackled. The prisoner wore a black sweatshirt, dark gray pants, and sandals. A white gym towel was draped across his lap to hide the handcuffs. Next to him on the wheelchair he kept a clear Ziploc bag containing pain medicine, several magazines, a Bible, and a book titled *The Life of Jesus Christ*.

"Were you going to crash the plane?" a TV reporter asked.

"Did you intend to blow up the FedEx hub?" said another.

Calloway's expression didn't change. His pained face was like a mask.

Calloway's uncombed hair and mustache were longer than usual, and stubble from uncut whiskers sprouted from his chin and cheeks. At the top left side of his forehead, just below the hairline, the photographers could see a circular imprint. It was concave, and about the size of a quarter—or the head of a hammer.

The attack had taken place seven weeks ago. Could the wound possibly have been inflicted then? Had it caused any permanent brain damage? If so, would Calloway be competent to stand trial and participate in his own defense?

The marshals moved Calloway quickly to the elevator without shielding him from the photographers. In a moment, the brown metal doors of the elevator closed tight and Calloway was on his way to court. Cameras were prohibited throughout the rest of the building. Just as well, the photographers reckoned. They had what they needed.

Angelique and brother Mark Calloway waited with Patricia, Keelah, and Burney in the federal magistrate's courtroom.

The bond hearing began at 2:10 P.M., and the wooden benches in the small courtroom were full of reporters, Calloway family members, and FedEx officials. None of the Flight 705 pilots or their families were there, however. Allen addressed the lawyers cordially. He welcomed Professor Ogletree to Memphis and said he hoped he'd enjoy his stay despite the rising temperature and humidity of the late spring season. The lawyer gushed that it was an honor for him to appear before such distinguished court officers.

The first witness, FBI agent Jennifer Eakin, recounted how she was summoned to The Med on April 7 to interview David Sanders. She had spoken with him in the hospital emergency room while doctors stitched gashes in his head and right arm. The DC-10 captain had told her that he heard a loud noise about fifteen minutes after takeoff from Memphis International Airport.

"He said it was a very loud sound, of something striking something," Eakin said. "The next thing he knew, he was being struck. He said he was overwhelmed by the blood. That was his first impression."

Calloway remained in his wheelchair behind the defense table, his face contorted. At times, he whispered to Ogletree. But his words were so faint the lawyer had to put his ear a few inches from his client's mouth to hear him.

On the witness stand, Eakin said the captain had told her that the defendant had pointed a speargun at him and shouted, "I'll kill your ass!" There was a furious struggle and the attacker was "exceptionally strong, determined, savage, and brutal." Eakin was reading from a report she had written the day of the attack. The plane could easily have crashed, she added, endangering many lives and many millions of dollars in property.

Fowlkes thanked Eakin for appearing, and the defense began presenting its witnesses.

Angelique Calloway testified that her brother was a peaceful man who would never intentionally harm anyone. She would oversee his medical care if he was released on bail. He could stay at her home in Virginia or she would move to Memphis temporarily. A teacher, she would have the summer months off to care for her injured brother. She would even pledge her home equity in order for her brother to make bail.

Auburn Calloway's ex-wife sat with Keelah, eleven, and Burney, seven. The handsome, well-dressed children from California sat behind the defense table while their mother testified.

"Auburn has always shown great affection for his family and especially his children," she said, adding that he visited them frequently at their home in San Diego and took them on vacations to Hawaii and Memphis. "I don't see him as being a threat to himself or other people. He's a good man. He has friends all over. I have no reason to believe that he would pose a threat to anyone."

On cross-examination, Fowlkes asked her to elaborate. And Patricia Calloway continued to extol her ex-husband as a kind, patient father and model citizen. The prosecutor opened a three-ring binder and removed two pages. They were stapled together.

"This is a copy of a note that was found aboard the FedEx DC-ten on April seventh after the crew returned to Memphis," Fowlkes said tersely as he walked to the witness box. "I'd like you to read it and tell me, if Mr. Calloway had written that note, would that change your mind at all about his mental stability? Would it make you alter your opinion about whether he was dangerous to himself or others?"

Patricia began reading the one-and-a-half page handwritten note. Her ex-husband's writing was as clear and distinctive as ever, with large, well-rounded letters. The photocopied letter was addressed to her, but the original version had never been delivered. Pat cast her large brown eyes down at the letter and tried not to show any emotion as she read.

Dear Pat,

I want you and the kids to know that I lived for you. I thought of your welfare every day, though, e.g. like how can I guarantee having enough money for Keelah and Burney's Stanford education, which today costs about $25,000 annually. Weddings cost an average of $16,000, all to the father or parents of the bride, etc. etc. (Burney's flying lessons!)

I have lived a good life, no, a great life really, but I've had some rough roads to travel. I don't mind, since, despite all the rough roads, I have accomplished a great deal, and seen even more. If I don't see my grandkids, well, I can't have it all. If I don't see Keelah and Burney grow up, that's okay too, because I will rest in peace knowing they are in good hands with you.

I have battle fatigue badly and a long life into old age is never guaranteed. I don't think I want to experience the pain and suffering of old age anyway. I would much rather go on a date, time, place and method of my own choosing.

I resolved quite some time ago that the next time my security and future is threatened or seriously jeopardized, it's time . . . my time to go."

Patricia was stunned by the letter but dared not show it. She measured her breaths, then exhaled deeply. Finally, she looked at the prosecutor.

"No," she answered, looking directly at him. "That wouldn't change my mind."

"It wouldn't change your mind at all?" Fowlkes repeated, incredulous.

"No," she added emphatically, lowering her eyes again to the photocopied pages.

Allen asked to see a copy of the letter. As soon as the magistrate read it, he announced that he was placing it under seal. The information it contained would make it impossible for Calloway to get a fair trial. If reporters got copies of it, the resulting publicity would likely prejudice the entire jury pool against the defendant. Releasing the letter, which had been marked as government's exhibit number one, presented an unacceptable risk to Calloway's right to a fair trial.

"This document will be ordered sealed," Allen said to the audience. "It will not be disclosed except on order of the court."

Calloway's family volunteered to surrender his pilot's license and passport if the magistrate set bail. After two hours of testimony, Allen had heard enough. He sipped a glass of ice water, then told the lawyers to be seated.

"In this case the government has the burden of establishing that the defendant, Auburn Calloway, should be detained," Allen began. "Evidence has been presented as to the incident involved and as to Mr. Calloway's ties to the community. I'm required to look at the factors outlined in the United States Code Section 3142-G in determining whether Mr. Calloway should be detained or released with conditions."

Allen knew the section by heart. But he opened his lawbook to the appropriate page and read the criteria as he announced his ruling.

"There are four general factors to be considered. They all have to be considered, and no one factor is given preference over the others. I take them all into account and more or less add them up, subtract, and come around with a general conclusion. The court must consider the nature of the offense charged, and obviously this offense involves a crime of violence. That factor is in the government's favor and is in favor of detention.

"The second factor is the weight of the evidence against the person. The evidence in this case appears strong, so that is a factor in favor of the government.

"The third factor deals with the history and characteristics of the person. The evidence indicates that he's a family man. He has no prior convictions or brushes with the law. He's been a neighbor and resident of this location, and his neighbors think highly of him. So, on balance, the third factor would be in the defendant's favor."

Calloway's brother and sister nodded in agreement with the magistrate's last finding. That left only one more factor for consideration: potential danger to the community if the defendant was released.

"Now, the only way that I can find that to be in the government's favor is to assume that it's likely that Mr. Calloway will do something, or there is probable cause to believe that he will do the same thing again if he is turned loose," Allen said, shrugging his black-robed shoulders. "I don't believe I'm smart enough to do that.

"I don't have any psychological training and I don't think I can draw any conclusion that Mr. Calloway is, from this point forward, by nature, a violent person. There is no indication that he was that way before this incident. And it is just as logical that this is an aberration as it is that it was an illustration of a tendency of character."

Allen sat back in his chair, then rocked forward and put his elbows on the elevated desk in front of him. He paused and sipped again from his water glass.

"What we have here is a number of factors in the government's favor, and a number of factors in the defense's favor. Which, of course, makes my life difficult. It makes it difficult for me to make a decision. And it is with a great deal of trepidation that I do make such a decision.

"I conclude that there are conditions, or a combination of conditions, that would reasonably assure Mr. Calloway's presence and would reasonably assure the safety of others in the community," Allen said. "First, I'm going to set a substantial bond."

The prosecutor was thunderstruck.

Fowlkes felt dizzy, and his heart pounded. When the hearing began, he believed there was virtually no chance Calloway would be released. But the magistrate had just announced that he was going to set bond. Maybe it would be a multimillion-dollar amount, Fowlkes thought wishfully. Maybe the bond would be so impossibly high that Calloway's family wouldn't be able to raise the 10 percent down payment most bail bonding companies require.

"Since the property residents own is out of state, I would prefer a secured bond," Allen said. "The bondsman and the relatives can work that out. I will set bond in this matter at seventeen thousand five hundred dollars."

Fowlkes could scarcely believe his ears. The magistrate ruled that Calloway need write a check for only 10 percent of that amount—$1,750—and he could walk away.

The prosecutor glanced at his watch. It was 4:05 P.M.

"Another condition which I will impose is that Mr. Calloway's travel be restricted to the Western District of Tennessee," Allen said. "If he has a passport, I want that to be surrendered. I will order that."

Calloway's lawyers quickly agreed and said his pilot's license also would be turned over voluntarily.

Allen said he would insist that the defendant begin psychological counseling, and that Calloway, not the government, pay for the counseling sessions. Again his lawyers voiced their approval.

The prosecutor rose to his feet.

"Your Honor, I do intend to appeal this decision."

"All right," Allen nodded. "I will order any release stayed until five o'clock."

"Thank you, Judge," Fowlkes said coldly.

"How about staying away from anybody at Federal Express?" Allen asked, almost as an afterthought.

Calloway's lawyers accepted the additional restriction. They would instruct their client to stay away from any FedEx employees as a condition for his release.

Allen began filling out the prisoner-release forms on his desk. They would only take a few minutes to complete. The magistrate asked Calloway for his mailing address. The forms required that information.

"My mailing address, sir, is Post Office Box 18163, Memphis, Tennessee, 38181," Calloway said, his voice clear and audible throughout the courtroom, the grimace suddenly gone from his face. "I normally check my post-office box every day."

Allen asked for the defendant's telephone number, but Calloway informed him the phone had been disconnected.

"Very well," the magistrate told him. "You are ordered to appear before Judge Julia Gibbons on Friday, June twenty-fourth, at nine-thirty A.M. If you fail to do so, it may be a violation of the Bail Reform Act. Court is adjourned."

The defendant's next scheduled court appearance was a month away.

The time was 4:15 P.M. Fowlkes had forty-five minutes to appeal before Calloway was released.

"A DANGER TO THE COMMUNITY"

MAY 23
4:20 P.M.

"You're not going to believe this," FedEx corporate lawyer Don Maliniak said apologetically. "I can hardly believe it myself. But it looks like they're going to let Auburn Calloway out of jail today. He's going to be released on bail."

Andy Peterson was at home with his three children when he got the late-afternoon telephone call from the attorney.

"Why?" the flight engineer stammered in disbelief. "Doesn't the judge know the guy tried to kill us?"

"I'm sure he does," said Maliniak, a self-effacing Pennsylvanian who specialized in labor relations. "But these bond hearings are strange. Judges don't decide whether a person did the crime or not. They just try to determine whether or not he's a danger to the community."

"Wait a second," Andy said. "I don't want to overreact here.

But the guy tried to smash our heads in with a hammer. He was going to crash our DC-ten. Those things are dangerous, right?"

The lawyer didn't want to get trapped into defending the magistrate's decision. It was as incomprehensible to him as it was to Peterson.

"Look, I'm really sorry," the lawyer began again. "I don't claim to understand what's going on here. It seems crazy. But I wanted to let you know and answer any of your questions before you hear about it on TV or the radio."

Andy tried to settle down. Prosecutors had told him and the other Flight 705 pilots that there was a chance a judge would set bail for Calloway. But they said it was an extremely remote chance.

"Well, do you think my family is safe?" the flight engineer asked. "Are we in any danger?"

"I don't think so," the lawyer answered quickly and confidently. "But if you'd like, if you'd feel better about it, we'll post a guard at your house. We'll have security there twenty-four hours a day for as long as you want. Frankly, I think once Calloway gets out, he'll want to stay as far away from you guys as possible."

Andy's wounds had healed to the point where he could walk normally, and the swelling of his face and head had receded. But each day new bruises seemed to appear on his body. Large yellow patches mysteriously welled up on his face, arms, and legs. Once they appeared, the bruises took weeks to go away. And there were deep aching pains that seemed to come from the marrow of his bones. He did his best to tough it out, but it was scary, especially for Susan and the kids. They weren't used to seeing him in this frail condition.

"Look," Andy concluded. "A guard probably isn't necessary. Calloway's probably not going to come to our house anytime soon. But I'm kind of weak right now. I get tired easy. And I'm just not a hundred percent sure that I could defend my family if I had to. Does that make sense?"

The admission wasn't easy for Andy to make. But he felt the FedEx lawyer should know the truth.

Andy kept a gun in his home. It was a forty-year-old .38 caliber police revolver. He had inherited it from a great-uncle years ago. He had fired the blue metal gun only once, and that had been more than a decade ago. It was packed away in a box, stuffed high in a closet so the kids wouldn't find it.

Andy wasn't even sure he or Susan could locate it if they had to.

The lawyer said that FedEx guards would be coming over right away. The security personnel wouldn't impose on the family. The guards would stay outside, in the driveway or across the street. The Petersons were told they should rest easy.

"ON THE RIGHT TRACK"

MAY 23

4:25 P.M.

The prosecutor was out of breath when he reached U.S. District Court Judge Julia Gibbons's chambers on the eleventh floor of the federal building.

Gibbons was the presiding federal judge in West Tennessee. She could overrule U.S. Magistrate James Allen's order to release Auburn Calloway on $17,500 bond if she chose. The judge listened to the prosecutor's arguments and quickly came up with a compromise.

She would not reverse the magistrate's decision right away. Instead, she would put a hold on Calloway's release, then review his decision the next day. If an error had been made, she would correct it after the hearing. Meanwhile, Gibbons picked up the black ballpoint pen on her mahogany desk and neatly filled out the one-page order that would prevent Calloway from being immediately released.

She handed it to the prosecutor, who ran back downstairs to Allen's courtroom. It was 4:45 P.M., just fifteen minutes before the magistrate was scheduled to release the defendant on bail.

Allen read the order, then read it again. He cleared his throat.

"There's been a change of plans," he said as calmly as he could. "A federal district judge has decided to block the entry of my bond order until the judge can review the decision. The defendant will remain in custody overnight, and a final bond decision will be announced tomorrow."

Ogletree was shocked. A few minutes ago, the Calloways were hugging and celebrating. Now, suddenly, their hopes were dashed. What could he tell them to ease their disappointment?

The next day, however, Calloway's family and friends received more bad news. Judge Gibbons overruled the magistrate's bond decision. The defendant would remain in prison until his criminal trial was over. That could take many months, maybe even a year or more.

"Based on the evidence, there is no condition or combination of conditions to reasonably assure the appearance of Mr. Calloway and the safety of other persons and the community," Judge Gibbons wrote by hand on a one-page form. "[He] is charged with a serious violent crime; the weight of the evidence appears substantial. Mr. Calloway's employment has given him great mobility, and he has no family ties to this community. The circumstances of the alleged offense and the fact that, if true, it represents a departure from the defendant's apparent earlier behavior, raise significant questions about his mental condition. The nature and seriousness of the potential damage to the community are great, if defendant is released."

Gibbons also granted a prosecution request to have Calloway undergo psychological tests to determine his competency to stand trial. Defense attorneys, however, would be allowed to have their own experts examine him first.

Ogletree would not comment to reporters who peppered him with questions about possible defense strategies. When asked about the prosecution motions to have Calloway undergo psychological tests, however, the defense team gave a cryptic response.

"Finally," the lawyer said, "the government is on the right track."

"MY LIFELINE"

MAY 26

11:00 A.M.

In the days that followed FedEx Flight 705's safe landing in Memphis, the crew members were deluged with media requests for interviews.

Television network producers, newsmagazines, newspapers—everyone wanted to talk to them. Especially David Sanders, the captain who successfully landed the aircraft. CBS planned a *48 Hours* show on workplace violence and sent a producer and camera crew to Memphis to interview the pilots. When all three declined, the network crews camped outside their homes with cameras and spoke to neighbors about them.

The three pilots had behaved as a crew on April 7. They were a team. When the appropriate time came, they would speak together. If it took months or years for Jim Tucker and Andy Peterson to recover, the media would have to wait. A few tabloid TV shows offered money, but David's decision, endorsed by Jim and Andy, was not negotiable.

FedEx and the union representing FedEx pilots also maneuvered for advantage. Company executives considered honoring the crew in public but decided such a spectacle might be seen as a cynical attempt to manipulate the injured pilots. Also, FedEx executives didn't want to draw attention to the fact that the attack was initiated by another company pilot, who nearly succeeded in taking over the airplane and might have committed one of the most destructive acts of terrorism in U.S. history.

While FedEx officials discussed their options, the pilots' union moved into action. Don Wilson, the ALPA chairman, nominated the crew for the Air Line Pilots Association's Gold Medal for Heroism, a seldom-granted award considered the highest civilian honor for commercial airline pilots. Only eighteen pilots had ever received the heroism medal since it was instituted in 1966.

There was just one problem. David was not a union member, and ALPA had never granted its highest award to a nonmember. Jim and Andy were members in good standing. The association risked cheapening the heroism award, however, if it ignored the highest-ranking pilot on the crew.

ALPA president J. Randolph Babbitt introduced a resolution to the union's executive council seeking to make nonmembers eligible for the heroism award. As news spread through the airline community about what the pilots aboard the FedEx DC-10 had accomplished, the resolution passed quickly and unanimously, and at the next union executive board meeting, Babbitt nominated the Flight 705 crew for ALPA's heroism award. The nomination too, passed without opposition.

Don Wilson, the ALPA chairman at FedEx, called David and told his old friend and fellow DC-10 captain about the rare honor. The union was locked in high-stakes contract negotiations with FedEx, but the union leader promised ALPA would not use the awards presentation as an antimanagement rally.

"It's going to be your show," Wilson assured him. "We'll do it when the crew wants it, the way the crew wants it. Just tell us when you're ready and we'll take care of the rest."

All three of the Flight 705 pilots were anxious to publicly acknowledge the people who had assisted them and their families after the attack. David told Jim about the ALPA award while visiting the copilot in the hospital.

"They're willing to wait to make the announcement until we're ready," David informed him. "There's no rush. Whatever we do, we'll do as a crew."

Judging from the critical nature of Jim's injuries and recent surgeries, David guessed it would be months until his copilot was ready to appear in public. He was shocked when Jim said he would be ready on May 26. Andy agreed to the date, too.

Jim was about to be released from the hospital after almost a month of intensive care and two delicate brain operations. He was making great strides in rehabilitation, but some days were better than others. He tired quickly, and fatigue sometimes turned to frustration. Flashes of anger only cluttered his thinking and made everything worse. Jim's doctors gave him the green light to attend the ceremony and thought it might help mend his spirit.

But Jim's family worried that a public ceremony might be emotionally overwhelming and physically draining. Jim still had difficulty walking, and the right side of his body was frequently numb. The loss of feeling in his right hand made it impossible for him to perform simple tasks such as writing his name or tying his shoes.

ALPA rented a ballroom at a Hilton Hotel in Memphis for the event. Until the day before the awards presentation, they wondered whether Jim would be up to it. Jim told them he would skip a breakfast ALPA was holding for visiting dignitaries that morning. But he would show up in time to be present at the awards ceremony.

On the morning of the event, the mayor of Memphis, FedEx executives, and friends of the Flight 705 pilots ate omelets and waffles at the Hilton while Jim and Becky prepared at home.

Becky poured a heavy dose of antibiotic medication into the tube doctors had inserted in her husband's chest. The veins in his arms had been poked and prodded by so many hypodermic needles in recent weeks that his forearms were beginning to show all the needle tracks of a heroin addict. The harsh medicine was simply wearing out the veins in his arms, so doctors had inserted the chest tube directly into one of the main arteries by his heart. Becky also prepared two bags of intravenous fluid and brought them in the car to the awards ceremony. If Jim became dehydrated or expended too much energy, she could replenish him immediately.

"I'm like a nicad battery," he told her. "I'll be doing great and feeling fine. And then, all at once, my power runs out. There's no warning. I'm just gone."

Becky was concerned about the timing of the awards presentation. She wondered if her husband was pushing himself too hard. Jim constantly set goals for himself and rarely failed to meet them. Run ten kilometers in forty minutes, replace the carburetor on the Luscombe before lunch, prepare for an awards presentation on the twenty-sixth.

That's the way he had always done things.

Becky drove the Dodge Caravan toward the hotel while Jim finished getting dressed. He wore a blue sport coat, gray slacks, and a collared shirt. But in the car, he had great difficulty knotting his tie. He couldn't remember how to do it, and he had trouble grasping the fabric with his right hand. Becky flipped down the sun visor on the passenger side of the car so that Jim could use the mirror. But when he looked at it, everything was backward and confusing. Using just his left hand, he finally formed an acceptable knot as the car was pulling into the crowded parking lot.

The Flight 705 crew met briefly in a conference room a few minutes before the ceremony was set to begin. David would speak first, then Jim, then Andy. Captain, copilot, flight engineer. None of them would discuss details of what had happened on the airplane. That would be left for future appearances in federal court when they were witnesses against Auburn Calloway.

In the back room, David, Andy, and their families marveled at how good Jim looked. Even though they had visited him in the hospital recently, they were astonished. Sure, the usual muscle mass was gone, and Jim looked a little gaunt. But otherwise, he seemed like his regular exuberant, personable self.

The organizers had not known how large a room to rent because the awards presentation was announced to other FedEx pilots less than a week in advance. Also, since it was to be held on a weekday, most FedEx pilots would be out of town on company trips. Organizers had estimated about a hundred people would be there.

When the three Flight 705 crew members walked into the room, however, it was packed shoulder to shoulder with more than four hundred people—mostly pilots in blue jackets and ties who stood and applauded in a thunderous ovation. The spectators exulted in shouts and cheers, refusing to be seated even when the first speaker came to the podium.

ALPA leader J. Randolph Babbitt made the presentations himself. Thin, telegenic, and six feet four inches tall, Babbitt had sharp features, clear blue eyes, and an even-keeled bearing that had served him well during his frequent appearances before Congress and TV cameras. As Babbitt addressed the group of FedEx pilots and their families, though, he had to pause to keep his composure.

"Today I have the honor of presenting the Air Line Pilots Association's highest award to three of the most professional and courageous airmen to have ever been members of the piloting profession," Babbitt began, his voice amplified by a microphone and public address system. "We've all read accounts of the terror and pain that these men experienced as they fought to save their lives, they fought to save their aircraft, and they fought to save the lives of a lot of people on the ground.

"Few of us can actually visualize the horror that these men survived or truly comprehend the extraordinary airmanship they employed in a life-threatening situation."

He recounted how FedEx Flight 705 took off normally on April 7 and headed west toward California. He mentioned that another FedEx pilot was riding one of the DC-10's two jump seats and that he had smuggled hammers, a diving knife, and speargun aboard the plane in a guitar case. But he avoided mentioning Calloway by name as FedEx executives had asked.

Babbitt told how the crew members were severely injured by hammer blows that rained down on them without warning from a coworker none of them knew personally.

"It's a pilot's tendency to place him- or herself into the cockpit when we hear the recounting of any flying incident to measure how we might have responded or reacted under similar circumstances. But this event transcends all of that. These aeronautical feats were performed in the context of the pure horror of hand-to-hand combat. Life-and-death combat. They are unimaginable, and I am in awe of the skill that brought this aircraft back home safely.

"Today we are honoring these three men for their courage, for their valor, and for their airmanship in thwarting the takeover and destruction of their aircraft."

The crowd couldn't be restrained. Spectators stood and hollered and cheered wildly for several minutes as the three pilots walked onto the stage to accept the awards, gold medallions about the size of silver dollars mounted on square wooden pedestals. Jim leaned on Becky for support as he negotiated the three steps onto the elevated stage.

Jagged wounds were still visible on the left sides of both Jim's and Andy's heads, where their hair had been shaved. Andy had recently undergone minor surgery to remove stitches that had become infected, and his hair was even shorter than Jim's. The stubble that had grown back could not hide the scars and suture marks on both men's pale scalps. TV cameras with bright lights focused on their injuries as the two pilots turned to watch the presentation.

The applause finally subsided as David stepped to the microphone. His eyes were moist as he surveyed the audience of friends and coworkers. He began to read from an index card on which he had written a few notes, but his teary eyes made reading impossible. He slid the card back into his breast pocket.

"The ultimate compliment to any pilot is recognition by his fellow pilots for a job well done," David began, slowly and softly, his eyes humbly lowered. "And on behalf of the crew of Flight seven-oh-five, we are very grateful to you for this rare award—and we thank you very, very much."

He looked up and scanned the familiar faces, drawing strength from the room full of friends. As their applause reverberated through the room, David had the sensation of feeling it more than hearing it.

"We thank all of you for being here today, families and friends, and all of you guys in blue suits with stripes on your sleeves. I think you all experienced Flight seven-oh-five in your own personal way." He swallowed hard and continued.

"On April seventh, aboard Flight seven-oh-five, the unthinkable occurred. And the crew on that day, in order to survive, had to do the unthinkable. With considerable restraint toward the attacker, we subdued him. All survived, including the attacker. We train as a crew, we fly as a crew, and unfortunately, on April seventh we fought as a crew.

"It was hand-to-hand combat. It was life or death. And we lived."

The captain's voice grew stronger and he spoke with increasing conviction. He was tempted to give details, to let people know exactly what happened aboard the DC-10 that day. There had been so much speculation, so much rumor, so much misinformation. Sanders wanted people to know the facts. Yet he had to refrain.

"I'd prefer today to tell the entire story; however, legal considerations prevent me from doing that. The pilots need to know, everybody needs to know, exactly what happened. Perhaps in the future we'll have an opportunity to do that.

"I must say now though that it is an honor, it is a privilege to have flown with, and now count as personal friends, two aviators whose professional skills and sheer determination to survive made it possible for us to be alive today."

David became more animated as he went on, and the words began to flow. He raised his hands from the podium and gestured as he spoke.

"Several times we took the airplane to the edge and brought it back in. On April seventh we were in every sense of the word a crew, a team. We did our jobs and more. We saved each other's lives, and we literally owe our lives to each other. I am thankful, I am blessed, to have had Jim Tucker and Andy Peterson on my crew that day.

"Jim and Andy, you are the best." David stepped back from the microphone and embraced Jim, then Andy.

The crowd erupted again, tears flowing freely.

David stepped back and gestured to Jim, motioning for the copilot to go to the podium.

Becky led her husband the few brief steps to the sturdy wooden structure. He could lean on the podium. She tried to back away, but Jim held firmly to her right hand. He kept Becky by his side as he cleared his throat. He looked at the ceiling and then at the floor. Like David, he had made notes to cue him during his speech, but they were equally useless. None of the prepared lines seemed appropriate anymore. Like the captain who had preceded him, Jim decided to wing it.

"This is very difficult for me," the thin, drawn copilot began. "Those of you who know me know that I am more frightened of public speaking, probably, than anything else."

There were some sympathetic chuckles in the audience as Jim paused.

"First," he said, "I have to mention my wife. She is my lifeline."

Still gripping Becky's hand, Jim turned and faced her.

"Becky, you are so strong. I thought I was strong, but you are the strongest. You have sustained me, and I love you for it. Thank you."

Many in the crowd wept, whether they knew the Tuckers personally or not. Even some of the reporters stopped taking notes, their eyes welling with tears.

"I can't thank everybody. You're going to have to read between the lines a little bit. I want you to know, you've watched over my children, you've cut my lawn, you've worked on my car," he laughed, a broad smile settling across his angular face. "I wouldn't let you fly my airplane.

"In short, you have been our daily bread. Everything we needed was provided for. You have to know that."

Then the smile receded. Jim took several deep breaths and steadied himself with both hands on the podium. "I have to talk about the crew, David and Andy. I can fly an airplane. Must of us here can do it second-nature. I think I was spared a lot of the trauma that day, and the reason for that is this: I flew the jet.

"David and Andy, you got up out of your seats after you'd been beaten severely about the head and shoulders. You faced our attacker, and you subdued him. You can't imagine the fear that I was suffering. I didn't know what was happening. I had no way of knowing what was going on.

"Stuck on a plane with an individual who could jump me at any time—I just had to put it out of my mind. It was too hard to even fathom. David and Andy, I stand before you and tell you without shame that I love you, I admire you, and I'm so glad to have had you with me."

Jim paused, still holding his wife's hand and leaning heavily against the podium.

"There's another matter I must address. It's the matter of divine intervention." Jim's voice cracked. For a moment the emotion overcame him. The articulate pilot was at a complete loss for words.

"Please bear with me just a minute," he said, looking down solemnly as if in prayer.

"We want to thank God for his mercy. His strength, His power. He sustained us. We were able to do all things through Him. There was no other way, no way. Please understand that."

The crowd roared again. Some gave up even trying to hide the tears that streamed down their cheeks as they stood on their chairs and clapped and cheered. The Tuckers stepped back from the podium. Now it was flight engineer Andy Peterson's turn.

With his crew-cut blond hair and compact build, Andy resembled the young astronaut John Glenn. He stepped to the microphone looking stiff and uncomfortable in a brown coat and a pressed shirt and tie. Just about everything he wanted to say had been said already.

"I'd like to thank all our fellow pilots who have honored us with this award," he began, glancing at Susan and their three young children seated beside the stage. "I especially would like to thank David and Jim.

"I'd like to thank all of our families for being so strong for us. They have suffered as much as we have, if not more. Also, I'd like to thank God for sparing our lives that day." Andy's voice was soft and smooth, his southern accent far stronger than the previous speakers'.

"I can't say it nearly as well as Jim did, but we all owe our lives to God."

Andy nodded stiffly toward the audience, signifying he was finished with his remarks. The crowd couldn't be contained. They stood again and cheered and shouted more loudly than they had at the conclusion of the previous speeches.

The ovation washed over the pilots and their families like a wave.

Babbitt returned to the podium. Never had he been so moved by a public ceremony. He invited the families of the three pilots to join them on the stage. Soon the elevated area was covered with wives, mothers, sons and daughters, their arms full of flowers and gifts from well-wishers.

"Although their families may not show the same physical scars, they bear the emotional wounds nonetheless. Although we don't have gold medals for their families, I want to commend each member of these families for the steadfast devotion and the never-ending support that they gave these pilots.

"You are all truly heroes."

PART FIVE

"ON TIME AND POLITE"

▼

▼

▼

The jury had deliberated for a day and a half when foreman Darro Robinson informed the bailiff that the panel had reached a verdict.

The courtroom on the eleventh floor of the federal building in downtown Memphis was filled to capacity when Robinson, thirty-two, a manager for the Internal Revenue Service, led fellow jurors from the conference room where they had decided Auburn Calloway's fate, through the doorway, and into the adjoining courtroom.

There were ten African Americans and two whites on the panel; nine women and three men. There were two teachers, two registered nurses, a machinist, a trucking-company dispatcher, a day-care worker, a federal government employee, a laborer, and a homemaker among them. They had three possible verdicts:

Guilty. Not guilty. And not guilty by reason of insanity.

If the jury found Calloway guilty, he faced a sentence of twenty years to life in prison. If not guilty, he would leave the courtroom a free man. If not guilty by reason of insanity, Calloway would be sent to a mental hospital until experts determined he was sane. That determination could take weeks, or it could take decades. The decision would be entirely in the hands of mental health experts.

Jurors had selected the quiet, reflective Robinson as their foreman soon after deliberations started. The IRS manager with a neatly trimmed beard was genuinely surprised by the honor. He hadn't wanted to serve on the jury, but unlike other busy professionals in the jury pool, he had been unwilling to lie or claim hardship in order to avoid it. Now, at the end of two weeks of testimony, he felt profound ambivalence about the jury's decision and his role in reaching it.

As the son of a career Army soldier and an African American

who had grown up near Memphis, Robinson identified with Auburn Calloway and admired many things about him. Robinson and Calloway both had humble family origins but prized education and had become college graduates; both had served in the military; both had two young children and wanted to open doors of opportunity for them.

Robinson also felt torn between the two talented African-American attorneys who tried the case from opposing sides. A. C. Wharton, the defense lawyer, was a Memphis community leader and a veteran courtroom strategist. He replaced Charles Ogletree when Calloway's college friend abruptly dropped the case after the preliminary hearings.

Ogletree's departure was an emotional setback for Calloway. But for Ogletree, Calloway's case was a loser. Instead of representing a victim, a persecuted minority member, or an underdog, in this case he was associated with the perpetrator of a violent crime. There were no broad constitutional issues to be decided. And the insanity defense that Calloway had insisted on using obligated his lawyers to prove their client couldn't distinguish the difference between right and wrong at the time of the attack. It was an uphill battle, and far removed from Ogletree's areas of expertise.

But Wharton, the lawyer Ogletree recommended as his replacement, didn't mind long odds. A legal scrapper and counterpuncher, Wharton had fought his way to the top of his profession through the gritty, streetwise ranks of the public defender's office. Now fifty-five, Wharton was at the pinnacle of his career. He had turned down prestigious judgeships and invitations to run for elected office many times in order to stay at the helm of his burgeoning legal practice. With distinguished silver hair, smooth ebony skin, and expressive brown eyes, he exuded a gentlemanly, learned air of confidence.

The prosecutor, Assistant U.S. District Attorney John Fowlkes, sat alone at a mahogany table opposite Wharton and Calloway. Fowlkes had handled the government's case by himself from the day Flight 705 landed. He oversaw the investigation, interviewed all the prospective witnesses, wrote every legal brief, and cross-examined all the defense experts. There were stacks of file folders and reams of printed information on the table next to him, but Fowlkes seldom referred to the written material. He knew the facts of the case by heart.

"There's a saying in basketball that applies here," Fowlkes told the jury in his opening statement. "I go for a layup and I get fouled, but the ball goes in, and I say, No harm—no foul. This case is going to be different from a basketball game, and you're going to have to apply the law. You can't say No harm—no foul."

Tall and slender with light-brown skin and a hint of silver in his curly hair, Fowlkes punctuated his speech with crisp, energetic hand movements. He spoke so fast that court reporters strained at times to keep up with him. Fowlkes had painstakingly retraced Calloway's actions leading up to Flight 705's departure from Memphis on April 7. He explained the problems Calloway faced at work and the financial transactions he had made before boarding the plane. He carefully laid out the evidence, and he called expert witnesses to testify about Calloway's state of mind. The defendant obviously knew what he was doing was wrong, the prosecutor said, because he went to such great lengths to conceal his true intentions.

But Fowlkes couldn't prove what Calloway had planned to do with the aircraft if he had been able to seize control of it. And although he had his suspicions, the prosecutor couldn't provide a clear motive. What could drive an outwardly successful man to such extremes? Why would the prospect of losing a job make such a person suicidal?

Wharton tried to exploit those unanswered questions and tear apart the carefully woven fabric of the prosecutor's case. He reacted quickly and tenaciously to prosecution witnesses, leading them into verbal corners during cross-examinations—then dissecting them patiently and persuasively. But he discouraged comparisons between the forceful personalities in the courtroom.

"This trial is not a contest between two lawyers, John Fowlkes and myself," Wharton told the jury the first time he addressed the panel. "This is not about Fred Smith versus Auburn Calloway."

He spoke slowly in soft, gentle tones, making eye contact with each of the jurors, a pair of tortoiseshell reading glasses in his left hand.

"Oddly enough, I'm not going to get into my version of what took place in the skies. The key is this: Mr. Fowlkes made the analogy of shooting a basketball and getting fouled. I'm not a basketball player, but even a spectator like me knows that when you watch a ball game, you keep your eye on the ball.

"There was a vicious attack, yes. Injuries, yes, terrible injuries. Lingering nightmares and memories. I've heard the tapes from the cockpit, and you'll hear them, too. It'll be hard to listen to. But as you listen, keep your eye on the ball. Ask yourself, Where is the proof? It will leave reasonable doubt."

U.S. District Court Judge Julia Gibbons presided in a gracious, informal manner.

At forty-four, Judge Gibbons had already been a federal judge for eight years. A native of a small town near Nashville, she was one of the youngest federal judges in the country when President Ronald Reagan appointed her. Now, legal experts speculated that she might soon be elevated to the federal Court of Appeals, and then, perhaps, the U.S. Supreme Court.

With shoulder-length reddish brown hair and blue eyes that sparkled behind oversized glasses, Judge Gibbons could fill the red-carpeted courtroom with her lilting southern accent and grandiose gestures. She refused to allow TV cameras in the courtroom, however, and she declined to sequester the jury. Time-consuming conferences with attorneys were kept to an absolute minimum.

The pilots had been the first witnesses to appear before the jury.

Defense lawyers had sought to delay the start of the trial as long as possible in order to give the pilots more time to heal. Wounded men, they knew, would gain more sympathy from the jury.

Now, almost a year after the attack, the defense tactic appeared to have worked. More than six months of postponements had allowed Jim Tucker and Andy Peterson to grow their hair back. Long, jagged scars on their heads looked like craggy fault lines, but the men seemed healthy and robust when they appeared in court. Jim was tanned and rested from recent days spent hiking outdoors, and none of the panelists could tell that a portion of his skull had been removed and that only a few thin layers of skin protected his brain.

Jim walked without a trace of the limp that had so clearly afflicted him during the ALPA awards presentation ten months before. But he still wasn't allowed to drive a car, and he had to wear a bicycle helmet whenever he went outside to protect against falling acorns and other small objects.

Jim worked out every day, and as he added muscle mass, his weight reached 210 pounds—about ten shy of his weight on the date of the attack. The workouts were unusually fatiguing, however, because Jim's mind would tire more than the rest of his body. After each workout, he would sleep for two hours, and powerful medication had debilitating side effects. But the jury was never given this information.

When David Sanders was called to the stand, the prosecutor asked him to authenticate the audiotape from Flight 705's cockpit voice recorder. Each of the jurors was given a headset, and Fowlkes played the thirty-minute tape for them.

David studied the jurors' faces as the recorded cockpit conversation instantly turned from a casual chat about the passing geography to a savage, life-or-death brawl. But the captain couldn't tell if jurors sitting in the dispassionate courtroom environment were able to understand the terror the pilots had known on the plane. How could anyone understand such an ordeal without having lived it?

Two psychologists testified for the defense that Calloway was legally insane on April 7. They diagnosed the flight engineer as suffering from a paranoid personality disorder, a long-standing condition that was exacerbated by a bout of depression in the days before the attack. These maladies combined in a "psychotic episode" in which Calloway temporarily snapped, they said. He lost control of himself and his senses. In his mind, the attack was a blur of conflicting images, voices, and emotions.

"A psychotic episode is basically a period of time in which one's behavior, or one's thinking or cognition, seems to be out of contact with reality," said psychologist John Hutson, an expert witness summoned by the defense. "An individual who is psychotic doesn't seem to respond well to external stimuli. He responds primarily to thoughts and ideas within his own head, oblivious a lot of times to the consequences, the situation in which he finds himself physically. On April seventh, Mr. Calloway suffered a combination of the depression imposed upon an existing paranoid state, which appears to have culminated in a psychotic episode."

But a psychologist and psychiatrist who testified for the prosecution claimed Calloway's mental illness was a pretense. They said his actions on Flight 705 had been carefully planned in advance and carried out ruthlessly. They accused Calloway of "malingering"—inventing phony symptoms in order to avoid taking responsibility for his actions. When Calloway told doctors he was hearing voices at the time of the attack or not remembering portions of the incident, prosecution experts asserted, he was simply lying.

Raymond Frederick Patterson, M.D., a psychiatrist and hospital administrator from suburban Maryland, was the main expert for the prosecution. An amiable African-American man with a self-effacing sense of humor, Patterson liked to explain complex theories by way of analogies to everyday life. The psychiatrist's dark hair was turning gray at the edges, and he spoke in a deep baritone voice.

The psychiatrist pointed out that his life contained some remarkable parallels with the defendant's. Patterson had enrolled at Northwestern University in 1970—the same year Calloway began at Stanford. Patterson graduated a year early and attended medical school at Howard University from 1973 until 1977. He didn't meet Calloway during Calloway's short stint in veterinary school there in 1974. Patterson had been a staff psychiatrist at St. Elizabeth's Hospital in Washington, D.C.—the mental facility where Calloway's mother had been institutionalized.

Patterson made eye contact with each of the jurors and spoke to them as if they were having a friendly chat in his living room. "Mr. Calloway reported to me that he heard voices, or a voice, and it varied between our two interviews," he said. "On the one interview, he told me he heard voices, plural. On the other interview he told me it was a single voice. That's significant. Now, I don't know if anyone here has ever heard voices, but if you have observed anyone who ever has, it's a very unpleasant experience.

"A patient once told me, 'Doc, it's like someone puts a telephone receiver against your ear and says stuff you don't like and don't want to hear, and you can't stop it.' That's disturbing. Mr. Calloway told me he heard the voice or voices for the first time on April seventh. He told another interviewer that he first heard the voice in January 1994. That's inconsistent.

"As I said, people who legitimately, truly, hear voices are suffering. They're in pain and distress. When Mr. Calloway was asked to tell about the voices, he responded by saying, 'Tell me what you want to know.' That's inconsistent. It's like coming to me with a terrible headache. When I ask 'Where does it hurt?' you're not going to say, 'Tell me what you want to know.' You're going to point here and tell me how long you've had it."

As Patterson explained his opinions, he extended his right hand toward the jury, palm upturned as though he were handing them something small and delicate.

"I don't believe Mr. Calloway hears voices," the psychiatrist concluded. "It's malingering, plain and simple. Everyone who has had a child who claimed to be sick to avoid going to school has some experience with malingering."

Angelique Michelle Calloway, the defendant's younger sister by three years, told about their unhappy childhood.

Their father, Earl Calloway, a postal worker, had been physically and verbally abusive to the children and their mother. Miriam Clara Waters had been a teacher in Maryland when she met Calloway. But soon after they were married, she developed symptoms of paranoid schizophrenia. She became secretive and withdrawn. She couldn't work and was institutionalized, first as an outpatient, then full-time.

Angelique and Auburn Calloway tried to protect their mother from the beatings she received, but they were powerless to help her. As their mother continued her irreversible slide into dementia, their father stayed away from their home.

"My father was at home frequently when I was a young child," Angelique said. "As I got older, age twelve and beyond, my father was rarely home. He came home—he came to our house—once a week on Fridays to get his mail, check on things, and leave. We didn't see him again for another week."

When their parents argued, Auburn tried to protect his mother, Angelique said. "Auburn would get between the two of them to try to protect her, to ward off the blows. We both did. We did that a lot growing up."

Angelique dabbed her eyes with a paper tissue as she recounted the painful memories in a soft, steady cadence. "I was miserable. I was miserable as a child and hated living there. I hated the way my father treated my mother. I hated the way he treated us. I was devastated when I learned he wished we had never been born.

"I saw Auburn in anguish over our parents," Angelique said. "I saw him in turmoil."

Ruby Yates was supposed to be a minor witness for the prosecution. The matronly African-American woman had lived in Memphis her whole life, and she had worked at FedEx almost since the company began flying. She was a jump-seat reservationist, and she was one of the last people to see Auburn Calloway before he boarded Flight 705.

Fowlkes asked her to confirm the dates and times she spoke to Calloway on April 7. The prosecutor was trying to firm up some of the small links in a very long chain of events.

On cross-examination, however, Wharton asked about Calloway's demeanor. Was anything different about him that day? Was he unusually agitated or distracted?

"Yes, there was something different," Yates answered. "He was on time, and he was polite."

Wharton presumed the witness had misspoke. You mean he wasn't normally punctual or mannerly? "No," Yates clarified. "He was arrogant and disrespectful—and he has been that way the entire five years I've been dealing with him. He was always in a hurry, and he was always rude."

Instead of eliciting compassion for his client, Wharton had allowed Yates to cast him as a conceited outsider who mistreated common folk.

The jury foreman handed the one-page verdict form to the bailiff, and he gave it to Judge Gibbons. She read it, then looked at the jurors seated across the room from her.

The panelists were expressionless, motionless.

Darro Robinson silently prayed that he and his fellow jurors had reached the right conclusion. Arriving at the verdict had been one of the most difficult experiences in his life. Now, he was about to share his decision with the world. The Flight 705 pilots and their families were seated on the wooden benches behind the prosecutor's table. The Calloways sat behind the defense table on the other side of the courtroom. Robinson recognized the Calloway children even though they hadn't testified or been introduced. There was a strong family resemblance.

Robinson hoped that the losing side would understand that he and the other jurors had done their best. They had taken an oath, and they had tried to live up to their obligations.

The judge began reading, her resonant, melodic voice filling the chamber. There were no dramatic pauses or flourishes. Her tone was serious and deliberate.

"In the matter of the United States versus Auburn R. Calloway, on the charge of attempted aircraft piracy, the jury finds the defendant guilty," she said without looking up. Judge Gibbons took a long, deep breath and she placed the rectangular piece of paper on her desk. Despite her prior instructions, some spectators embraced in joy and celebration.

"Yes!" one shouted. "Thank God!"

At the insistence of defense lawyer Wharton, the jury was polled one by one. Each juror answered yes when Judge Gibbons asked if they agreed with the verdict.

The judge thanked the jurors for their service and dismissed them. She ordered the bailiff to keep all spectators in the courtroom for at least five minutes so that jurors would have time to leave the building through a back exit if they didn't want to talk to reporters. All of the panelists quickly departed. Judge Gibbons set a sentencing date sixty days hence. Then she, too, disappeared into her chambers.

In the spectator area, friends of the Flight 705 pilots gathered around them. The three men held their wives and hugged each other, tears welling in their eyes.

Behind the defense table, Calloway showed no emotion as the verdict was read or afterward. Burney and Keelah leaned against their mother, and Patricia gently stroked their hair. Angelique sobbed. She walked forward to the low wooden barrier that separated participants from spectators. She leaned across to speak with her brother.

"I'm sorry," she cried. "I'm so sorry."

Calloway patted her on the shoulder.

"It's OK," he said. "We expected this."

As two federal marshals stepped forward to lead him away, Calloway looked over his shoulder at Angelique.

"I'll call you tonight," he said.

Escorted by the marshals, Calloway began to walk—but his

knees were wobbly. One of the marshals moved to support him, but Calloway pulled away. Defense lawyer Wharton was talking to several reporters in the spectator area. They busily wrote in thin notebooks as the lawyer spoke.

"It will be my advice to Mr. Calloway to appeal this decision," Wharton said, seemingly unfazed by the verdict. "However, the final decision will be his. We're glad this phase of the trial is behind us. We would have wished, in the interest of justice, that there had been a different result."

In the guarded parking lot outside the federal building, Robinson stepped into his car and closed the door.

Feeling drained and tired, he removed the red "Juror" button from his shirt for the last time. He was anxious to go back to work and leave the memory of the grueling trial behind him. He hoped that the twenty federal workers he supervised wouldn't know that he had been on the jury. He suspected the verdict would be unpopular with them. But he didn't feel he had to make excuses.

He had just voted to take away the most productive years of a talented man's life, and Robinson knew he would carry that burden with him forever.

The most troubling aspect of the case for Robinson had been that he was never able to figure out Calloway's motivations. Why had he hurt those innocent men? Why did a gifted man with two beautiful children want to kill himself? And why would he send all the money to his ex-wife? His ex-wife?

As a manager, Robinson prided himself on being able to understand the things that drive people, that make them perform. But Calloway was as much a mystery to Robinson at the end of the trial as he had been at the beginning. Maybe someday Calloway would provide the missing pieces of the puzzle. Maybe not.

But Robinson was done thinking about him.

He hadn't looked Calloway in the eyes the entire two weeks of trial. When the jury was polled after the verdict was announced, Robinson stared straight ahead. He believed that the jury had made the right choice for the right reasons.

But he was troubled by his inability to answer the most basic question: Why did this happen?

PART SIX

''RECOVERY AND RENEWAL''

▼

▼

▼

**JULY 25
1:30 P.M.**

Andy and Susan Peterson were driving down a rural highway with their five-year-old daughter, Anna, and one of her kindergarten friends.

The radio was off and the windows of the white van were rolled up. Andy and Susan listened to their daughter's soft voice in the backseat as she recounted recent events. Anna's friend had moved away the previous summer, and this was the first time they had seen each other in months.

Anna told about her new teacher at school, the bedroom her father had built for her in the attic, and Flight 705. Without prompting, Anna effortlessly recounted the date, the flight number, the names of the victims and the attacker. She told about seeing her father in the hospital, and how she and her older sister shrieked and cried, refusing to approach their dad's bedside.

"He looked scary and yucky," Anna explained.

The Petersons had never heard their children talk about the tumultuous events of the previous year. They always tried to answer their children's questions about their father's injuries frankly and directly. They expected the kids to be curious, and they knew that there was no way to shelter them from the facts of the hijacking attempt. They lived in a small community. People talked, and the children were bound to be influenced by the things they heard. But considering their young ages and their hectic lives, Andy and Susan doubted that the facts about FedEx Flight 705 ever really sank in.

Riding in the car on this summer afternoon, however, the Petersons learned otherwise.

Andy and Susan held hands and smiled, in awe of a child's perceptiveness and ability to distill a year's worth of confusing facts and emotions into a short monologue.

*   *   *

A few weeks later, Andy and Susan learned that their oldest child, eight-year-old Mary Margaret, could be equally succinct.

For one of the first writing assignments of the fall semester for third graders at Chickasaw Elementary School in Olive Branch, teacher Pam White told her students to draft a composition. It could be about any subject—summer vacations, new brothers or sisters, favorite pets. But whatever their focus, students should consider their words carefully because some of the finished essays would be published next week in the *DeSoto County Tribune* on pages purchased by the school's P.T.A members. Parents hoped to give students a practical lesson in the power of their written words and make them proud of their writing through the newspaper program.

Mary Margaret decided to write about her father.

Tall for her age, the slender seven-year-old with ribbons in her straight blond hair wrinkled her nose as she wrote, concentrating intently on forming perfect letters. Each character fit neatly between the wide blue lines on the rectangular piece of paper. Mary Margaret and the other students in White's class began their writing assignment at 2.00 P.M. Twenty minutes later, they were finished and White collected the assignments.

As she expected, some of the writing was illegible. There were frequent misspellings, but that was normal, especially so early in the academic year. Some of the young writers jotted down scattered, incoherent thoughts. But for an early attempt, the prose was remarkably solid. Maybe one of her students would become a novelist like John Grisham, the DeSoto County lawyer who had become such a hit in Hollywood. Mississippi prided itself on its history of producing great authors like William Faulkner, Hodding Carter, Willie Morris, Shelby Foote, and Eudora Welty.

White flipped through the stack of handwritten pages. Several students had written about family trips to Disneyworld. Another went to Mexico.

One of the written pages caught White's attention.

My daddy was one of the pilots that got hijacked on April 7, 1994.
It was really sad for our family, but he is OK now. He has a gold
medal and a gold clock! I am very proud of him.
MARY MARGARET
MRS. WHITE

The author printed her name in block letters, and White was surprised to find her eyes suddenly brimming with tears.

The teacher knew Andy and Susan Peterson. They went to the same church, and they had many mutual friends. White found herself touched by their eldest child's simple, hopeful message. The attack must have been torture for the little girl and her siblings. People in their community had been concerned about them, but no one knew exactly what they could do to help. The teacher was overjoyed to hear from Mary Margaret that things were better now. And that she wrote about the incident in the past tense—as an episode that now was behind her.

White marked the page with a happy face—her highest possible grade.

A week later, Mary Margaret's letter was printed in the newspaper with those of dozens of other students. Susan Peterson clipped her daughter's first published words and mailed copies to family members. Susan recognized that Mary Margaret had summed up the painful, complex, tumultuous recent events with rare brevity and clarity.

There had been injury and sorrow. That was true. But recovery and renewal had followed. Susan taped her daughter's first press clipping to the door of the family's refrigerator.

"CONSUMED BY HATE"

Auburn Calloway had made the trip from the federal correctional institute in Mason, Tennessee, to downtown Memphis so many times during his two-week trial that he knew the drill by heart.

Prisoners with court dates ate an early breakfast. Then guards took them to a holding area and patted them down, searching for weapons. U.S. marshals then met the prisoners, searched them again, fastened a long chain to their ankles, and loaded them into a van bound for Memphis.

The forty-mile drive down two-lane Highway 70, then Interstate 40, always seemed to pass quickly. The van's windows were covered with wire mesh but sunlight still poured through, and the humming tires conveyed the pleasant sound and feel of motion. Calloway had enjoyed the same pleasing sensation hundreds of times when the massive airliners he flew at FedEx began their takeoff rolls. In the Navy, he had always looked forward to the exhilaration of being launched from steam catapults on aircraft carriers—a mind-numbing sensation that propelled him from zero to 140 miles an hour in two seconds.

When Calloway was in Navy flight training at Meridian, he used to zoom along at 400 miles an hour over the land where his slave ancestors had toiled and suffered such unspeakable deprivations. Calloway used to wonder if it would bring them peace to know that one of their descendants was looking down on those same verdant farms and fields from a bird's perspective.

Now, prison life was so sedentary that a ride in a ten-year-old Ford van seemed exciting. But even though the routine was familiar, when Calloway boarded the van for Memphis, he knew his situation was different this time.

The landscape had certainly changed since he had come to Memphis each morning during the trial. Then, the spring air was sweet and wildflowers bloomed purple and blue along the heavily wooded roadsides. Now, the sky was obscured by a listless haze and the oppressive summer heat and humidity pervaded everything. The U.S. marshals in the front seats claimed the van's air conditioner was going full blast, but even so, it was powerless to provide relief to the steamy prisoners in the rear.

The biggest difference in today's trip wasn't the change of seasons, though. It was the change in attitude by the guards who escorted him. During the trial, the men and women with the guns and badges had quit talking among themselves when Calloway neared. They seemed to regard him with fear and suspicion, and they treated him with caution and deference. Now, the U.S. marshals laughed at each other's tasteless jokes and kept up their aimless banter in his presence. They were still wary of him. They treated him as a potential physical threat. But they certainly didn't seem to care what Calloway thought or said anymore.

During the trial, Calloway had been allowed to change into civilian clothes in the basement of the federal building each day before the proceedings. His attorney, A. C. Wharton, took pains to make sure jurors never saw Calloway in prison garb. Wharton didn't want them to picture his client as a criminal. Every time Calloway appeared before the jury, he wore custom-tailored suits that he had purchased during FedEx trips to the Orient. He wore monogrammed shirts with his initials A. R. C. on the pocket, wide-rimmed glasses—the kind favored by young business executives and cuff links.

The silky feel of those fine garments had been an unwanted reminder of his previous life.

Today, Calloway left the suits and ties behind. He was about to be sentenced. Judge Julia Gibbons would give him the same punishment no matter what his apparel. This morning, like every morning in federal prison, Calloway wore tan hospital-style pants with a drawstring at the waist, a long-sleeved cotton undershirt, and a tan, short-sleeved V-neck hospital-style T-shirt on top.

Wharton was standing at the doorway to the elevator when it reached the eleventh floor. The lawyer was dapper as ever in a deep-blue suit and red-striped tie. He escorted Calloway into the courtroom and they walked to the familiar mahogany defense table. They sat in the same overstuffed wood and leather chairs they had occupied during the trial. John Fowlkes, the prosecutor, was seated next to the podium—right where he had been when the jury convicted Calloway back in April. Today, however, the jury box was vacant.

Calloway scanned the audience. He had expected to see the Flight 705 crew members and their wives but, astonishingly, all of them were absent. Calloway knew his own family would be elsewhere. He had asked them not to come. But he expected to see the three pilots and especially their wives—the women whose presence at trial had been so constant. Where were they now? Didn't they want to gloat at his defeat?

Calloway expected the pilots and their wives to show up at any moment. He was counting on it. Calloway had urged Wharton to call the pilots back to the witness stand prior to sentencing to ask them about their injuries. Had the pilots played golf recently? Had they been hunting, or flown in small airplanes? Wharton could compel them to answer the questions under oath.

The passage of more time must have aided the pilots' recoveries. By minimizing their injuries, the artful lawyer could argue there was no need to severely punish his client. No harm, no foul.

About forty spectators were present in the courtroom, fewer than at trial. Calloway recognized a pair of FedEx lawyers seated directly behind the prosecutor's table and a few TV reporters. Judge Gibbons was in her chair already. She was wearing the same black robe and large-framed glasses that had become so familiar to spectators.

During the trial, Calloway had noticed that the more deferential the judge seemed toward the defense, the more patient and indulgent she had been to his lawyer, the more adverse her subsequent rulings were likely to be. It was as though she sought to give the appearance of bending over backward to favor the defense right before she clobbered them.

When she smiled at Wharton and, in her flowery regional prose, asked him to expound on his motions or objections, it was an invitation to disaster. Wharton would carefully construct his legal arguments, and Calloway would begin to feel they were making headway. Then Wharton's points would be rejected, completely and totally. The sweeter the judge's disposition, the more likely she was to deny defense motions or overrule objections.

Now, with the trial over, her demeanor also changed. She was less patient, more irritable. Her normally dulcet voice had a harsh edge. When Wharton introduced a motion for a new trial, a standard postconviction tactic, Judge Gibbons summarily dismissed it before he had even finished his statement. When Wharton objected to a prosecution move to introduce photos of the wounded pilots, she impatiently cut him off again.

"I'll give you every opportunity to test or dispute the evidence introduced today," she told Wharton curtly. "These photographs are part of the evidentiary base upon which I'm going to base my decision. Anything else that you want to present, I'm happy to consider. Now, is there anything else you'd like to present?"

Icy silence.

Wharton suggested the sentencing be postponed in order to give the defense more time to examine evidence. Gibbons turned him down flat.

She told prosecutor Fowlkes to submit the hospital photographs as Exhibit Number Four. The tall prosecutor approached the bench and handed the judge a file folder containing a dozen eight-by-ten-inch color photographs of the three wounded men. They had been taken a few hours after the attack by FBI agents at The Med.

Judge Gibbons began leafing through the file, examining the pictures individually. She wanted to make sure the photos were clear and properly labeled. The images were shocking, however, even to a federal judge accustomed to grisly crime-scene pictures.

There was Andy Peterson, the soft-spoken flight engineer, white as chalk from losing two thirds of the blood in his body. His scalp was ripped and grotesquely swollen, exposing the ivory white pieces of his fractured skull. There was Jim Tucker, the muscular and athletic copilot, paralyzed and semiconscious, his head shaved, barely clinging to life. There was David Sanders, the dignified airline captain, his wavy brown hair caked in dry blood, and his pressed blue uniform stained deep crimson.

Judge Gibbons closed the folder, took a deep breath, and handed it to a clerk.

"Please label this Exhibit Number Four," she said calmly. Next, she turned to Wharton and, as dispassionately as possible, asked the lawyer to make a statement on his client's behalf. Wharton stood, buttoning the top of his suit jacket as he rose.

"Your Honor. This is an individual who could not sustain the insanity defense but clearly was functioning at a diminished mental capacity at the time of the incident," he said. "The court is not precluded from considering a downward departure—a reduction in his sentence—based on his diminished mental capacity at the time of the offense. This is a single act of aberrant behavior. My client has no history of criminal behavior."

Wharton spoke about the law, how attempted aircraft piracy was a serious crime with already stiff penalties. The laws on attempted air piracy made no distinction about the size of the airplane, so, as far as the letter of the law was concerned, his client shouldn't get a longer sentence just because the crime took place aboard a DC-10 instead of a Piper Cub.

Wharton was about to conclude but Calloway urged him to continue. The lawyer consulted his notes and went on.

"Mr. Calloway has never denied the physical acts that brought injury to these men. It's been the insanity defense throughout. He never said he wasn't there or that he didn't do it. Mr. Calloway accepts responsibility for the fact this act occurred. Someone has been injured, and he accepts responsibility for that."

Judge Gibbons asked Calloway whether he had a statement to make. The former flight engineer handed his lawyer a letter, and Wharton took it to the judge. Wharton then repeated his request for a new trial and asked that the sentencing be delayed in order to introduce new psychiatric evidence. The lawyer said his client planned to appeal his conviction, but Wharton didn't intend to remain as his attorney.

Gibbons read Calloway's letter silently. It was dated August 9 and addressed to the Flight 705 crew members:

Dear Dave, Jim and Andy:

This heartfelt letter expressing my sympathy for each of you is long overdue. On April 7, 1994, I was severely mentally ill according to two highly experienced clinical psychologists. That the "Insanity Defense" (a legal term) failed in a sensationalized courtroom drama in no way diminishes the presence of my medical "psychiatric impairment" on that day or any other day.

I and my family will be forever grateful to each of you three for sparing my life on board Flight 705 when you could have justifiably killed me. I extend my special gratitude to you, Dave, for your heroic and safe landing of the aircraft under such extraordinary circumstances.

To the greatest extent that I can, I offer each of you and your families an apology for my bizarre behavior which resulted from me being severely mentally ill on April 7, 1994. There was no "well thought out plan" as the prosecutor speculates. I was unaware of what I was doing on board Flight 705 that day. I deeply regret your injuries and I hope you are back in the cockpit soon.

Finally, I ask your forgiveness and understanding of my mental illness just as much for yourselves as for myself while I remind you of MATTHEW 6:14 and 6:15. Please do not let your hatred and bitterness destroy you as Susan Peterson alludes to in her written statement "We pray for healing . . . that we would not be consumed by hate."

I also pray for your healing and that you are not consumed by hate.

Judge Gibbons asked Calloway a second time whether he wanted to make a statement in his own behalf. "No," he whispered, the word barely audible to the judge twenty feet away.

Then prosecutor Fowlkes rose. He had intended to speak slowly for the benefit of the court reporter, who struggled to keep up with his rapid-fire speech. But Calloway's letter galled the prosecutor, and when he got angry, he automatically talked faster.

"There has been no showing of personal responsibility here," Fowlkes began. "No contrition, no remorse. There has been nothing of the kind in this case. As far as the letter goes, it is dated August ninth—after the government [in written motions] suggested a higher penalty be imposed, based on the defendant's failure to take responsibility for his actions. It would be a joke for the court to accept this self-serving admission of responsibility at this time. The defendant was a malingerer and has tried to manipulate people throughout the trial. Any additional information you receive will be highly suspect."

Fowlkes had spoken with each of the Flight 705 crew members by phone before the sentencing began. The prosecutor knew the letter was a sham because none of the pilots had even received a copy.

Fowlkes asked the judge to remember the photographs she had just seen, the $135,000 in medical bills that the pilots had already received, and the additional care they would require for years into the future. He reminded her of the testimony at trial, the horrific audiotapes that proved that Calloway had continued to struggle even as the plane approached Memphis to land.

"At any time, that plane could have crashed," Fowlkes said. "Every person in this community was endangered. This was a huge aircraft that almost crashed upon landing. This was a unique situation unlike anything any other court has considered."

The hearing had lasted almost an hour. Then Judge Gibbons raised her hands like a traffic cop to stop the lawyers from making any more arguments.

On her desk, she had a eighteen-page report from the U.S. Probation Office that contained a sentencing recommendation. The recommendations aren't binding, but trial judges almost always tailor their sentences to fall within the range that the probation office suggests.

For Calloway, the probation office recommended a penalty between 235 months (19 years, 7 months) and 293 months (24 years, 5 months).

"On the subject of acceptance of responsibility, Mr. Calloway has not accepted responsibility," Judge Gibbons said with finality. "The proof at trial with respect to the insanity defense showed the defendant using the best possible means to avoid responsibility. Moreover, in this case, a defendant who accepted responsibility would have displayed a far different demeanor during the trial. There has been nothing about Mr. Calloway's conduct that shows he feels concern for anything other than his own legal situation."

Calloway sat with his head down, his arms crossed, elbows on the table. He closed his right fist and pressed it against his lips.

"There is no basis for a downward departure in the sentencing guidelines in this case," Judge Gibbons continued. "Every individual has certain psychological characteristics, and those characteristics can contribute to criminal conduct. The jury in this case found this was not a situation in which the insanity defense applied. And really, nothing else about this case provides for a lessening of the sentence based on mental condition. In fact, in this case there are several aggravating factors. There are multiple victims, specifically, the three pilots.

"There is physical injury. It's plain that very significant physical injury did result regardless of how permanent in nature. The photographs graphically depict those injuries. And the injuries were inflicted as a result of calculated, intentional conduct.

"There is property damage, although frankly, the property damage is of less importance to the court in determining the punishment.

"Finally, and most importantly, is the potential danger to the public. Only through the skill, courage, and training of the victims were they able to avoid a disaster in this situation. It was through their display of these attributes of character that a catastrophe was avoided. The court does think an upward departure is warranted, and the sentence will be *life in prison*."

Calloway didn't move when the penalty was announced. He stared straight ahead, immobile. He had expected the worst. This was it. Life in prison. In the federal system, there was no chance for parole. Judge Gibbons had imposed a sentence far beyond the suggested maximum range.

To Calloway, the punishment was worse than death. He had sought to end his life April 7 on his own terms. Now he was condemned to live it according to rules set entirely by others. Every minute of every hour of every day, Calloway would be controlled by individuals he regarded as less intelligent, less educated, and less worthy than himself.

"This is a very sad situation," Judge Gibbons continued, her voice subdued. "Obviously, Mr. Calloway is a person of great ability who could have contributed much if he had directed himself differently. There is no lesser sentence that adequately addresses the real injury, potential damage, and the extent that tragedy was only avoided through some very fortuitous circumstances.

"It's true that Mr. Calloway had no prior criminal record and that this was an unexpected course of conduct. The court will not impose a fine based on the defendant's lack of ability to pay."

Gibbons glanced at the clock on the wall. It was six minutes until noon.

"We're adjourned," she said, tapping her wood gavel on the desk.

Two U.S. marshals moved forward from their seats behind the defense table and handcuffed Calloway. They led him to the elevator at the side of the courtroom while the television and radio reporters scurried for the elevators. They had to rush outside to waiting cameras and microphones in order to get the news of Calloway's life sentence on their noon broadcasts.

A few reporters and photographers were waiting in the basement of the federal building minutes later when the marshals escorted

Calloway back to the prison van. "Too many black men are being sent to prison!" he shouted. "Does anyone care about that?"

Calloway shook his head in apparent disgust.

"I am not a criminal!" he yelled in the direction of the small crowd gathered there as the marshals opened the door of the prison van. "I'm mentally ill!"

"HIS SPIRITUAL LINK"

OCTOBER 5, 1996
9:00 A.M.

Jim Tucker had been sitting at his kitchen table on the winter morning he first felt the troubling, tingling sensations in his right hand, shoulder, and leg.

He had watched in quiet consternation as his right hand felt as if it was forming a tight fist but remained immobile. Jim tried to open and close his hand, but it was totally unresponsive. The hand seemed to belong to someone else. A tide of numbness slowly spread across the entire right side of his body. A few minutes later, however, the frightening, phantom sensations receded and gradually disappeared.

The surgery to replace the missing piece of Jim's skull five months ago had seemed like a total success. A molded, hardened piece of composite material now protected his brain, and there had been no sign of infection. Jim's weight had climbed back to normal, and he had resumed vigorous morning workouts. He looked as healthy as ever, but somehow he didn't feel quite right. And he couldn't explain the odd numbness that occasionally overcame him.

The episodes were reminiscent of the loss of physical control Jim had experienced on board Flight 705. He told his doctors about his troubles, and neurologists tried to halt the infrequent spells with ever increasing doses of medication. However, the powerful drugs put Jim's mind in a scary twilight. He had nightmares for the first time in his life, and the anxiety and lack of sleep made Jim increasingly tense, moody, and withdrawn.

In order to determine the exact cause and severity of Jim's episodes, doctors set up a test. They kept him awake for thirty-six hours, then connected him to sensitive monitors. By examining the electrical impulses within his brain during a time of induced stress, they hoped to pinpoint the source of Jim's problems and treat them more effectively.

After the exhausting examination, the doctors gave Jim and Becky a disquieting diagnosis. Small amounts of abnormal electrical activity were emanating from the injured portion of Jim's brain, and the spiked lines on a computer printout showed a mild seizure disorder. Jim's central nervous system had been permanently damaged, and now, they explained, he had developed epilepsy.

"Epilepsy is fairly common for people with serious head injuries," the neurologist said. "But don't worry. It can be treated quite effectively with medication, diet, and sleep management."

Jim's epilepsy was relatively benign, and with proper treatment, doctors told Jim he could probably ward off the convulsive types of seizures that characterize more severe cases. But Jim also knew that being diagnosed with any type of seizure disorder would permanently end all hope of resuming his flying career.

"You know what this means for me professionally, don't you?" he asked the neurologist.

"Yes, I do," the specialist answered flatly. "But don't worry. There are plenty of other things you can do."

Jim shook his head. The doctor didn't get it. Flying wasn't a job that Jim did for a paycheck. It was a calling, it was a gift. Aviation had shaped him, defined him, and allowed him to provide for his family. Now, that cornerstone of his life was slipping away. Jim didn't intend to let it go without a struggle.

He worked harder than ever at physical rehabilitation and stubbornly forced himself to use his clumsy right hand for tasks that he could accomplish easily with his more dexterous left hand. Jim began playing the drums again, just as he had in his youth. He started with a single snare drum, two sticks, and a sheet of simple music. Playing a percussion instrument seemed as good a way as any to improve his motor skills and coordination. He set up a punching bag in the garage and worked out twice daily.

At the same time, Jim bought a CD-ROM for his computer that contained reams of the most current information on epilepsy and its treatments. The more he learned, however, the more convinced Jim became that he would never be allowed to fly professionally again. Even if he was able to show that he could remain free of seizures for years at a time without drugs, as far as the FAA was concerned, he would always be damaged goods.

Some of Jim's fellow FedEx pilots suggested Jim might someday return to the company as a ground-based flight instructor. Jim had always enjoyed teaching other pilots the finer points of flying in the company's realistic, computerized cockpit simulators. But being so close to commercial aviation without being able to actually perform it would be cruel and unusual punishment, Jim decided. The most valuable information that instructors can pass along to their students is how complex aircraft technology applies to real-world scenarios. Being restricted to a simulator would quickly make Jim's operational knowledge obsolete.

If he was going to be forced out of professional flying, Jim knew he had to get all the way out. Although it would be the most difficult part of his healing process, Jim knew he had to say good-bye to the career he had loved.

But what about private flying? What about his Luscombe? Medical requirements for private pilots are far less stringent than for airline captains. Perhaps someday he could get permission to fly his sporty little airplane again. ALPA psychiatrists had warned Jim and the other pilots that flying might never be fun for them after the attack. Instead of a joyful expression of freedom, for many pilots who had lived through aerial emergencies, aviation became a nerveracking chore.

Jim didn't believe that would apply to him, though. Sure, he had been the victim of a violent, brutal crime. And yes, the crime had taken place on an airplane. But the savage assault could just as easily have happened in a parking lot or an alley. Why should the fact that it occurred on an airplane ruin his passion for airplanes?

Ever since April 7, 1994, Jim's Luscombe had been in storage at Colonial Air Park, a tiny grass strip a few miles from his home. Jim had hardly seen the plane since he was injured, and now it was overdue for its annual airworthiness inspection.

Should he sell the Luscombe? Jim wondered. Would he ever fly it again? Jim knew he was capable of it, but without approval from FAA doctors, he knew he might never be allowed back in the cockpit. Jim was concerned that if he kept the plane, the Luscombe might become a constant source of irritation and frustration; an object that was tantalizingly close but forever out of reach.

Finally, Jim decided it was time to make some tough choices about his little airplane—and his future. On a fall morning in 1996, he drove to Colonial Air Park and stopped his Ford Bronco in front of the rustic barn that contained his airplane as well as a pair of yellow Piper Cubs.

For years, Colonial had been the home of the Memphis Soaring Society, a group of glider pilots who used the barns and grass runway as their base of operations. But as the airspace around Memphis International Airport became busier, glider pilots became hemmed in. Finally, the glider club abandoned Colonial altogether and moved across the Mississippi River to rural Arkansas. The number of weekly takeoffs and landings at Colonial diminished to a trickle. But on this particular morning, Jim didn't mind the isolation.

He opened the creaky doors of the dusty red barn and looked at his forlorn Luscombe. Jim's friends had prepared it for long-term storage, just as he had asked. The plane's vents and exhaust ports were plugged with broad strips of duct tape and rags. The battery and spark plugs had been removed, and so had the engine oil. A thick layer of dust covered everything. Jim patted the metal cowling sympathetically. His airplane had been neglected lately, but its hibernation was about to end.

Jim pulled open the east-facing barn doors, and sunlight filtered into the damp, musty building. He took hold of the airplane's left strut and pushed it slowly outside. The balloon tires rolled easily over the concrete floor and onto the wet grass.

Jim peeled off the thick strips of duct tape that covered the vents and removed the protective rags from the exhaust pipes. Next, he rinsed the entire airplane with water from a garden hose. The dust slid off to reveal the shiny yellow airplane with black trim. He filled a bucket with soapy water and began scrubbing the plane in earnest. A few minutes later, the Luscombe was covered from spinner to tailwheel with foamy white bubbles. Jim could reach the tops of the wings without a stepladder, and he left no part of the airplane's skin untouched. A clean airplane, Jim had always believed, is a safe airplane. In washing the airframe, it's easy to see loose cables, hinges, and small cracks that might otherwise go unnoticed.

Jim rinsed the airplane again. He was creating a puddle of mud underneath, so he pushed it a few feet farther out from the barn. Water droplets beaded on the sparkling metal surface, and he dried them with a cotton beach towel.

Jim had purchased the Luscombe in 1992. It was the only private airplane he had ever owned. Other professional pilots might prefer modern, expensive aerial status symbols. But Jim gravitated to this relatively simple stick-and-rudder flying machine. It could fly slowly and land anywhere. His tiny Luscombe was like an aerial sports car—noisy, impractical, and with very limited baggage space.

The plane had two seats, but for the long-legged Jim, it was more comfortable to fly solo. The twins were still small and skinny enough that either of them could fit neatly into the passenger seat, but when Jim took his burly father for a ride, they had to wedge themselves together just to get the doors closed. Jim senior rode with his left arm wrapped around his son's broad shoulders.

Jim had first heard about this particular aircraft while looking through *Trade-A-Plane,* a no-frills list of airplane classified ads distributed nationally three times each month. The plane sounded perfect, with a 150-horsepower engine instead of the regular 65, relatively few flying hours in its log, and meticulous maintenance from one owner. Best of all, it was located in Raymond, Mississippi, about 130 miles straight south of Memphis. The plane cost a little more than Jim planned to spend, but still less than a new car, and after all the sacrifices he had made to launch his flying career, he decided to splurge.

He had gotten a one-way commuter airline ticket to Jackson, and the Luscombe's owner picked Jim up at the passenger terminal. They drove together to the tiny municipal airport west of the city. The owner loved the Luscombe, he confessed. But his wife didn't like riding in the cramped, noisy cabin. Besides, the smooth-talking Mississippian pointed out, if Jim bought the plane, the former owner could rest assured that the trusty machine had gone to a good home.

Jim was enamored with the Luscombe model 8E from first sight. He had planned to drive a hard bargain. But when he saw the jaunty plane waxed and ready to go, its black tires chocked inside the drafty metal hangar building, he agreed to pay the asking price. The two pilots went through the formalities of examining the log books, checking under the cowling, and shining flashlights under the inspection plates in the wings and fuselage. Everything looked perfect.

Jim learned how to start the plane. A couple of shots of primer pushed gasoline into the engine's four cylinders. Open the throttle a quarter inch. Then flip the electrical switch on, engage the magnetos, and press the starter button. The two-bladed metal propeller turned over three times; then the engine barked enthusiastically to life.

A strong winter wind was blowing from the north the day Jim bought the plane and flew it home to Memphis. The headwind made the flight almost three hours   not much quicker than driving. But Jim enjoyed every moment. When he landed at Arlington Municipal Airport about fifteen miles north of his Collierville home, even the initial touchdown went smoothly.

Now, on this autumn morning at Colonial, all of those memories came back.

How much his life had changed since then.

Jim had come perilously close to being killed on Flight 705. And there were times during his recovery when he feared he would spend the rest of his years in a feeble, debilitated state—a burden to his wife and children. The ordeal had tested his family's courage and faith to the limit. Yet now, looking back, everyone seemed stronger because of it. They faced the future knowing they could handle adversity when it came.

Also, in ways that were difficult for Jim to define, his close brush with violent death had deepened his love and admiration for his father. Jim senior was a World War II veteran who had fought aboard PT boats at Midway, Tulagi, Iron Bottom Sound, Guadalcanal, and the Solomon Islands. Jim knew that his father had survived battles during his years of combat in the Pacific that must have been more traumatic than the struggle aboard the FedEx jet. He had certainly faced the prospect of his own violent death many times and known the same kind of terror and desperation the Flight 705 pilots felt. Jim senior had faced fanatical kamikazes, too.

Jim recalled a night when he was just eleven years old and lightning had struck a stand of bamboo in the backyard of his family home. The brilliant white flash and earsplitting explosion made young Jim vault out of bed and run to the living room, where his parents were watching television. Jim had been amazed to find his normally placid father shaking uncontrollably. Post-traumatic stress syndrome hadn't entered the popular lexicon then, but the sudden flash of lightning had instantly transported Jim senior seventeen years back in time. He stared off into the distance with glassy eyes while his wife, Evelyn, placed a blanket around his shivering shoulders and fed him warm tea.

Now, Jim could empathize with his father, and he could learn from his example: Jim senior never harbored ill-will toward his former enemies, and Jim promised himself not to become bitter, either. Jim couldn't even hate Auburn Calloway. When he saw Calloway in court during the trial, Jim felt nothing toward him. No hostility, no fear. Calloway was a stranger, just as he had been that day he boarded the DC-10 in Memphis.

During Jim's convalescence, an African-American nurse in Memphis had tearfully asked him not to hate her race for the crime that had been committed against him. She needn't have made such a plea. How could Jim hold a grudge against prosecutor John Fowlkes, prosecution witnesses, jurors, or the other African-American professionals, friends, and coworkers who had helped him and his family through the ordeal?

A newspaper photograph that had been published a day after the attack on Flight 705 showed Jim being whisked into The Med on a stretcher while a battered David Sanders emerged from the ambulance. It was a dramatic image. It had been reprinted in newspapers and magazines around the country. But when Jim looked closely at the photograph, when he really examined it, he saw African-American firefighters and paramedics assisting him. An African-American paramedic gently supported the injured captain, holding his arm as the bloodied flier stepped from the emergency vehicle.

Jim took comfort in the knowledge that in the end, the judicial system had worked. It had been a difficult process for everyone, but the investigators, the lawyers, the jurors, and the judge had done their jobs. The outcome had hardly seemed assured, but when the trial was over, Jim felt that justice had been served.

Jim walked to the back of the barn/hangar and found a case of aircraft engine oil, Aeroshell 100, his customary brand, in dust-covered black plastic bottles. He took seven quarts and a funnel to the Luscombe and began pouring the clear, golden fluid into the engine. The job was done in five minutes. The dipstick confirmed the lubricant was at the proper level. He installed a new battery and fastened it to a metal tray in the engine compartment. He replaced the eight missing spark plugs with brand-new ones.

Jim made sure the plane's electrical system was turned off, then pulled the propeller through one blade at a time. Moving the propeller helped circulate the oil through the engine. Despite the plane's long period of inactivity, all four engine cylinders felt as if they had good compression.

Jim stepped around to the left side of the aircraft and climbed into the cockpit. He primed the engine and flipped the main electrical switch on. Magnetos on, then press the starter. The propeller turned three times, and the engine came to life with a few puffs of black smoke. Jim pulled the thin metal door closed, and he watched the engine instruments carefully. Oil pressure was fine, steady as a rock. The oil temperature came up just as it was supposed to.

He sat and listened to the engine warm up. Hearing the engine purr, feeling the steady rhythm of the pistons, was better to Jim than sitting in the front row at a symphony concert. A few minutes later, he increased the throttle and the gauges held their proper positions. All the needles were in the green. Jim decided to test the brakes, too. He taxied forward, then tapped the heel pedals. Luscombe brakes are notoriously unreliable, but these seemed firm and even. He went a few feet farther and tapped them again with the same result.

Despite his forced absence from the cockpit, Jim felt immediately at home in the Luscombe. He was more comfortable flying airplanes than driving cars. Some of the happiest moments in his life had been spent alone in airplanes.

In the Navy, he loved flying on moonlit nights at sea. Night carrier landings were treacherous—even under ideal conditions. Yet on clear nights with moonlight glistening off the ocean surface and the fast-moving ship churning a phosphorescent, V-shaped wake in front of him, Jim was filled with the purest self-assurance. It was as though he controlled everything, the entire world around him, from his high perch in the cockpit. Those moments had been magical.

He taxied the Luscombe to the south end of the grass runway

at Colonial. There was a slight downhill grade for the next thirty yards; then the wide runway became almost perfectly flat. A tattered orange windsock atop the red barn showed a light northerly breeze. After all the agonizing setbacks and torment, finally, Jim Tucker was beginning to feel like himself again.

His future was uncertain. Jim accepted that. But he felt sure that God would continue to guide his recovery, just as he remained positive that He had enabled the Flight 705 crew to bring their plane home safely.

Jim decided then and there to keep his Luscombe.

For Jim, the antique airplane wasn't just a possession. It was his new goal for the future, his reward for complete physical healing, and his spiritual link to his past.

"WORK TO BE DONE"

OCTOBER 26

11:00 A.M.

It took only two hours for David Sanders to hitch his family's mobile home to the moving trucks, and on a cool autumn morning, the job was done.

David, Susan, and Lauren cheered and waved as the brown-sided structure that had been their temporary quarters for two years—far longer than they'd expected—made its way down the long gravel driveway and onto the paved road that led to the highway. Now they occupied their permanent home, the one that David had designed and helped build.

There was some interior painting and carpentry, decorating and wiring to be done. But David and Susan planned to live in the house the rest of their lives, so there was plenty of time to install the aquarium, the billiard table, the stereo speakers in the walls and to take care of other details. For now, the structure had heat, air conditioning, running water, and a wood-burning stove downstairs. The fireplaces worked, and so did the hot tub. The new home was as comfortable and magnificent as David had envisioned it would be.

A sturdy wood porch wrapped around the entire ground floor of the two-story house, and electric fans kept the shaded areas comfortable even in summer. Mature trees dotted the property, and huge windows on the south and east sides of the house spread sunlight throughout its spacious interior. The kitchen was open and expansive, and upstairs balconies provided a hilltop view of the twenty-acre lake to the west where a flock of Canada geese had settled in for the winter.

During the long, methodical construction process, David had developed a familiar daily routine that gave his life a pace and a rhythm that his irregular flying schedule had never allowed. Even without an alarm clock, he would awaken each morning a few minutes after dawn. He'd brew a pot of coffee and drop some wheat bread in the toaster oven. Then, after the light snack, he'd walk to the construction site and begin the day's chores.

David labored alone during those few, quiet early morning hours before the subcontractors arrived to perform their specialized tasks. During that solitary time, David would review plans for the day ahead. He made sure the subcontractors' work areas were clear, that they had the materials they needed, and that they understood their instructions perfectly. Nothing was to be overlooked.

Once the subcontractors had begun their jobs, David, Susan, and Lauren had time for a quick breakfast together. Sometimes the meal was a bit rushed since Lauren usually caught an early bus to high school. But it was David's favorite time of day.

After breakfast, he would carry a mobile phone back to the construction site. In addition to allowing him to take calls from subcontractors and material suppliers, the phone was a critical link to the FedEx universe. About a year after he brought Flight 705 safely back to Memphis, a group of pilots had recruited David to lead a political struggle. This time, their foe was the Air Line Pilots Association.

ALPA leaders seemed to be getting more bellicose toward FedEx management, and the harsh rhetoric and confrontational tactics were causing deep rifts among company pilots. Contract negotiations between ALPA and FedEx had droned on fruitlessly for more than a year. ALPA claimed about half the pilots at FedEx were members of the national union, but that percentage was the lowest among all the airlines that ALPA represented. The union was dealing from a position of fundamental weakness, David suspected, and ALPA leaders were lashing out.

As the peak pre-Christmas shipping season approached in 1995, ALPA threatened the first organized work slowdown in FedEx history. The union placed ads in national newspapers warning FedEx customers that their Christmas shipments might be delayed. ALPA pilots in uniform picketed outside company offices in Memphis, New York, Anchorage, Los Angeles, and Indianapolis. Arguments between pro- and anti-ALPA pilots became so acrimonious they ruined long-standing friendships. The situation threatened to destroy the kinship and camaraderie that had made working at FedEx so rewarding.

David jumped back into the fray and turned his tiny trailer office into an electronic clearinghouse for the FedEx Pilots Association (FPA), a newly founded group that intended to replace ALPA with an independent union. The FPA would have no national structure or agenda. Its leaders would become the quiet, reasonable voice of loyal FedEx fliers. FPA founders like David intended to deal with managers calmly and constructively, in keeping with their corporate traditions.

If the FPA attracted support from the vast majority of FedEx pilots, as David was sure it would, then there would be no reason for angry accusations or destructive strikes. Leaders could speak softly, knowing that high membership numbers among FedEx pilots would ensure their message was heard.

David worked tirelessly to launch the FPA. He was elected chairman of the group's first steering committee, and he researched and helped write the FPA's constitution and bylaws. He led pilot meetings, met with lawyers and accountants, wrote newsletters, sent faxes, and recorded telephone messages.

David had hoped to be back on flying status during the independent union campaign, but he was still prohibited from flying. Even though his physical injuries weren't as severe as the other Flight 705 pilots', doctors wanted to know that he was not at risk of a seizure. In head injury cases, the FAA often requires pilots to remain free of seizures without medication for years before the agency will consider returning them to flying the cockpit. David's test period was still in progress.

Despite a psychiatrist's warning that David might someday feel guilt or excessive remorse that his crew had been injured on Flight 705, his appraisal of events on the plane remained stark and analytical. He wished the incident had never taken place, but he was proud of the way that he, Jim, and Andy had responded, and he was glad to have contributed to their victory, their survival.

Being barred from flying was painful, but David threw himself into the construction of his new home as well as building the new union among his peers. Susan worried at first that her husband was taking on too much, working too hard, and spreading himself too thin. As she watched him swing into action, however, she saw his spirit rebound. Construction kept him physically active. David was stronger and trimmer than she had seen him in years. His hands were calloused from carpentry and painting. His skin was a reddish tan from days spent working outdoors, and the exhausting manual labor helped him sleep soundly at night. Mentally, the political battle against ALPA brought back his competitive instincts. And the detail-oriented research and technical writing kept him focused and sharp.

It was a welcome contrast to the weeks and months following Flight 705. For David, preparing for trial, then testifying in court, had been a stressful, draining, and emotionally taxing ordeal.

David could not control those events. He was an actor in those dramas—not a director. Building the FPA allowed David to plan, to set strategy and take decisive action. He had a mission again, and he was determined to accomplish it. If he seemed preoccupied or distant in the bewildering days that followed the attack, now he was his normal vibrant, confident, opinionated self. Other FedEx pilots sought him out for advice and guidance. And David responded in a way that both relieved and gratified Susan.

On November 25, 1995, negotiations between FedEx and ALPA broke down, and ALPA pilots launched a series of job actions designed to disrupt the company's time-critical shipments. It was exactly the situation that David and other FedEx veterans had sought to avoid. ALPA declared that any pilots who volunteered to fly overtime during the hectic pre-Christmas season would be regarded for the rest of their careers as scabs—strikebreakers.

If David had been allowed to fly, he gladly would have been the first to cross ALPA's "invisible picket line" and deliver DC-10s full of packages himself. He considered himself a FedEx employee first. The company's success ensured his success. Despite the ongoing pilot labor troubles, David still believed that FedEx was unique, just as it was when he aligned his future with the company in 1974.

David visited the FedEx flight-training department frequently to meet with other pilots, explain the FPA, and ask them to support the fledgling independent union drive. After six weeks of job actions, FedEx and ALPA went back to the negotiating table. Unionized pilots had been unable to disrupt deliveries on a broad scale, and ALPA's attempted work disruptions were widely regarded as failures. The confrontation convinced more pilots than ever to answer the FPA's call for an alternative union. And in the spring of 1996, seven months after it was founded, the FPA collected enough voter authorization cards to demand a new union representation election.

David felt at that moment that he had done as much as he could for the young organization. He had hoped to return to the flight line by now, but since his medical status remained in limbo, he decided to step down as leader of the FPA. It was critical, he argued, for active FedEx pilots to set the group's direction. There were 3,200 FedEx pilots now, and most participants and observers expected the contest between ALPA and the FPA to be extremely close. But David confidently predicted the independent group would win by a huge margin.

On October 25, 1996, the day the ballots were scheduled to be counted, David and Susan drove to Memphis to await the results along with hundreds of other FPA supporters. Most of them believed their independent union would win, but regardless of the outcome, they vowed to back the victor and put an end to the acrimony that had clouded their workplace in recent years.

The election turned out to be a stunning win for the FPA. The final tally was 1,589 for the independent FPA and 1,133 for ALPA. To David, the results confirmed the self-reliance of FedEx pilots and their eagerness to chart their own course. The election marked the first time a pilot group had split with ALPA since 1963.

David and Susan drank red wine at the FPA party and savored the victory, knowing it had been launched, in part, on their mobile phone and fax machine. David's way of doing business—the soft-spoken, gentlemanly way—had prevailed. Future discussions between FedEx fliers and managers would be cordial and civil, and each side would seek to earn the trust and respect of the other.

David was uncertain of his role in the fledgling union's future. According to the constitution and bylaws he had helped write, only active FedEx pilots were allowed to hold union offices. And David had no way of knowing when, or if, he would ever be allowed to return to flying.

The new era at FedEx would surely present extraordinary challenges. Contract talks were bound to be demanding, and being the guardian of thousands of careers was an awesome responsibility. But David was convinced that if pilots and managers stayed true to their beliefs, they could enable FedEx, a company that had revolutionized the way Americans did business, to become a leader in labor relations, too.

There was a tremendous amount of work to be done, but David felt that he and his fellow pilots were up to it.

EPILOGUE

JANUARY 1997

Due to the injuries they sustained on April 7, 1994, the three crew members aboard Flight 705 have not been allowed to return to commercial aviation. All of them have asked for medical clearance to fly again, but so far doctors have not approved their requests.

FedEx still does not require pilots who board planes in Memphis to pass through metal detectors. The FAA proposed new rules in the wake of Flight 705 that would have required weapons screening for all pilots, but after extensive lobbying by the air cargo industry, the agency quietly dropped the measure in 1994.

David and Susan Sanders, Jim and Becky Tucker, and Andy and Susan Peterson still reside in the Memphis area.

Auburn Calloway is prisoner number 14601–076 at the federal penitentiary in Atlanta. He is seeking to have his conviction and sentence overturned by the Sixth Circuit Court of Appeals in Cincinnati. As of this writing, his case is still pending.

The crew of Flight 705 received awards for airmanship from the Daedalions, Lloyds of London, and Federal Express Corp. A portrait painting of them hangs on permanent display in the FedEx pilot training building in Memphis.

I was plotting an early escape from my newspaper office that spring afternoon in 1994 when *The Commercial Appeal*'s Metro editor came through my door. The business news department where I work is far removed from the main newsroom, so editors seldom wander back there by accident.

"We heard something on the police radio scanner about a hijacking on a FedEx plane," he began with a skeptical look that told me he thought the call was bogus. "The plane's supposedly on its way back to Memphis. We've got some people checking it out, but would you mind making a few calls?"

I rolled my eyes.

A hijacking attempt? So much for my quick getaway. Now I was going to be stuck in the office for hours chasing some ridiculous tip. Why would anyone want to hijack a cargo plane in Memphis, the geographic center of the United States?

I cover FedEx on a day-to-day basis, so I talk to the company's spokesmen regularly with predictable questions about package volume, financial information, and corporate strategy. Our conversations usually begin with some lighthearted banter. But on this day, the spokesmen were unusually tense and distant. They didn't have any information about a hijacking—but they might have something to say later that evening. I called the president of the airport, and his secretary said he was out on the tarmac somewhere. Something big was going on. I ran to my truck and made the familiar eight-mile drive to Memphis International Airport.

So began, for me, the most fascinating story I've ever covered.

But Flight 705 has become far more than a news event.

The more I learned about the crew of Flight 705, the twists of fate that brought them together and the boldness, creativity, and skill they showed under the most extreme circumstances, the more amazing their accomplishments became. With the encouragement of my wife, Martha, and the permission of my newspaper editors, Darrell Mack, Deborah White, Robert Hetherington, Otis Sanford, Henry Stokes, and Angus McEachran, I began writing this manuscript in my free time.

I'll always be grateful to each of the Flight 705 pilots and their wives for their trust, patience, and candor. Andy and Susan Peterson are delightful and funny. David and Susan Sanders are people of deep thoughtfulness and character. Jim and Becky Tucker are courageous beyond measure. I respect and admire each of them.

A unique and talented band of aviators also made invaluable contributions to this project: Gary Austin, Don Henry, Loree Hirschman, Fred and Julie Johnson, David Peeler, Jimmy and Penny Price, Don Ray, Morris Ray, Pat Rooney, Colin Ruthven, Herb Sanders, Dennie Stokes, and Gary Zambito all gave their expertise and enthusiasm generously. My brothers, Jason, Harry, and Micah, also gave advice and encouragement, as did my stepfather and mother, John and Wilma Melville, and my father, Henry Hirschman.

Coworkers Lawrence Buser and Robert Cohen plowed diligently through my most primitive first drafts and made helpful suggestions. So did Robert and Carole Bazzell, Kit Boss, John and Jenny Branston, Barbara Deal, Charlie and Laurine Fite, David Gish, Armand Schneider, Anya Silecky, and Jess Walter.

Special thanks to Alice Fried Martell, my agent and trusted adviser. Her wit, determination, and willingness to bet on a long shot made this book a reality. Henry Ferris and Ann Treistman, editors at William Morrow and Company, have been fantastic partners. They provided crucial guidance and insight, and they improved the final version of this manuscript immensely. And Joan Amico's skill, pre-

cision, and diligence as copy editor saved me from many embarrass-
ments.

While the people listed above helped in the creation of the text,
as the author, I accept full responsibility for its accuracy. Any errors
or omissions are mine alone.

—DAVE HIRSCHMAN